Understanding Disney

Understanding Disney

The Manufacture of Fantasy

Janet Wasko

polity

First published in 2001 by Polity Press in association with Blackwell Publishing Ltd

Reprinted 2002, 2003, 2005

Polity Press
65 Bridge Street
Cambridge CB2 1UR, UK

Polity Press
350 Main Street
Malden, MA 02148, USA

A catalogue record for this book is available from the British Library.

Library of Congress Cataloging-in-Publication Data
Wasko, Janet.
    Understanding Disney : the manufacture of fantasy / Janet Wasko.
        p. cm.
Includes index.
    ISBN 0-7456-1483-3 (hc)—ISBN 0-7456-1484-1 (pb)
    1. Walt Disney Company.   I. Title
PN1999.W27 W37 2001
384'.8'06579794—dc21
                                        00-010448

Typeset in 10.5 on 12.5 pt Bembo
by SetSystems Ltd, Saffron Walden, Essex
Printed in Great Britain by T. J. International, Padstow, Cornwall

Contents

Preface and Acknowledgments

1 On writing a preface while 36,000 feet in the air between Singapore and Tokyo It seems difficult, if not impossible, to escape Disney's "magic." Even here, 36,000 feet above the South China Sea, I am inundated by Disney products. The featured film is *Mission to Mars* (a Touchstone/Disney production), followed by several classic Mickey and Pluto cartoons and *Goof Troop* episodes. The audio program includes one entire channel featuring Disney's Hollywood Records' recording artists (Duran, Duran, BBMak, and Jessica Riddle), while the inflight magazine displays a prominent advertisement for Walt Disney World's 2000 celebration. The Sky Mall catalogue (shop while you fly) offers classic animation art pieces featuring Mickey, Pluto, Winnie the Pooh and gang, priced from $99 to $325, as well as a board game for *Who Wants to be a Millionaire*, an ABC/Disney television program.

Meanwhile, the screaming child in the seat in front of me is sporting Pooh pajamas and clutching a Mickey Mouse plush toy. Well, at least the airline is not owned by The Mouse House. Not yet, anyway.

2 Disney and me: the requisite ritual of placing one's self in one's research Growing up in southern California in the 1950s and 1960s meant a good deal of exposure to Disney's world. Disneyland was just up the freeway from where I lived in San Diego, and *The Wonderful World of Disney* and *The Mickey Mouse Club* were essential television viewing. For me, as for most American children, more than a few family memories involved Disney, in one way or another.

For this reason, I dedicate this book to my family, especially to my brother, Jack, whose first girlfriend moved from San Diego to Los Angeles to become one of the minor Mousketeers, with whom I shared many of these childhood memories, and who still finds pleasure and delight in trips to Disney's "magical worlds."

I also must admit that, once upon a time, I found myself working "down on Uncle Walt's farm" (AKA Disney's studio) in Burbank, California. It was the final in a series of film/television industry jobs that propelled me back to academe to try to understand why the entertainment industry behaved the way it does, and to question its role in society.

And, finally, I now find myself at a university that has a Disney character as a mascot. But more on that later . . .

3 Whither cometh this book? A few years ago, it thus seemed like a good idea to offer a course on Disney at the University of Oregon. The course became known by the same title as this book, and has covered some of the same territory. Initially, it was an attempt to expand upon a political economic approach to the media, as well as to respond to all those critics who say that political economists are uninterested in texts, audiences, or culture. But it also seemed like it would be a potentially popular course on media – and it has been. Over the years, literally hundreds of students have helped to sort through many of the questions posed in the book, offered their thoughts about the Disney phenomenon, as well as sharing their own Disney memories (some of which are included in chapter 7). My thanks to all of them – whether they liked the course or not.

4 More thanks (and no thanks) Many other acknowledgements are due – and some are not. I made few attempts to illicit support from the Walt Disney Company, being familiar with the many rebuffs experienced by researchers doing critical work on Disney. However, a plethora of people offered valuable insights during this project, for there seems to be an abundance of interest in Disney these days. Early on, colleagues in the University of Oregon's Telecommunication and Film Deptartment provided ideas and encouragement, especially Carl Bybee (for the title), Ellen Seiter, Ron Sherriffs, Chris Purdie, and Ron Gregg. During a Fulbright appointment at the University of Copenhagen, I also received useful comments from faculty and students who enrolled in the Danish version of the Disney course. Later on in the process, I received invaluable feedback on specific issues and rough drafts from Susan Davis, Mark Phillips, Bill Kunz, Eileen Meehan, Kim Sheehan, Francis Coogan, Jeremy Alden, Liz James, and Randy Nichols. Research assistance was provided by Ellen

Riordan, John Groves, and Mark Phillips; while a small grant from the University of Oregon's School of Journalism and Communication supported a visit to Disneyland Paris. Thanks also to Matt Dyste, head of Licensing and Merchandising at Oregon, for talking with me about the university's mascot. My appreciation also goes to Tom Guback for handing over his invaluable Disney files, including 30 years of annual reports. Over the last few years, many, many thoughtful individuals (too many to be named here) have forwarded articles, clippings, and email stories, and others have passed along a wide range of Disney paraphernalia (especially Bill Kunz, Jörg Becker, Deb Merskin, and Andrew Jakubowicz).

Photographs were provided by Carlos Calderon, Jeremy Alden, and Andrew Jakubowicz, although many other colleagues also snapped interesting shots in various places around the world, which we were unable to use in the book. My special thanks to Martina Russial, for the use of her Lion King drawing; Peter White, for his special Hidden Mickeys illustration; George "The Tattoo Man" Reiger, for the use of his photo; and, James Victore, for sharing his poster, Disney Go Home.

Again, the people at Polity Press and Blackwell have been patient, professional, and efficient. Special thanks to Jean van Altena, Pam Thomas, Sandra Byatt, and Gill Motley.

1 Introducing the Disney Universe

Special wish: choosing, chasing his final dream.
Thanksgiving: James Simpson just wants to take his family to Disney
World before he dies, which could be within a year.

Register Guard

It was a touching story on the front page of a local newspaper on
Thanksgiving Day, 1997.[1] A man dying of cancer wanted to take his family
to Disney World. His "final dream" could have been almost anything, but
he chose something that has come to represent the ultimate family event.

Apparently, hundreds of local readers recognized his dream and contributed to making it come true. A little over a month after the original story
appeared, the newspaper announced in another headline: "Wish comes
true for dying man, family: Vacation: Donations from hundreds of people
give the Simpsons a trip to Disney World."[2]

How is it possible to understand the significance and meaning of this
phenomenon? What is it about the Disney theme parks in particular, but
Disney in general, that attracts so many children as well as adults? How can
we come to understand the appeal of Disney products?

It cannot simply be magic, as portrayed in Disney stories, or as the
company would like us to believe. For even though Disney provides an
important source of pleasure and entertainment for children and adults, it
is also necessary to understand the process by which Disney's magic and
fantasy are deliberately manufactured – they are produced by one of the
largest media and entertainment corporations in the world.

Since the early 1930s, the Disney company has manufactured stories, characters, and experiences that reinforce the key elements in mainstream US culture. Over the years, Disney stories and images have represented the USA in other countries around the world. Today, Disney films, comics, books, toys, theme parks, and other products are sources of pleasure for many – if not most – young American children, who learn and have reinforced ideas and values that may last a lifetime. Many adults join their children in these forms of leisure, dutifully introducing them to the same stories, characters, values, and ideals, or revisiting these sites on their own, renewing the pleasure and satisfaction experienced as children. Indeed, Disney holds an almost sacred place in the lives of many Americans.

The Disney company started in the late 1920s, as a small entrepreneurial enterprise when Walt Disney and his brother Roy Disney began producing Mickey Mouse cartoons. The company grew gradually, sometimes experiencing financial difficulties, but eventually establishing itself as an independent production company in Hollywood. Never one of the major studios (in fact, the company relied on other companies to distribute its film products), the Disney brothers built a reputation for quality animation, utilizing cutting-edge technological developments such as sound and color.

Despite the independent status of the Disney company in Hollywood, the popularity of Disney's products and characters was instantaneous and unmistakable. Indeed, the image of Mickey Mouse was a global phenomenon by the mid-1930s. Thanks to the international distribution of Disney films and the merchandising efforts that accompanied them, the Disney company developed a reputation that was magnified far beyond the relatively small company's resources.

And that reputation has continued. The aggressive marketing of a multitude of Disney products through a wide range of distribution channels all over the world has contributed to a proliferation of Disney images and characters that could hardly have been imagined in the 1930s. Disney products are almost everywhere.

Disney now represents a far more dominant player in the entertainment business, as the company has successfully diversified far beyond the arena of children's programming. Yet it still maintains its reputation for producing family entertainment that is safe, wholesome, and entertaining. This reputation is even further enhanced by increasingly more vivid and overt portrayals of violence and sexual content in other media fare, some even produced by Disney under other labels. Thus, Disney is able to remain extremely influential, if not dominant, in the marketing of children's and family entertainment, even as it expands into other lines of business.

In 1973, in his book *Mass-Mediated Culture*, Michael Real discussed what had by then become known as the "Disney universe."[3] He argued that the term was appropriate because (1) the Disney organization used it, (2) it signified the "universality" of Disney's products, and (3) the Disney message created "an identifiable universe of semantic meaning."

Despite claims that it merely produces entertainment, the Disney company has created a self-contained universe which presents consistently recognizable values through recurring characters and familiar, repetitive themes. The Disney brand is represented by its products – everything from films and television programs to theme parks and resorts – as well as by the philosophy of the company.

It is possible, then, to identify a "Disney universe" and to study something called "Disney" – the company, its parks, products, and policies, the individuals who manage and work for the company, as well as Disney characters and images, and the meanings they have for audiences.

However, studying Disney can be a challenge. When it is introduced as a topic for discussion, Disney is most often accepted with unqualified approval, and even reverence, by the American public. Many feel that the Disney company is somehow unique and different from other corporations, and its products are seen as innocent and pleasurable. There is a general sense that its product is *only* entertainment, as Walt Disney constantly reminded everyone. It is as though the company and its leaders can do no wrong – after all, they're making so many people so happy. And they do it so well – how can one not be awed by their success?

There is also some hesitancy to discuss Disney as a business, despite the overwhelming emphasis on stockholder value and corporate goals by the company itself. In some settings, calling Walt Disney a "capitalist" would be considered risky, despite his role as head of a profit-motivated company. Furthermore, taking a critical stance towards the company that has created the happiest places on earth may be considered overly pessimistic, not to say downright un-American. After all, why should it be taken so seriously? As we're told continuously, it's *just* entertainment.

Nevertheless, it is important to consider the Disney phenomenon seriously and to insist that it is a legitimate focal point for cultural and social analysis. It is appropriate not only to look more closely at the Disney company and its products, but also to critique their role in our culture. Indeed, with the proliferation of Disney products and the diversification of corporate activities, one must insist that Disney is fair game for serious critical review.

Why another book on Disney?

This is not to say that the Disney phenomenon has gone unnoticed. Indeed, the attention that Walt Disney, the Disney company, and Disney products have received in print is staggering. Several books consist mainly of references to Disney material,[4] while a recent search on the amazon.com website identified 2,922 books with "Disney" in the title. (Of course, many of these are Disney products.) To this list must be added the constant attention that the company and its products receive in the popular press, which has contributed to the Disney phenomenon.

In some academic circles, the study of Disney in particular, and popular culture in general, has been perceived as an irrelevant, frivolous, "Mickey Mouse" occupation. Nevertheless, Disney has been the focus of study in a wide variety of disciplines, with countless books, essays, and articles on Walt Disney, his contribution to animation, the history of the Disney company, and the analysis of its products and their creators.

In the 1930s, cultural pundits and film critics celebrated Disney as art, while members of the Frankfurt School often used Disney characters such as Mickey Mouse and Donald Duck as examples in their discussions of the culture industry. In addition to Michael Real's study, the Disney empire attracted the attention of communications scholars in several classic studies in the 1970s, specifically Ariel Dorfman and Armand Mattelart's *How to Read Donald Duck* and Herbert Schiller's *The Mind Managers*.[5]

More recently, there has been a boom in "Disney studies," as numerous scholars have directed attention to the phenomenon and joined in "the fashionable sport of Disney bashing." Analysis has featured rhetorical, literary, feminist, and psychoanalytic critiques, stressing social issues, such as race and gender representation. Anthropologists, architects, historians, and geographers are also seriously discussing the impact of Disney's worlds (especially the theme parks), considering their aesthetic, cultural, and social implications.

But despite all of this attention and analysis, there is still a need to look at the *entire* Disney phenomenon from a critical perspective.[6] This book will look at the wide range of perspectives that have been used – and must be used – to understand the Disney universe. The overall objective is to encourage analysis of popular culture and its role in society by exploring a specific popular culture phenomenon through various approaches and methodologies.

The continued expansion and popularity of the Disney empire calls for the deliberate integration of political economic analysis with insights drawn from cultural analysis and audience studies or reception analysis, or, in other words, analysis emphasizing the economic as well as the ideological, or production as well as consumption. In the case of Disney, this approach is expressed in the notion of *manufacturing fantasy*.

In chapter 2, different versions of Disney's history will be discussed, as well as the issue of Walt Disney's contribution to the company's development. A political economic analysis of the different sectors of the current Disney empire will be presented in chapter 3, followed by a discussion of the way the company works in chapter 4. Chapter 5 will review the wide range of analysis that has focused on the content of what we will call Classic Disney products, and chapter 6 will consider how some of the same techniques have been applied to the Disney theme parks. Chapter 7 will discuss the reception of Disney by different types of audiences or Disney fans, as well as presenting some examples of how individuals respond to Disney.

Although every detail of the Disney universe cannot be discussed thoroughly, we can still come closer to understanding its significance by looking at the whole phenomenon and utilizing interdisciplinary analytic tools. An integrated, interdisciplinary approach can help us to further understand the popularity of Disney over the years, as well as the significance of Disney as a major contributor to consumer culture in the USA and internationally.

Disney History(ies)

In the truest American Tradition, Walt Disney rose from virtual obscurity to become, through his beloved character creations, film-land's greatest success. . . . by virtue of his unsurpassed imagination, native genius, determination, and resourcefulness, he has utilized all so effectively as to become a world renowned, self-made pioneer in creating highly entertaining, thoroughly delightful, colorful, and edu-cative motion picture spectacles.

Wisdom, 1959

As indicated in the epigraph above,[1] the history of the Disney company has almost always been the story of Walt Disney. From the early 1930s until his death in 1966, Disney received an enormous amount of public attention – probably more than the movie moguls who distributed his cartoons. But the fascination has continued, with numerous biographies appearing since his death, as well as the more expected glorification by the Disney corporation itself. As William McReynolds has observed, there is a "pseudo-religious aura which has come to surround his name before and since his death."[2]

Much of the story was deliberately constructed by Walt Disney himself and was carefully repeated over the years by Disney, his family, and the Disney company.[3] In 1968, Richard Schickel concluded that "Walt Disney's greatest creation was Walt Disney."[4] Joel Taxel echoed these sentiments: "His success in building an empire based on the animated film and in making his name one of the best known in the world was, to most, far more intriguing than any of the products he created."[5]

It may not be surprising that the story of Walt Disney seems to have special, almost sacred, meaning for Americans. Not only does the Disney company actively present him in this special, sacred way, but the legends of Walt and Mickey Mouse have been picked up and repeated endlessly by journalists, historians, and biographers.[6] Even the more critically oriented biographies often attempt to psychoanalyze the man through the products, inevitably concluding with consummate praise for Disney's genius.[7]

Not only does this perpetuate the "great man" version of history, but this ongoing fascination with Disney and his accomplishments tends to deflect attention away from the corporate nature of his enterprise. For example, Leonard Maltin, one of Disney's well-known chroniclers, asks: "why and how did Walt Disney get to the top of the heap and stay there? Most of the answers are to be found in the man himself."[8]

To establish a foundation for understanding the Disney phenomenon, it is necessary to sort through the hagiographies of Walt Disney that rely heavily on this great man approach and attempt to discover his actual impact on the company and its products. Disney obviously owned and clearly controlled the company during his life, as well as playing a very strong leadership role in the company's management for most of that time. Thus, it is sometimes difficult to separate the history of Disney the man from that of Disney the company. Nevertheless, understanding both these Disney histories is essential.

It is also necessary to establish the social context in which Disney and his company developed. It is thus crucial to study the history of the Disney company through the interweaving of instrumental and structural analysis. In brief, instrumental approaches have been used to understand corporations by focusing on individual capitalists, while structural analysis considers corporate activities within the context of more general economic and political contexts. As Graham Murdock has argued, to understand the full dynamics of media corporations, it is essential to use both approaches, examining "the complex interplay between intentional action and structural constraint at every level of the production process."[9]

Drawing on the many biographies and the few corporate histories, this chapter will present an overview of the Disney company during Walt Disney's life, thus establishing a foundation for understanding the Disney universe at the beginning of the twenty-first century.

Walt Disney, the man

Once upon a time . . .

Walter Elias Disney was born in Chicago in 1901, the fourth son in a
family of five children.[10] Struggling to gain financial security, his father
moved the family from Chicago to a farm in Missouri (1906), to Kansas
City (1910), and then back to Chicago (1917). Later in his life, Disney
often referred to his memories of the farm and rural life in Marceline,
Missouri. But the irony, pointed out by some biographers, is that the
family lived in Marceline only a few years; thus Disney's rural roots were
relatively shallow. Nevertheless, Disney "idealized and romanticized" these
memories, which provided the basis for his attachment to small-town
America and its values.

When the family moved to Kansas City, Walt and his older brother,
Roy, apparently suffered from long hours of hard work delivering newspapers for their father's new business, and were also reportedly subjected to
some physical abuse from their straitlaced father. Roy served as an ally and
protector of the younger Walt but, upon reaching maturity, left the family
as two other older brothers had done previously. Thus, despite his fondness
for warm, happy families, Walt Disney's own family life lacked these
qualities. His biographers note that he developed a "creative and lighthearted personality," an inclination towards commercial activities, an
intense desire to succeed, a strong rejection of organized religion, and a
loathing of poverty, as well as faith in practical education and experience.[11]

Disney left home when he was 16 years old, falsifying his age so that he
could join the Red Cross Ambulance Corps. Even though World War I
had virtually ended, he served as a driver and performed other duties in
various locations in France. When he returned to the USA in 1919, he
pursued his interest in drawing at a commercial art firm in Kansas City,
rather than finishing high school. After dabbling with animation for a few
years, he formed his own company, Laugh-O-Gram Films, in 1922, and
started producing the Alice's Wonderland series, which combined animation with live action. It was also the beginning of his collaboration with
the talented artist Ub Iwerks, who joined the Disney enterprise and became
an important part of Disney's future success.

Walt joined his brother Roy in Los Angeles in 1923, as an official
history distributed by the Disney company explains, "with a lot of hopes
but little else." After failing to gain employment with one of the film

studios, Disney started where he had left off in Kansas City by reviving the Alice series. After a New York company agreed to distribute the cartoons, Walt convinced Roy to become his business manager, and the Disney company was officially formed on 16 October 1923. Although at first the company was called The Disney Brothers Cartoon Studio, it soon became the Walt Disney Studio, reflecting the roles that the two brothers would play throughout the history of the company – Walt as the primary, "creative" force, who received the public attention and acclaim, and Roy, who worked behind the scenes, handling finances and tending to the organization.[12]

While the studio produced 56 Alice shorts, another animated series based on a character called Oswald, the Lucky Rabbit, was created in 1927 for Universal Pictures. However, after brief success with ten Oswald shorts in 1927 and 16 in 1928, the Disney brothers discovered that the rights to the character were actually owned by Universal. In addition, the majority of his animators had been lured away from the Disney company to work for the New York distributor. This story is an oft-repeated one in the Disney legend, as it was said to have taught Walt an important lesson: never lose control of your creations. Any number of events in Walt's life and in the Disney histories are explained by this one story.

"It all started with a mouse"

What followed the loss of Oswald also became part of the Disney legend: the birth of Mickey Mouse. The most famous version of the story features Disney and his wife (whom he had first employed at his studio and then married in 1925) traveling by train from New York after learning that Oswald had been lost. Disney created Mickey, at first called Mortimer, and returned to Hollywood with the first cartoon in mind. It is amazing how often this story is repeated.

Another version is presented by one of the official histories distributed by the company: "It was at the Hyperion Studio, after the loss of Oswald, that Walt had to come up with a new character, and that character was Mickey Mouse. With his chief animator, Ub Iwerks; Walt designed the famous mouse."[13] The more careful biographies agree that the creation of The Mouse was a collaboration between Disney and Iwerks; however, Disney took the credit in public. Iwerks animated two cartoons featuring the new character, *Plane Crazy* and *Gallopin' Gaucho*. Yet, the first Mickey Mouse cartoon released was actually the third film produced. *Steamboat Willie* appeared in November 1928 after synchronized sound had been added. Many of the Disney histories credit the addition of sound to Walt, after he viewed the first feature film with sound, *The Jazz Singer*, in 1927. However, another version of the story is that he was "unable to sell (the cartoons) because they were silent films, and sound was revolutionizing the movie industry."[14]

What is indisputable is that Mickey Mouse was an instant success, not only with distributors and theater owners, but also with the public. In his controversial biography of Disney, Marc Eliot notes that there were more sophisticated animated shorts being made at the time. "However, what set Disney's films apart was his ability to produce cartoons that not only talked but made lots of money, and that combination made them highly desirable to the industry leading distributors."[15] The Disney company was able to secure a distribution contract with Columbia Pictures to produce additional Mickey Mouse cartoons, even though the amount received often did not cover the costs, which had increased from around $5,400 to $13,500 for each cartoon by late 1931.[16]

Thus, the Disney brothers found that they needed additional revenue to survive and turned to other sources, especially merchandising. The first arrangement to produce a Mickey Mouse product was a $300 offer to feature The Mouse on writing tablets in 1929, but it was quickly followed by many more. The first formal merchandising contract was with the George Borgfeldt Company in 1930, although apparently there was also a good deal of unlicensed merchandise, especially in Germany, France, England, Italy, Czechoslovakia, and Spain.[17] In 1932, the company hired a dynamic salesman and innovator, Herman "Kay" Kamen, to head the merchandising division, leading to a proliferation of Disney products. An indication of the growing importance of merchandising for the company was the reorganization in late 1929 into four divisions: production, film recording, real estate, and licensing and merchandising (later called Walt Disney Enterprises).[18]

Early Mickey Mouse products were mostly toys and dolls but subsequently expanded to every imaginable kind of product. Especially popular were watches and clocks produced by the Ingersoll–Waterbury Company. By January 1930, Mickey appeared in a comic strip distributed by King Features. Mickey and his friends were also featured in *Mickey Mouse Magazine* (from 1933 to 1940) and numerous books, as well as in a newspaper comic strip. Similar publications appeared in other countries, as Mickey was featured as *Topolino* in Italy and in *Le Journal de Mickey* in France.

Even before the merchandising efforts, Mickey Mouse Clubs had appeared around the country and the world, organized around Saturday movie matinees for children. The company distributed bulletins to theaters explaining how to start clubs in their towns. By 1932, there were one million members worldwide of the Mickey Mouse Clubs, which also served to promote the Disney cartoons and merchandise.[19]

With the success of Mickey Mouse, the studio began production of the Silly Symphonies, a series of short films that experimented with sound, music, and images to create moods and emotions, rather than humor as in other Disney productions. The first of the Silly Symphonies was *The Skeleton Dance* in 1929, followed by *Frolicking Fish*, *Monkey Melodies*, and *Arctic Antics*. Disney was one of the first companies to use Technicolor's color process, producing the first full-color cartoon, *Flowers and Trees*, a Silly Symphony that won the Academy Award for the Best Cartoon for 1932.[20] Another of the Silly Symphonies that attracted special attention was the Disney version of *The Three Little Pigs*, released in 1933. The film not only grossed $125,000 during its first year of release but also became a national sensation. (More discussion of this film is included in chapter 5.)

Other characters emerged from the company's films to become part of the Classic Disney stable, including Minnie Mouse, Mickey's dog Pluto, Goofy, and, to a lesser extent, Clarabelle Cow, Horace Horsecollar, and the villain Pegleg Pete. Donald Duck appeared in one of the Silly Symphonies in 1934 and became one of the company's most popular characters, with his own line of merchandise, including Donald Duck bread, Donald Duck peanut butter, and Donald Duck orange juice.

By 1934, the company employed around 200 people at its Hyperion Avenue location, which was continuously expanding with the addition of offices, stages, and labs. By all accounts, the company had become successful.

Hooray for Hollywood

Only a few of Walt Disney's biographers attempt to establish any context for the company's achievements. Indeed, many profiles give him so much credit for animation innovations that one would think that animation originated with Walt Disney.[21] But, as Watts suggests:

> Disney's success cannot be understood as an isolated event. It unfolded as part and parcel of much larger cultural changes in the early twentieth century. Shaped by the rise of consumerism in the economic realm,

bureaucracy in the social structure, and corporate liberalism in politics, an enormous historical transformation had reworked the meaning of entertainment and the definition of success.[22]

Indeed, motion pictures in general and Disney in particular represented examples of these changes. The Disney company was part of the growing motion picture business that had emerged in the Los Angeles area from around 1910. What is also overlooked in many of the Disney histories is how small the Disney company actually was by comparison with the corporate giants that controlled the film industry at the time. In the early 1930s, the industry was dominated by five fully integrated corporations – Fox, Paramount, Loew's, RKO, and Warner Brothers – that produced and distributed motion pictures to their theater chains around the country. Meanwhile, three smaller companies – United Artists, Columbia, and Universal – produced and distributed films in cooperation with the Big Five.[23]

Although the Disney studio received an enormous amount of public attention and was proclaimed to be an amazing success, it was only a pint-sized midget compared to these other incorporated giants that produced hundreds of films each year and amassed sizable revenues and profits. Under its distribution agreement with United Artists, the Disney company produced between 20 and 25 short films annually, for about $50,000 each, with expected revenues of around $120,000 each. However, distribution costs reduced the ultimate profits for the Disney firm. During the 1930s, the Disneys rarely made a profit of more than $500,000 per year, and this was poured back into production.

Gomery reminds us that the Disney brothers were able to survive for three reasons: (1) distribution deals with some of the major film companies (Columbia, 1929–31, United Artists, 1931–36, and RKO, 1936–54); (2) product differentiation, including short subjects which took advantage of technological innovations such as sound and color; and (3) revenues from merchandising contracts (the company received 2.5 percent royalties on inexpensive products, 5 percent on expensive items).[24] For these reasons, the Disneys were able to hang on as a small Hollywood independent in an industry controlled by much larger, integrated corporations.

Hollywood's Horatio Alger

In spite of the company's small size, the Disney legend grew to become larger than life. The company's success was magnified because of the widespread popularity of its products, as well as the abundant praise heaped upon its leader.

Bryman describes Walt Disney as one of those rare charismatic leaders "who dream up a vision about the need for a product, attract others to that vision and build the organization into an enthusiastic group of adherents."[25] Bryman characterizes him as extremely ambitious, with a perpetually positive attitude and a strong belief in hard work and high-quality products.

But even the most laudatory biographies point out that Disney was also authoritative, moody, and demanding. Some of his employees called him a benevolent dictator and reported various scare tactics that he used to get his way. The more critical histories reveal that "Uncle Walt" (as he became known in later years) was extremely controlling and obsessive in various ways.[26]

There is no doubt, however, that Disney's attributes included a "remarkable capacity to sell his product and himself."[27] He was especially adept at projecting his own image as someone who had become successful through hard work and perseverance. The press picked up his story and ran with it, repeating endlessly the saga of "the Horatio Alger of the cinema" and the self-made man image that Disney cultivated. In 1934, *Fortune* observed that "Enough has been written about Disney's life and hard times already to stamp the bald, Algeresque outlines of his career as familiarly on the minds of many Americans as the career of Henry Ford or Abraham Lincoln."[28]

In spite of his image as a talented artist, Disney actually did little drawing after 1924, when he started working with Ub Iwerks.[29] Disney is reported to have been more than a bit frustrated when asked to sign autographs, as he struggled to duplicate the famous Disney signature that the public came to recognize and expect. However, most accounts agree that Disney's talent was in story editing and development; he seemed to have an innate sense of what would entertain the public and an ability to communicate his ideas to his staff.

Above all, Disney was committed to mass culture. He explained, "I am interested in entertaining people, in bringing pleasure, particularly laughter, to others, rather than being concerned with 'expressing' myself or obscure creative impressions." His attitude, as well as his products, were well-suited to the era described above. For Disney's products incorporated elements of other commercialized forms of entertainment and mass culture: "music, mischief, dance, comedy and heroic melodrama" drawn from popular music, vaudeville comedy, and dance.[30]

Disney's driving passions have been summarized especially well by Watts:

> The imperatives of success and mass culture always directed Disney's path. From the earliest days of his career, he repeatedly confessed the great passions of his life: he was in love with his work and in love with the idea of entertaining a mass audience. His meteoric rise in the 1920s and early 1930s had made him a dynamic success story and a wildly popular entertainer for millions of American consumers.[31]

Disney's Folly

The Silly Symphonies set the stage for animated feature films, an innovation that was accompanied with the usual fanfare and praise for Walt's foresight and ingenuity. As the official history tells us, "Walt Disney was never satisfied with what he had already accomplished."[32]

Actual work on *Snow White and the Seven Dwarfs*, the company's first animated feature, began in 1936, with an estimated budget of $150,000. By the time it was completed in 1937, the cost was $1.5 million, and the film was known as "Disney's Folly." Though many doubted the wisdom of producing an animated feature, *Snow White* was an immediate hit, setting attendance records around the USA, with box office grosses of $8.5 million within its first three months of release. The film industry was pleased as well, awarding Disney a special Academy Award in 1939.

The merchandising and tie-in campaigns that accompanied the film may surprise those who think of such activities as a more recent Hollywood phenomenon. As early as 1936, the company granted over 70 licenses to various companies to produce a wide range of items, including clothing, food, toys, books, phonograph records, and sheet music.[33] Comic books, painting and coloring books, and picture books were sold before the film was released. Also featured were Snow White radios produced by Emerson, Snow White-print corsets, Snow White sliced bread, and Snow White treasure chests for all the Snow White toys. In fact, the merchandising campaign was noted as a "dramatic example of a new force in merchandising."[34] The multitude of products not only brought in revenues but importantly helped to publicize the film and build the Disney reputation.

While continuing to produce several cartoon series based on Mickey Mouse, Donald Duck, Pluto, and Goofy, the studio also worked on new animated features. *Pinocchio* and *Fantasia* were both released in 1940, followed by *Dumbo* (1941), *The Reluctant Dragon* (1941), and *Bambi* (1942).

The animation factory

With the success of *Snow White*, the company grew dramatically. By May 1940, the company's 1,100 employees had moved into a new $3 million studio in Burbank, with 20 separate buildings for the different stages of the animation process. For instance, the Animation and Story departments were separated from the Camera and Inking and Painting buildings, although all were connected via underground tunnels. The new studio represented not only the success of the company, but also the growing rationalization of the animation process. While this specialization was intended to make the operation more efficient, it also increased the bureaucracy at the studio.

Other innovations were incorporated into the animation process, including the pencil test (a method of projecting pencil drawings) and the Leica reel (a method of projecting both completed and uncompleted parts of a project). The studio also adapted the story board, a series of drawings used to depict an entire film, rather than just segments. Other technological developments included the multi-plane camera, a device that incorporated multiple layers of animation, thus providing increased depth and contributing to Disney's constant quest for more realism. The famous artists' school set up at the studio was another innovative feature that helped to eliminate waste, though it also enforced a kind of "uniform technical mastery" among the animators.

Many of these innovations were attributed to Disney, but it is arguable that others at the studio were more responsible for their development. McReynolds noted that Disney had an "unerring appreciation of technical developments and how to use them for profit."[35] As Schickel pointed out, "Disney's gift, from the beginning, was not as is commonly supposed a 'genius' for artistic expression; if he had any genius at all it was for the exploitation of technological innovation."[36]

The company received a good deal of publicity for its new studio, which became known as the "fun factory." People seemed fascinated with the industrial process that created Disney's films, apparently finding it hard to believe that fantasy could be manufactured. Much less attention, however, was focused on the commercial orientation of Disney's fantasy production.

Along with the company's success, its debts had grown as well. So before completing the move to the new Burbank headquarters, the company issued 155,000 shares of preferred stock and 600,000 shares of common stock. Though the company had incorporated in 1929, until now, all its stock remained privately held. In 1938, 45,000 shares were owned by Walt and Lillian Disney, and 30,000 shares by Roy and Edna Disney. While the stock sold quickly and provided needed capital for the company, it diluted the Disneys' ownership control of the company.[37] Yet, by all accounts, Walt was still very much in control of the company's operations, at least until the dramatic events that started unfolding in the early 1940s.

Conflict in Wonderland

By most accounts, the growth of the studio and the move to the new Burbank facilities led to changes in the working conditions at the company. The Disney studios had previously been depicted as a "democratic, collective, creative paradise."[38] Many of the employees agreed that the Disney plant was unique during the 1930s, with a family atmosphere that inspired creativity.

However, by the early 1940s, the studio had lost its charm for at least some of its workers. Salaries were often out of balance, with new animators hired at higher salaries than seasoned veterans. And although the studio was known for its creativity, it was always Walt's personal visions that prevailed. Furthermore, screen credits were provided only for the company's feature films, with "Walt Disney" as the only name attached to the cartoons.

By the end of the 1930s, there was increasing dissatisfaction at the studio, especially due to the inconsistent wage scales, the erratic distribution of bonuses and other forms of compensation, and well as the lack of professional screen credits. The dissatisfaction finally erupted in 1941.

Hollywood had experienced a wave of unionization during the 1930s, with most of the industry's workers being represented by the end of the decade by labor organizations both from within and outside the film industry.[39] The Screen Cartoonists Guild (SCG) had been founded in 1936 to organize the growing number of animators in the industry and, by the early 1940s, had gained contracts at MGM and Schlesinger's animation unit at Warner Brothers. Meanwhile, at the Disney studio, the Federation of Screen Cartoonists was formed as a company union in 1937.

The SCG started organizing at Disney in late 1940 and, by January 1941, was recognized by the National Labor Relations Board (NLRB) as the bargaining unit for animators, story men, directors, and production workers at the studio. The SCG filed formal charges with the NLRB, charging the company with unfair labor practices (including supporting a company union). After Disney fired a group of union activists, the SCG voted to strike in May 1941. At least one-third of the company's employees supported the strike, although it has also been claimed that one-half of the company's workers went out.[40]

By most accounts, the nine-week strike at the fun factory was no fun. Tension grew as physical and verbal conflicts increased the hostility between workers and management. Disney (who almost became involved in a fist fight with the strikers at one point) accused the union leaders of being Communists and "bad seeds." The conflict became especially bitter when the company called on the assistance of infamous labor racketeer Willie Bioff, who was working with the conservative International Alliance of Theatrical Stage Employees (IATSE) at the time.

After the studio closed down completely for nearly a month, the conflict was finally settled in September with assistance from Labor Department arbitrators. It probably helped that Walt had departed in early August on a government-funded tour of South America, which later served as the basis for several films, including *Saludos Amigos* (1943) and *The Three Caballeros* (1945), as well as a wide range of educational films for the Coordinator of Inter-American Affairs.[41]

In the end, enormous damage was done during the labor conflict. As Watts concludes:

> Socially, the strike had destroyed the image of a workers' paradise.... Creatively, the strike exploded the spirit of camaraderie, innovation, and participation that had inspired the wonderful creations of the 1930s. Financially, it blew a large hole in the studio's profits, as production, already curtailed by the growing world crisis, was further reduced.[42]

As labor troubles had surfaced at the studio, so had Disney's more conservative nature. During the Depression, he had adhered to a type of populism that distrusted bankers and the monopolistic practices of big business. But increasingly, he moved from a sentimental to a more paranoid version of populism, becoming vehemently anti-Communist. As Watts explains, he became "a conservative Republican whose intense patriotism, loyalty to the work ethic, suspicion of regulatory government, and support for American individualism had grown steadily more intense."[43]

A lesser-known chapter of Walt Disney's legacy is his role in the formation of the Motion Picture Alliance for the Preservation of American Ideals (MPA), the organization that set the foundation for the Hollywood blacklist. Disney served as the MPA's first vice-president and was featured prominently in publicity about the organization. The MPA has been acknowledged as the inspiration for the House Un-American Activities Committee (HUAC) investigation of Hollywood, which examined film industry notables on their adherence to the Smith Act, which made support of certain political parties illegal. The act was declared unconstitutional many years later, but not before the Hollywood Ten (a group of writers mostly who refused to cooperate with the committee) had been sent to prison, and hundreds of Hollywood workers had lost their jobs, sometimes for being "named" by those who chose to cooperate with the committee and the organizers of the blacklist.

Disney testified at the second set of HUAC hearings in 1947, along with other friendly witnesses such as Ronald Reagan, Gary Cooper, and Adolphe Menjou. Disney explained that the strike at his studio had been organized by Communists, and "throughout the world all of the Commie groups began smear campaigns against me and my pictures." He also stated that communism was "an un-American thing" and had infiltrated labor groups, especially. The well-known Hollywood blacklist had already been established, but Disney's testimony was said to have strengthened it. Meanwhile, the MPA served as "the bulwark of anti-communism in Hollywood" through the 1950s, a period in which hundreds of Hollywood workers lost their industry jobs.[44]

Another aspect of his life that is neglected by most of his biographers is his collaboration with the FBI from at least the 1950s until the end of his life.[45] Disney's FBI file includes a 1954 memo offering the agency "complete access to the facilities of Disneyland for use in connection with official matters and for recreational purposes." The file also includes evidence that Disney was on the agency's Special Correspondents' List. Watts generally downplays the relationships and explains that this was "a largely honorary designation given to friendly community leaders who were willing to talk with the agency's special agent in charge for their region." In other words, he did not serve as a spy, but "simply endorsed the agency's broader agenda of anti-communism during the tense days of the Cold War."[46] Whether or not Disney actively assisted the FBI, his well-documented cooperation with the agency clearly establishes his strong conservative credentials.

World War II: Disney and the government

The bitter labor strike marked the end of what many have called "Disney's golden age."[47] Both *Pinocchio* and *Fantasia* had entailed high costs and suffered at the box office in 1940 due to the loss of foreign markets because of World War II. Several other feature projects even had to be suspended.

And then the war hit home, for both the USA and the Disney operations. The day after Pearl Harbor, US Army troops took over the Disney lot, using the studio (the only one in Hollywood occupied by the military) as a repair and storage facility over the next eight months.[48] But the company also became involved with the war effort through a large number of government films contracted during the conflict. By 1942, over 93 percent of the studio's production was devoted to government projects, including a wide range of animated and live-action films produced for at least six branches of the government.

Military training films included a series of aircraft identification films for the Navy, plus other titles such as *High-Level Precision Bombing*, *Glider Training*, as well as *Dental Care* and *A Few Quick Facts about Venereal Disease*. The studio also produced a number of educational films, such as *Food Will Win the War*, *The Grain that Built a Hemisphere*, and *The New Spirit* (encouraging Americans to pay income taxes).[49]

The company also produced a few propaganda films, primarily satirical pieces such as *Education for Death* (1943) and *Der Fuehrer's Face* (1943). *Victory through Air Power* (1943) was a full-length feature promoting long-range bombing as a key military strategy. However, it was Donald Duck who became the wartime hero at the studio, and was featured as a loyal, dedicated American citizen in short films such as *Commando Duck* and *Home Defense* (1943).[50]

The studio also released a few features during the war, including the South American films and *Bambi* (1942); however, the box office grosses were disappointing. The government work during the war, while ultimately unprofitable, served to keep the studio alive, as well as to diversify the company's filmmaking activities. The ongoing support from the company's primary bank, the Bank of America, also helped the studio through these difficult years.[51]

Postwar period

Disney and his company were shaken by the war, as well as by the damaging labor strife earlier in the decade. In addition, the declining film markets at the end of the 1940s were taking their toll on the entire industry. Watts summarizes the postwar period, observing that "Creativity was blunted, profits disappeared, and the old spirit of joyful innovation nearly evaporated."

To gain some quickly needed revenue, the studio released a few "packaged" features, such as *Make Mine Music* (1946) and *Melody Time* (1948), consisting of recycled bits from previously released cartoons. Live-action productions also became more profitable than animation, although the first one – *Song of the South* (1946) – included some animation. Another economic move was the production of nature films in the *True-Life Adventures* series, beginning with *Seal Island* (1948), which made as much money at the box office as many of the company's animated features. (These films will be discussed further in chapter 5.)

Finally, the studio returned to animated interpretations of fairy tales with *Cinderella* (1950), the first new animated feature since *Bambi* in 1942. Other successes followed, with the live-action feature *Treasure Island* (1950), the first of 63 live-action films produced by Disney over the next 16 years. The late 1940s were a transitional period, as the company recovered from the war and made necessary adjustments to a changing entertainment market. The changes that the Disney company made ultimately allowed them not only to survive but to prosper during the next few decades.

Diversification, Disney-style

During late 1940s, Walt gradually pulled away from the day-to-day management of the studio, relying on his senior animators to develop most of the studio's films. His enthusiasm was reignited, however, by a few projects that evolved during the early 1950s.

Television was becoming the hot, new medium, with 90 percent of American homes having sets by 1960. At first, the Disney company produced a few Christmas specials, beginning with "One Hour in Wonderland," broadcast on NBC in 1950. In October 1954, the weekly series *Disneyland* appeared on ABC, moving to NBC seven years later as *Walt Disney's Wonderful World of Color*.

Disney is often acknowledged as the first executive in Hollywood to recognize the potential of television. The claim is understandable, in that many of the studios did not become active initially by producing television programming or selling their films to the new medium. However, some of the film companies were involved with television technology as early as the 1920s, and many attempted to secure television stations in the late 1940s.[52] Nevertheless, Disney certainly deserves credit for moving into television when it finally became established in the early 1950s and for recognizing its potential value in promoting and diversifying the film business. Walt explained, "Through television I can reach my audience. I can talk to my audience. They are the audience that wants to see my pictures."[53] The television series also allowed the studio to recycle its already released products, just as it rereleased its animated features in theaters every few years, thus reaping further profits at little additional cost.

But television also proved helpful in several ways for Disney's most cherished project – an amusement park that would appeal to adults as well as children. The arrangements with ABC for the Disney television series were apparently prompted by Disney's need for capital to build Disneyland, which eventually opened in Anaheim, California, in 1955. ABC invested $500,000 in the park and became a 35 percent owner, as well as guaranteeing loans of up to $4.5 million. Disney apparently received little support from the Disney company itself but raised the funds from the ABC deal and from loans on the strength of his insurance policies. In 1952, he formed a separate company called Walt Disney Inc., later to become WED Enterprises, to develop the park without involving company funds. Disneyland ultimately cost $17 million, but it was an instant success with one million visitors during its first seven weeks of operation. (More discussion of the development of Disneyland and the other theme parks is included in chapter 7.)

In addition to providing financial backing, *Disneyland*, the television series, became a terrific promotional vehicle for the park, even before it opened. The show was organized around the same four divisions as the park – Fantasyland, Adventureland, Frontierland, and Tomorrowland – and constantly featured updates on the new park. Of course, new content was also developed for the show. For instance, *Davy Crockett* started as a three-part episode, inspired a national merchandising sensation, and was then recycled as two feature films.[54] However, a good deal of the show featured the studio's recycled cartoons and feature films.

In 1955, the company also introduced a daily afternoon television show designed exclusively for children and proclaimed as a "new concept in television programming." *The Mickey Mouse Club* featured the mouse-eared singing and dancing Mousketeers, plus other features that often involved Disney's other products (e.g., Disney cartoons, news about Disneyland). Despite its enormous popularity (at one point, reaching 75 percent of the television sets in the USA and attracting lots of advertising) and the longevity of its theme song, *The Mickey Mouse Club* lasted only three seasons.

In addition to these developments, the company decided finally to distribute its own films, creating Buena Vista Distribution. The move was attributed to Disney's deep concern about maintaining control over his own products, again recalling the earlier Oswald, the Lucky Rabbit episode. But the move into distribution signaled the Disney company's transition from a marginal independent film company to one of the Hollywood majors.

Even though the company may have been slow to take control of its own film distribution, it led the way in the diversification that would characterize the industry for the next few decades. As Schickel argues, the Disney company had a head start on the rest of the industry. While the larger, integrated majors were dealing with the rising competitive threat of television, as well as the loss of their theaters due to the Paramount decrees, the Disney company was diversifying its film products, as well as its overall business.[55] Furthermore, by the beginning of the 1960s, the company was integrating its film, television, theme park, and merchandising businesses, thus laying the foundation for the Disney synergy that blossomed in the 1980s and 1990s, which will be discussed further in the next few chapters. In addition, while the US film industry was also extremely active in international film markets, often dominating the screens in some countries, the Disney company was especially successful at selling and promoting its products globally. By 1954, it was estimated that one-third of the world's population had seen at least one Disney film.

By the 1960s, the market for short cartoons had diminished, and the company moved much more aggressively into live-action films. Disney established a regular cast of stars who appeared in "wacky comedies" such as *The Shaggy Dog* (1959), *The Absent-Minded Professor* (1961), and *Follow Me, Boys!* (1966), literary adaptations such as *Swiss Family Robinson* (1960), and animal adventures such as *That Darn Cat* (1965). However, the most successful film of this period was *Mary Poppins* (1964), a live-action/animation version of the novel, which made $31 million in the USA, and $45 million worldwide, as well as being nominated for 13 Academy Awards. Animated features also continued, with *One Hundred and One*

Dalmatians (1961), *The Sword in the Stone* (1963), and *The Jungle Book* (1967).

Walt Disney's reputation blossomed yet again with the success of *Disneyland*, the television series, as well as with the continued success of the studio's animated features. Even before the opening of the park, *Time* magazine called him "one of the most influential men alive." Indeed, Uncle Walt's face and "homespun voice" became especially well known due to his role as weekly host of *Disneyland*.

Another development around this time was, as the official history notes, "the culmination of all Walt Disney had learned during his long movie-making career." The company had created its own version of robotics, called Audio-Animatronics, enabling lifelike robots to speak, move, sing, and dance. People could be brought back to life in an Audio-Animatronic production. For instance, Abraham Lincoln could recite the Gettysburg address again, and do it perfectly 100 times a day.

The technology made its first appearance at Disneyland with the Enchanted Tiki Room. Disney then made arrangements for exhibits featuring the Audio-Animatronic technology at the New York World Fair in 1964. General Electric, Ford, and Pepsi-Cola agreed to fund exhibits featuring their names, as well as moving them to Disneyland after the fair ended. The corporations gained promotion, but the Disney company gained revenues as well as new attractions for the theme park without the cost of creating them. (Further discussion of these kinds of corporate alliance will be presented in chapter 7.)

By 1965, plans had begun for another Disney theme park. The aim was to build a park that would serve the East Coast, but without the physical limitations of the Anaheim site. Using several assumed names, Disney purchased 28,000 acres of land near Orlando, Florida, at around $200 per acre – a price that would have been considerably higher had Disney involvement been known. (More discussion of the company's Florida operations will be presented in chapter 6.)

Walt Disney World opened in October 1971, with enough space to create not just one park, but an expansive "resort destination." It would eventually include EPCOT, but not in the form originally envisioned by Disney, who imagined the Experimental Prototype Community of Tomorrow as a futuristic city where people would actually live. (His dream emerged many years later, however, as the community called Celebration, which will be discussed further in chapters 3 and 6.) EPCOT became an exhibit featuring snapshots of different countries in world pavilions and corporate visions of the future at Walt Disney World. However, Walt Disney did not live long enough to see the world that would bear his name.

Genius on ice?

Walt Disney was 65 on 15 December 1966, when he died after an acute circulatory collapse following surgery for lung cancer. His death prompted extensive adulation worldwide, as the popular press sang his praises once again. Jackson cites Eric Sevareid's eulogy on *CBS Evening News*:

> He was an original; not just an American original, but an original, period. He was a happy accident; one of the happiest this century has experienced; and judging by the way it's been behaving in spite of all Disney tried to tell it about laughter, love, children, puppies and sunrises, the century hardly deserved him. He probably did more to heal or at least to soothe troubled human spirits than all the psychiatrists in the world. There can't be many adults in the allegedly civilized parts of the globe who did not inhabit Disney's mind and imagination at least for a few hours and feel better for the visitation.[56]

The acclaim that Disney received during his life was far-reaching. As reported in one of many biographies of Walt on the company's website:

A pioneer and innovator and the possessor of one of the most fertile imaginations the world has ever known, Walt Disney, along with members of his staff, received more than 950 honors and citations from every nation in the world, including 48 Academy Awards® and seven Emmys® in his lifetime. Walt Disney's personal awards included honorary degrees from Harvard, Yale, the University of Southern California, and UCLA; the Presidential Medal of Freedom; France's Legion of Honor and Officer d'Académie decorations; Thailand's Order of the Crown; Brazil's Order of the Southern Cross; Mexico's Order of the Aztec Eagle; and the Showman of the World Award from the National Association of Theatre Owners.[57]

However, certain aspects of Disney's life have been consistently under-emphasized or simply left out of most accounts. As Bryman suggests, there was some "ambiguity about Walt's status as a businessman"; for instance, in most accounts, the company's extensive merchandising activities are neglected.[58] Yet, there is considerable evidence that Walt Disney was interested and involved in the business side of the company, not merely in artistic or other kinds of success. Disney once advised: "Don't create potboilers. Create masterpieces. There's such a big market for master-pieces."[59] In 1953, over the objections of his brother, Roy, he set up a company to control the rights to his name. Retlaw – Walter spelled backwards – received 5 percent of the income received by the company from merchandising and, by the 1960s, was drawing around $500,000 each year.[60] Disney died a rich man.

Jackson writes: "Walt Disney, the man, may be gone. However, the myth he created remains very much alive." As noted at the beginning of this chapter, many of the myths have been perpetuated through biographies that accept the Disney legacy without question. Given the ongoing predilection for "great man history," as well as the growing fascination with celebrity biographies, the pseudo-religious profiles of Walt Disney will probably continue.

As Bryman observes, " 'Walt Disney' is also in a sense a social construc-tion – a product of his own and others' efforts at creating a public face and a personal biography that would serve his business's aims."[61] In other words, the Walt Disney myth benefits the company and will continue to be promoted as such. Indeed, the company's website now includes the "Walt Disney Family Museum," which includes "Walt's Story," "Walt's Thoughts," a "Family Album," film clips, a "Walt Disney Dictionary," more detailed biographical material by historians Katherine and Richard Greene, and other special features. The site is produced by the Walt Disney Family Foundation, a non-profit organization that was founded in 1995 "to promote and produce serious discussion, writing, and scholarship about the life, work, and philosophy of Walt Disney."[62] Of course, there is also a gift shop, where various Disney biographies and other books can be purchased on-line.

There is a fairly widespread rumor that Walt's body is on ice some-where, waiting to be revived cryogenically when medical science becomes capable of healing his fatal affliction.[63] Whether or not this is true, it is hard to believe that among the 1,700 robots at the theme parks, there are not Audio-Animatronic versions of Disney, strategically placed at each theme park to greet guests and tell them his version of Disney history.

Table 2.1 Disney company profits, 1941–1970 (in $ million)

1941	(0.8)	1951	0.4	1961	4.5
1942	(0.2)	1952	0.5	1962	6.6
1943	0.4	1953	0.5	1963	7.0
1944	0.5	1954	0.7	1964	7.0
1945	0.4	1955	1.4	1965	11.0
1946	0.2	1956	2.6	1966	12.4
1947	0.3	1957	3.6	1967	11.3
1948	(0.1)	1958	3.9	1968	13.1
1949	(0.1)	1959	3.4	1969	15.8
1950	0.7	1960	(1.3)	1970	22.0

Source: "Mickey Mouse is 50," *Economist*, 7 July 1973, pp. 68–9, from Moody's Industrial Manual and Annual Reports

The Disney corporate legacy

Of course, even without Audio-Animatronic Walts, the Disney myth, as well as the Disney corporation, lives on. Even though the years immediately following Walt's death may have been uninspired, the corporation survived. By the late 1960s, the company had established a strong diversified base, distributing its own films and television programming and generating revenues from merchandising and theme parks. By 1965, the company reported profits of $11 million (see table 2.1).

However, around this time, only 45 percent of the company's revenues were from film rentals. By the mid-1970s, the company had become even more reliant on park revenues and was proving to be rather sluggish, both in moving into newly developing distribution technologies (such as cable and home video) and in producing a wider range of media products. Perhaps Walt would have inspired the company to adjust to these changes. Perhaps not.

The aim of this chapter has been to sort out the background of the Disney company that emerges from the inflated and mythical depictions of its namesake. Accordingly, Douglas Gomery's summary of the Disney company provides fitting closure:

> The Disney company has not been a success story from the beginning. Like other capitalist operations it has had its ups and downs, heavily influenced

by the uncontrollable factors of technical change, the business cycle, and war.

In the end we need to abandon the "great man" version of history. Walt was no genius, nor is Michael Eisner. We are the fools if we ascribe all the actions and strategies of a company to one man or woman. The Disney company is simply another capitalist enterprise with a history best understood within the changing conditions of twentieth-century America.[64]

The next chapter discusses how the company adjusted to the entertainment world of the late twentieth century and established the Disney empire.

The Disney Empire

Disney's overriding objective is to create shareholder value by continuing to be the world's premier entertainment company from a creative, strategic and financial standpoint.

www.disney.com/Investor Relations

Success tends to make you forget what made you successful . . . We have no obligation to make art. We have no obligation to make a statement. To make money is our only objective.

Michael Eisner, 1981 staff memo

To understand the Disney phenomenon, it is crucial to study Disney, the corporation. In other words, to understand Disney's brand of fantasy, we must understand how it is manufactured and marketed, and by whom.

Political economy is one of the approaches that has been used to examine these issues. A few general definitions may be helpful in understanding how political economy has been applied to the study of media. In the 1960s, Dallas Smythe argued that the central purpose of applying political economy to communications was to evaluate the effects of communications agencies in terms of the policies by which they are organized and operated, and to study the structure and policies of communications institutions in their social settings. Smythe further delineated research questions emanating from policies of production, allocation or distribution, and capital, organization, and control.[1] In the 1970s, Murdock and Golding defined political economy of communications as the study of communication and media as commodities produced by capitalist industries.[2] In *The Political Economy of Communication*, Vincent Mosco has defined this version of political economy as "the study of the social relations, particularly power relations, that mutually constitute the production, distribution and consumption of resources."[3]

Although analyzing the political economy of media is not sufficient to fully understand the meanings and impact of cultural products, to many it is an indispensable point of departure. Especially for popular culture production, economic factors set limitations and exert pressures on the commodities that are produced (and influence what is not produced), as well as how, where, and to whom these products are (or are not) distributed.

These issues have everything to do with the products manufactured by the Disney corporation. As Michael Eisner once explained to Disney stockholders, "I have always believed that the creative process must be contained in what we call 'the financial box' – financial parameters that creative people can work in – but the box is tight, controlled and responsible. Finance has the key to the box."[4] In yet another lesson in political economy, the handbook used at The Disney University explains: "Disney is a business. As a business we are accountable to our stockholders to produce a profit. But in order to make money, we have to get the public to consume our product. And once we do that, we have to invest our money wisely to maintain our business."[5]

While some of the academic studies of Disney acknowledge the commercial character of the Disney phenomenon, unless the study is primarily oriented to a business audience, relatively little context is provided to understand the extent of Disney's empire or its corporate strategies. Grover and Taylor offer detailed financial discussions of the transition period during the 1980s, but their discussions are aimed mostly at the business community. Meanwhile, Gomery and Lewis have presented useful discussions of the corporate characteristics of the company through the early 1990s.[6] A few other studies firmly ground their analysis in economic considerations – for instance, Fjellman's interesting and refreshing discussion of Disney, commodities, and consumption, and Bryman's coverage of economic factors in his discussion of Walt Disney World.[7] However, these are rare examples among a glut of analyses that overlook the business side of the Disney universe.

This chapter will present the Disney empire at the end of the twentieth century – its holdings, its owners, and its managers. The framework for this discussion is drawn from political economy, which sets the stage for analyzing the allure of Disney's brand of fantasy. The chapter presents an overview of the various types of activities encompassed by the Disney enterprise, briefly discussing the period after Walt Disney's death, but emphasizing the 1990s – or, as company promotional material calls it, the Disney Decade.

The evolution of corporate Disney

In Walt's shadow

As noted in the last chapter, the company had developed a diversified foundation by the 1960s, with the Disney brand firmly established in a wide range of film products (live action and animation), as well as television, theme parks, and merchandising. The Disney firm also benefited from a policy of rereleasing its popular (already amortized) feature films every few years, thus reaping additional profits with minimal additional expenditures. For instance, *Snow White and the Seven Dwarfs* was rereleased in 1952, 1958, and 1967, amassing an additional $50 million.

Roy Disney, Donn Tatum (previously vice-president of administration), and Card Walker (formerly in marketing) served as the management team until 1971 with some success. Film releases included *The Jungle Book* (1967), *Winnie the Pooh and the Blustery Day* (1968) – the beginnings of a franchise that would become especially lucrative during the 1990s – and *The Love Bug* (1969). Roy Disney saw Walt Disney World open in October 1971 but died a few months later.

After Roy's death, Tatum moved into the chairman position, and Walker became president. By that time, however, the company had become even more oriented to recreation and real estate than to entertainment, as exemplified by the theme park expansion and an ambitious plan to develop a mountain resort in Mineral King, California (which eventually failed).

Meanwhile, the film division was turning out mainly box office duds, including the not very notable *The Apple Dumpling Gang*, *The Unidentified Flying Oddball*, *Night Crossing*, *Something Wicked This Way Comes*, and *Trenchcoat*. Even more successful films, such as *Tron* and *The Black Hole*, as well as animated features such as *Robin Hood* (1973), *The Rescuers* (1977), and *The Fox and the Hound* (1981), fell far short of previous Disney successes. Part of the reason may have been the attempt to cling to the past, attempting to reproduce successful Disney films and avoid the changes

Table 3.1 Walt Disney Productions: revenues, income, and stock values, 1970–1983

Year	Assets (in $ million)	Revenues (in $ million)	Net Income (in $ million)
1970	275.2	167.1	21.7
1971	505.2	175.6	26.7
1972	617.2	329.4	40.2
1973	687.2	385.0	47.7
1974	751.5	429.8	48.5
1975	782.6	520.0	61.7
1976	873.9	583.8	74.5
1977	964.4	629.8	81.9
1978	1,083.1	741.1	98.3
1979	1,196.4	796.7	113.7
1980	1,347.4	914.5	135.1
1981	1,610.0	1,005.0	121.4
1982	2,102.8	1,030.2	100.0
1983	2,381.1	1,307.3	93.1

Source: Walt Disney Productions, Annual Reports, 1970–1983

being adopted by the rest of the industry. For instance, the management turned down proposals for *Raiders of the Lost Ark* and *ET: The Extra-Terrestrial* – both films that became huge box office hits. By the early 1980s, Disney's share of the box office was less than 4 percent.

Moreover, the company seemed to be moving into new media outlets at a leisurely pace. By the early 1980s, much of the film industry had started to adjust to the introduction of cable and home video, seeing them as new opportunities for distribution of theatrical motion pictures, as well as opportunities for new investments.[8] The Disney company made a few moves in this direction, with the launching of the Disney Channel in April 1983 and an adult-oriented film label, Touchstone, inaugurated in 1984 with the release of *Splash*. However, by the mid-1980s, most analysts agreed that the company's management was basically "sitting on its assets," trying to "do what Walt would have done" and not doing a very good job of it. (See table 3.1.)

Finally, in 1984, Disney's uninspired management was challenged by a group of outside high-profile investors and eventually lost control of the company. Grover, Taylor, and Lewis have presented detailed descriptions of this complex period, however, so only the highlights will be covered here.

By November 1983, the Disney company appeared to be a likely takeover target because of its weak condition and undervalued stock. Roy Disney Jr, who held 1.1 million shares of the company, made the first move by resigning from the board in March 1984, as well as buying more of the company's stock. The feeding frenzy was on, as the company appeared ripe for takeover. A group of corporate raiders who recognized the value of the enterprise started accumulating huge blocks of Disney stock and jockeying for position to take over the company. In the end, the billionaire Bass brothers of Fort Worth, Texas, invested nearly $500 million in Disney, preventing a hostile takeover and the possible dismantling of the company. Bass Brothers Enterprises ended up with around 25 percent of the Disney stock, enough to control the company and to appoint their own managers.

The New Disney

A new management team was installed by the new owners, who looked to experienced players in the entertainment business to help turn the company around. Most of the new executives, who became known as "Team Disney," came from either Paramount Pictures or the Marriott Company (Bass interests). Michael Eisner, former head of Paramount, was appointed Chief Executive Officer, although other studio heads were reported to have been considered.[9] While some viewed Eisner as a surprising choice, one writer observed that he was "more Walt than Walt Disney." In fact, several accounts have compared the two men, observing that both represented (or at least projected the image of) strong family men and charismatic leaders.[10] Although in many ways, Eisner is not at all like Walt – he is upper class, from the East Coast, urban, and Jewish – he assumed the role of company leader and spokesman and has been credited with much of the company's success since the mid-1980s. (Plenty of detail on Eisner's rise to glory is provided in his highly promoted autobiography, *Work in Progress*.[11])

Team Disney also included former Warner Brothers' vice-chairman Frank Wells, a Rhodes scholar and lawyer who served as Disney's President and Chief Operating Officer until his death in 1994. Also from Paramount were Jeffrey Katzenberg, who became head of the Film Division, and Helene Hahn, who took over the Business and Legal Affairs Department.

As major stockholders, the Bass brothers assured these managers that

Table 3.2 Walt Disney Company: revenues, income, and stock values, 1984–1999

Year	Assets (in $ million)	Revenues (in $ million)	Net income (in $ million)
1984	2,739.4	1,655.9	97.8
1985	2,897.3	2,015.4	173.5
1986	3,121.0	2,165.8	247.3
1987	3,806.3	2,876.8	444.7
1988	5,108.9	3,438.2	522.0
1989	6,657.2	4,594.3	703.3
1990	8,022.3	5,843.7	824.0
1991	9,428.5	6,112.0	636.6
1992	10,861.7	7,504.0	816.7
1993	11,751.1	8,529.2	299.8
1994	12,826.3	10,055.1	1,110.4
1995	14,605.8	12,151	1,380.1
1996	36,626	18,739	1,214
1997	38,497	22,473	1,966
1998	41,378	22,976	1,850
1999	43,679	23,402	1,368

The company changed its name from Walt Disney Productions to The Walt Disney Company in 1986.
Source: Walt Disney Company, Annual Reports, 1984–1999

they would receive support for at least five years. And over those five years and beyond, Team Disney has (for the most part) done a bang-up job of managing the Disney company for its owners. Immediately after the team was put in place, it proceeded to break a strike at Disneyland and fire 400 employees. Other cost-cutting measures and strategies were also introduced, as will be discussed below. But the real evidence of Team Disney's achievements for Disney's owners is in the value of the company's stock and its balance sheets. From 1983 to 1987, annual revenues more than doubled, profits nearly quintupled, and the value of Disney's stock increased from $2 billion to $10 billion; by 1994, it was worth $28 billion. By 1998, the company revenues totaled nearly $23 billion, assets were over $41 billion, and net income was $1.85 billion.[12] (See table 3.2.)

Since the new ownership/management team took over in 1984, the

Disney empire has extended its tentacles more widely and tenaciously than ever before. While drawing on valuable assets and previous policies, Team Disney also introduced new strategies which must be understood in the context of the entertainment business of the 1990s.[13] As with the other major Hollywood companies, Disney's expansion did not depend solely on motion pictures, but on a wide array of business activities in which the new management team aggressively exploited the Disney brand name, as well as diversifying outside the traditional Disney label.

Team Disney rejuvenated the sagging corporation through a variety of new policies, which are summarized quite well by Knowlton:[14]

- reviving the traditional Disney (by repackaging existing products and creating new animated features)
- modernizing some Disney characters (for instance, "Modern Minnie" and Goofy as a father)
- introducing more diverse product lines (for instance, adult films released by Touchstone)
- implementing severe cost cutting (especially on feature films)
- introducing dramatic price increases at the theme parks
- employing new technological developments (such as computer animation)

However, Team Disney also emphasized at least four other related strategies that the Disney company had already developed.

1 Corporate partnerships   The company became especially reliant on various kinds of strategic alliances in the 1950s with the construction of Disneyland. As more theme parks and diverse activities were added, more partnerships emerged. Examples abound at the theme parks, especially at EPCOT, where exhibits are sponsored by AT&T, Exxon, and General Motors. (The company received about $100 million each year from EPCOT alone at the time Team Disney took over.) The company has also relied heavily on revenues from licensing their characters to other companies, which might be considered as a kind of corporate alliance.

Team Disney milked these partnerships even further, rearranging the EPCOT licenses to add further benefits for the Disney company and moving to more advantageous partnerships when possible. Gomery reports that, within two years, funds from these participatory agreements had doubled.[15]

Other important examples include the agreement between Disney and

McDonald's, establishing a ten-year formal relationship. Disney tie-ins are featured at McDonald restaurants, which also were added at the theme parks. Meanwhile, Delta Airlines represents the "official airline of Disney World," while National Car Rental is Disney's official car rental company. And while technically not a "strategic alliance," it is interesting that Disney is still involved with the Bank of America, a relationship that has existed since the 1930s.[16] The company maintains credit agreements with the bank, and the Bank of America is the official bank at the theme parks.

2 Limiting exposure   While the Disney company has relied on corporate partnerships as a way of limiting investments in some projects, other sources of funding have been pursued. One example was the US government contracts for film production during World War II. Even though the company may not have made large profits, the work sustained Disney through difficult times. Team Disney has implemented an even wider range of strategies to use other people's money and to limit the company's exposure. For instance, after the transition period in the late 1980s, the company's financial experts arranged several schemes for limited partnerships to produce feature films. Another example was the funding of Euro Disneyland, which was possible with the assistance of the French government. (More in the next chapter.)

3 Diversified expansion   In Disney's *1996 Annual Report*, Eisner listed the businesses that had been added to Disney's operation since 1984, which provides a good index of the company's diversification activities during the last decade. They included the following:

> international film distribution; television broadcasting and station ownership; expanded ownership of cable systems; radio and radio network broadcasting and ownership of radio stations; newspaper, magazine and book publishing; the Disney Stores; the convention business; live theatrical entertainment; home video production; interactive computer programs and games; online computer programs; sites on the World Wide Web; ownership of professional sports teams; telephone company partnership (Americast) to produce and provide programming for distribution over home telephone lines; Disney Regional Entertainment, and Disney Cruise Lines.[17]

Many of these kinds of businesses have also been added by other film and entertainment companies, in attempts to take advantage of new and emerging technologies. But Disney has been especially active in diversifying its business activities.

4 Corporate synergy Not only has Disney added this wide range of corporate activities, but the company has linked these different business endeavors under the Disney brand (and, more recently, the ABC and ESPN brands). Their aim has been clearly stated: to "exploit the most profitable niches and synergies in the franchise." So, not only was Team Disney busy diversifying, they became masters at business cross-fertilization, and perhaps the quintessential masters of synergy, as we will explore in the next chapter.

In these ways, Team Disney rebuilt the Disney company. However, it might also be noted that the management team was able to extend the company's assets because this was a particularly strong economic period, in which government deregulation allowed new media and entertainment technologies to multiply and prosper. Team Disney was able to take advantage of these factors, building the Mouse House (as the company became known in Hollywood) into a diversified and profitable media and entertainment giant.

The Disney Decade

When Team Disney boldly proclaimed the 1990s as "The Disney Decade," some may have scoffed at their effrontery. Who would have guessed what the Mouse House would accomplish in only ten years?

During the early years of the Disney Decade, the company continued to expand and prosper, utilizing the strategies noted above. In 1991, the company ranked in the top 200 US corporations in terms of sales and assets and was forty-third in terms of profits. The company's stock was worth $16 billion.

But despite $1.1 billion in profits, over $10 billion in revenues, and becoming the first film company to gross over $1 billion annually in domestic box office, a gloomy shadow fell over the Magic Kingdom in 1994. Wells died in a helicopter accident, Eisner had heart surgery, Euro Disney (which opened in 1992) was suffering huge losses, and a proposal for a new historic theme park was getting hammered by nearly everyone. (More on these last two developments later in this chapter.) It looked like the company was running out of magic and the Disney Decade was doomed.

Then in July 1995, the company stunned Wall Street and the media with the dramatic $19 billion takeover of Capital Cities/ABC. The move greatly enhanced the company's position in television, sports programming, and international marketing, as well as adding publishing and multimedia to its operations (more on all of these areas to follow). Thus, Disney became – at least for a short while – the world's largest media company, with $16.5 billion in annual revenues. As a financial analyst noted after the takeover, "Disney is the benchmark that all other entertainment companies are going to have to value themselves off."[18]

During the last few years of the Disney Decade, the company continued to expand, adding more on-line activities and additional features at Walt Disney World, including the Animal Kingdom. The company also sold off most of the publications that had been acquired as part of the Capital Cities deal. And even though a few clouds had appeared by the end of the Disney Decade, the company was quietly confident and looking forward to the new millennium. Eisner's 1998 letter to stockholders ends on an atypically cautious note, yet still reiterates the primary goals of the corporation:

> To be sure, the years of the 21st century will include ups and downs, just as did the years of the 20th. But, through all our fiscal seasons, I am confident that, over the long term, Disney will continue to be a leader in offering creative new ways – and creative old ways – for people to spend their most precious possession: their time.[19]

Before we look more closely at the company's businesses, we need to return to the often-neglected question of ownership and control, as well as consider the primary objectives of the Walt Disney Company.

Owners and managers

As a rule, Walt Disney and others downplayed his role as a capitalist, presenting him and his company as interested primarily in creating innovative forms of entertainment, diverting attention away from the Disney company as a profit-motivated enterprise. Although the new Disney company attempts to perpetuate the traditional Disney image, other goals seem far more apparent.[20]

The company's website states plainly, "Disney's overriding objective is to create shareholder value."[21] But who are these shareholders? Who actually owns the Disney company? And who benefits from Disney's accumulation of wealth? We might also ask who actually makes decisions for the company, the owners or the managers?

According to a widely accepted myth, corporate America is said to be controlled by millions of individual stockholders. But even though stock ownership may be widely dispersed over a large number of different

Table 3.3 Dominant Disney shareholders, 2000

Shareholder	No. of shares
Bass Brothers	(unavailable)
Warren Buffett	22.5 million
Roy E. Disney	17.7 million
Michael Eisner	12.3 million
Thomas Murphy	3.2 million

Source: Walt Disney Company, 2000 Proxy, p. 4
(does not include shares held by family members or other shares in which ownership is "disclaimed")

shareholders, an extremely small group of individuals still own the bulk of the stock in American corporations. Furthermore, control of specific corporations is often in the hands of those who control the largest blocks of stock.[22] Numerous Congressional studies in the 1970s found that control is possible with ownership of as little as 5 percent of the shares of a corporation. Thus, the Securities and Exchange Commission (SEC) still requires publicly-held corporations to report those stockholders with more than 5 percent shareholdings.

But what about Disney's stockholders? Who are they? A Disney executive once told a group of potential filmmakers that decisions about Disney films were made to benefit "all of those children who will finance their education through their Disney stock." The audience cheered. It was a touching moment. Of course, it is possible that many of the 588,000 shareholders benefit handsomely from their holdings in the Disney company, even to the point of financing their expensive college degrees.[23] However, some of Disney's stockholders benefit more than others, and only a few have the potential for controlling the corporation's decision-making process due to their ownership of large blocks of stock. These owners possess far more control than is typically acknowledged by the company, the popular press, or some academic sources. The focus of attention is nearly always on Michael Eisner and other managers, rather than on the owners of large blocks of Disney stock. But this may not be that unusual, as it is often a difficult task to track large blocks of stock, even for publicly held corporations. Table 3.3 includes some of Disney's largest shareholders; however, the difficulties of obtaining accurate information must be emphasized.

As noted previously, Bass Brothers Enterprises became the largest shareholder in the company in 1984, controlling around 25 percent of Disney's stock. The family includes four brothers, who have used the fortune of their oil man father to invest in oil, casinos, and real estate, as well as for corporate raids on Wall Street companies. In 1997, *Forbes* reported the family's net worth as $6 billion, though it is difficult to identify many of their actual investments, because the brothers are obsessively secretive and generally remain out of the limelight (as opposed to the Hollywood crowd, who thrive on it). However, Sid Bass appears to have been the brother most involved with the family's Disney interests.

The initial investment in Disney – which was reported to be $478 million – immediately boosted the Bass fortune, as a capital gain of $850 million was reported only two years later. Taylor concludes that the Disney investment turned out to be "the single most lucrative deal they ever put together, and it is undoubtedly one of the most successful financial maneuvers in modern times."[24] The family has sold some of its interest in the company over the years. In 1991, the Bass holdings were reported to represent 18.6 percent of Disney's stock, valued at $5.5 billion. The 1995 Disney Proxy Statement reported that the Bass Management Trust owned 6.02 percent of the total common stock, while the next year, a SEC 13D document reported that the trust owned 4.6 percent. It is possible that the Bass family was still the largest stockholder in the Disney corporation in early 1999, even though the Proxy Statement claimed that no single person or group was beneficial owner of more than 5 percent of the company's stock. This was contradicted by information included in material from Disclosure Inc. (31 Jan. 1999), which listed one owner with 14.4 percent holdings.

While none of the Bass family has served on the board of directors or as a manager of the Disney company, the power they have held should not be underestimated. In fact, the Bass brothers' ownership involvement in the company represents a good example of the allocative control that major stockholders typically hold over corporations. It is clear that the Bass interests approved Eisner and Wells as chief managers of the corporation, as well as receiving continuous reports from Eisner about the company's activities. Initially, the Bass brothers provided their own representative to the management team when Al Checchi, formerly with the Marriott company, became a Disney executive. Their involvement in decision making has not been in the day-to-day operations of the corporation (or operational control), but in major decisions involving mergers, acquisitions, and other key events. For instance, many sources reported that Sid Bass was involved in the decision to take over Capital Cities/ ABC in 1995.

Another major stockholder has been Warren Buffett, who had a large investment in Capital Cities stock and thus became a major player in Disney after the merger. In late 1998, Buffett's Berkshire Hathaway Inc. was reported to hold 22.5 million Disney shares. Both Buffett and Sid Bass were powerful enough in December 1997 to be called "ex officio board members" by Eisner, who invited them to attend at least one board meeting that year. Eisner explained: "You have a pretty large shareholder representation there, making sure we do it as good as we can."[25]

Eisner's comments should be seen in light of the criticism launched against him for the composition of Disney's board of directors. After 13 percent of Disney shareholders voted against the reelection of five directors at their annual meeting, *Business Week* named the company the worst board of directors in America in its second annual analysis of the state of corporate governance in 1997. The publication cited institutional investors and other experts who noted that the Disney board was a "meek, handpicked group, many of whom have long ties to Eisner or the company." (See table 3.4.)

Technically, corporate boards are elected by the stockholders; yet again, some stockholders have more clout than others. It is possible to find major stockholders represented on corporate boards; however, this is not always the case, and it has not been the case with the Bass brothers, for instance. Nevertheless, the allegations made about Eisner's chosen few is relevant not only to the question of control and power within the corporation, but also to the distribution of corporate profits. These issues have been the focus of attention at several recent annual stockholders' meetings, when institutional investors have proposed changes in the board's composition and have challenged the colossal executive compensation that the Disney executives regularly receive.

Large stockholders are not the only beneficiaries of the Disney company's financial success. Like many executives of large corporations these days, some of Disney's managers receive sizable salaries, in addition to stock options pegged to improvements in the value of the company's stock. However, Disney's executives have received special attention because of the size of their compensation. While Michael Eisner's salary has been set at $750,000 per year, he also receives bonuses pegged to the company's net income.

The amount that this one executive has received is staggering, to say the least. In 1992, Eisner sold $32.6 million in Disney stock and held remaining

Table 3.4 Walt Disney Company Board of Directors, 2000

Board member	Affiliation	Previous positions or ties to Michael Eisner
Reveta Bowers	Head of School, Center for Early Education	Principal of elementary school attended by Eisner's children
Roy E. Disney	Vice-chairman, The Walt Disney Company	
Michael D. Eisner	Chairman and Chief Executive Officer, The Walt Disney Company	
Judith Estrin	Chief Technology Officer and Sr VP, Cisco Systems, Inc.	
Stanley P. Gold	President and Chief Executive Officer, Shamrock Holdings, Inc.	
Sanford M. Litvack	Sr Exec VP and Chief of Corporate Operations, The Walt Disney Company	
Ignacio E. Lozano, Jr	Chairman, Lozano Communications	
George J. Mitchell	Special Counsel, Verner, Liipfert, Bernard, McPherson and Hand	Former US Senator; consultant to Disney for $50,000 in 1997
Thomas S. Murphy	Former chairman, Capital Cities/ABC, Inc.	
Leo J. O'Donovan	President, Georgetown University	
Sidney Poitier	Chief Executive Officer, Verdon–Cedric Productions, Ltd.	
Irwin Russell	Attorney	Eisner's personal attorney
Robert A. M. Stern	Senior Partner, Robert A. M. Stern Architects	Designed Eisner's home, parents' apartment, and Disney buildings
Andrea L. Van de Kamp	Chairman, Sotheby's West Coast	
Raymond L. Watson	Vice Chairman, The Irvine Company	
Gary L. Wilson	Chairman, Northwest Airlines Corp.	

Source: The Walt Disney Company, *1999 Annual Report to Stockholders*, p. 72.

options reported to be worth around $350 million. In 1993, he received more than $203 million in salary and stock options, becoming the highest paid executive in the country. In 1995, he managed only $8 million in cash bonuses and $6.8 million in restricted stock, in addition to his regular salary. However, in June 2000, he was cited as the CEO who "gave the least relative to his paycheck," which amounted to over $636.9 million over three years.[26]

Other Disney executives also seem to be accustomed to hefty compensations. Even those who do not fulfill their contracts are mightily rewarded, as in the case of Michael Ovitz, Eisner's longtime pal, who served as Disney's president at a salary of $1 million per year and, upon leaving the company after 14 months, received $38 million cash and 3 million stock options (said to be worth more than $200 million in early 1998). And then there is the case of Jeffrey Katzenberg, who left the company after not being promoted to Frank Wells' position but still managed to receive around $100 million from the company through a legal settlement.

It is obvious that some of Disney's executives and large stockholders are richly rewarded. The same may not be said for other workers for the Disney empire, who will be discussed in the next chapter. But, first, what is the basis for all this wealth? What does the Disney company actually produce other than stockholder value?

Dissecting the Disney empire

The Walt Disney Company encompasses a wide array of domestic and international investments, which overlap and reinforce each other. To understand the company's diverse activities, as well as the connections between them, it is helpful to look more closely at Disney's operating segments, as well as the company's activities and investments in international markets. Without a doubt, there will always be changes in corporate structure and activities. Likewise, it is impossible to include all of this enormous corporation's products and businesses. However, it is still important to look more closely at the extent of Disney's far-flung empire.[27] The following discussion provides a snapshot of the corporation, based on company reports as well as other sources.

Table 3.5 Creative Content Division

	Revenues (in $ million)	Operating income (in $ million)	Percent of operating income
1995	7,736	1,531	
1996	10,159	1,561	
1997	10,937	1,882	44
1998	10,302	1,403	35
1999*	9,784	630	17

* Split into three different operating segments in 1999: Studio Entertainment, Consumer Products, and Internet and Direct Marketing.

Creative Content

The Creative Content division has covered a wide range of products and distribution outlets, including film, television, cable TV, home video, recorded music, theatrical productions, and consumer products. (See table 3.5.)

Theatrical films Since the 1984 management shuffle, the Disney company has greatly diversified its repertoire of theatrical film releases. In the Disney tradition, the company has continued to periodically reissue classic Disney films (to be defined further in chapter 5) in theatrical releases. But, perhaps more importantly, the company has reinvigorated its animated film business, thus adding stories and characters to the Disney stable. Animated features, such as *The Little Mermaid*, *The Lion King*, and *Beauty and the Beast* have been wildly successful, not only as theatrical films, but as home videos, television series, merchandise, and Broadway productions.

In addition to animated and live-action films under the Walt Disney label, the company owns the Touchstone, Hollywood, and Caravan labels (or, as the company calls them, "banners"), thus providing opportunities to distribute films that are not associated with the family-oriented, PG-rated Disney brand.[28] To further this type of diversification, Miramax, a successful independent distribution company, was acquired in 1993, followed by the purchase of Merchant-Ivory, an independent production company, in 1994. These two acquisitions extended the Disney film empire even further into markets for adult and foreign films, again providing diversification beyond the family-oriented market.

Table 3.6 Theatrical film box office market share, USA and Canada, 1998

Distributor	Number of films	Gross (in $ million)	Share (%)
Buena Vista	28	1,103.3	16.0
Paramount	19	1,084.0	15.8
Warner Bros	32	749.7	10.9
Sony	37	748.5	10.9
Fox	17	730.2	10.6
New Line	24	539.1	7.8
Dream Works	7	473.3	6.9
Miramax	38	403.6	5.9

Source: Variety, 11 Jan. 1999, p. 9.

While it may be surprising and even shocking to find that the Disney company has distributed films such as *Pulp Fiction*, *Scream*, *Judge Dredd*, and *Armageddon*, the distribution of a diversity of films has led to Disney's leadership of the Hollywood majors' box office revenues for nearly two decades. Including Buena Vista's and Miramax's revenues, the company received over $1.5 billion, or nearly 22 percent of the market share in the US and Canadian markets in 1998. (See table 3.6.)

In addition to theatrical releases, Disney films are seen in other settings – everywhere from airplanes to classrooms. While the revenues garnered from movie theaters represent a sizable income, further revenues are gained from these ancillary markets.

Home video   During takeover discussions in the early 1980s, the value of the Disney film library was estimated to be approximately $400 million, but the same reports observed that, if exploited more aggressively, it could be worth even more. Team Disney was aggressive, to say the least. Many of the classic (and even not-so-classic) Disney films were pulled from the vaults and released on video, resulting in quick cash for the new management team. Gomery notes that, in 1986 alone, video revenues raised more than $100 million of "pure profit" for the firm.[29]

The company has continued to exploit its film library, carefully releasing already amortized products in home video formats, as well as promoting them in other ways, thus maintaining the stable of classic Disney characters for exploitation throughout the company's various businesses.[30] For

Table 3.7 Buena Vista home video top-selling domestic titles, 1997

Title	Industry Rank
The Lion King	1
Snow White and the Seven Dwarfs	2
Aladdin	3
Beauty and the Beast	4
Cinderella	5
Toy Story	6
Bambi	7
Pocahontas	9
101 Dalmatians (animated)	11
Pinocchio	12
The Fox and the Hound	13
Fantasia	15
Sleeping Beauty	18
The Aristocats	19

Rankings as of 30 Sept. 1997.
Source: The Walt Disney Company, *1997 Fact Book*, p. 12.
http://www.disney.com/investors/factbook97/index.html. 27 Aug. 1998.

example, the philosophy was clearly stated in the company's *1997 Annual Report*: "More Disney Classic re-releases are planned, including *Peter Pan* and *101 Dalmatians*, with marketing campaigns aimed at a whole new generation of children and parents who have yet to collect these titles." And, of course, the "new" Disney classics that have been created, such as *The Little Mermaid* and *The Lion King*, have been sensational hits not only at the box office, but in video release.

Buena Vista Home Entertainment manages Disney's home video business and interactive products around the world and, thanks to the video release of its popular animated features, has consistently been the top video company in the USA. According to *Variety*, the company accounted for $1.6 billion and 19.83 percent of the retail market share in 1998.[31] Meanwhile, the list of top-selling titles for many years has been virtually monopolized by Disney. (See table 3.7.)

During 1999, the company announced "a new worldwide strategy" for releasing its classic library feature animation titles on DVD and VHS home video. The year-round video catalog was expanded, while a special Disney

Platinum Collection was created to include ten classic animation features that would be held "in moratorium" for a specific time. One of the Disney classics is to be introduced in DVD and VHS each fall, "supported by a worldwide marketing effort that will include cross-promotion initiatives by Disney's various business units." As Joe Roth, chairman of the Disney Studios, explained:

> This new cycle will allow us to maximize each film's performance by reaching an entirely new generation every 10 years. We will treat each Platinum Collection release as a company wide – and worldwide – event each fall. In addition, by creating a predictable, once-a-year, high-profile release, we will maximize consumer and retail excitement for each title. And as we've seen in the past, major campaigns such as this have a "halo effect" that stimulates demand for all Disney products.[32]

The company offers so many releases that video stores often set aside special sections for these products – a feature that is unique to the Disney brand.[33] Follow-up, direct-to-video versions of successful animated features have also become common, thus adding further value to the characters. Examples have included *The Return of Jafar*, *Aladdin and the King of Thieves*, *Beauty and the Beast: The Enchanted Christmas*, *Lion King II: Simba's Pride*, *Pocahontas: Journey to a New World*, and *The Little Mermaid II: Return to the Sea*.

Television   Disney has diversified its television business in the same way as its film offerings, producing and distributing a variety of programming under the Buena Vista, Touchstone, and Walt Disney labels. Walt Disney Television and Television Animation produce and distribute a wide array of appropriately "Disney" programs. Team Disney revived the network prime-time *The Wonderful World of Disney* on Sunday evenings on ABC, featuring mainly original television movies, but also highlighting new events in the Disney empire (such as the opening of the new Animal Kingdom in 1998).

New animated television programming has been added as well. In addition to the Disney Afternoon – a one and a half hour block of Disney animated programs, such as *Ducktales*, *Mighty Ducks*, *Quack Pack*, etc. – the company expanded its Saturday morning offerings with the takeover of ABC. *One Saturday Morning* is a two-hour live-action show that serves as a "wrap-around" for other Disney-produced animated series, such as *Disney's Doug*, *Recess*, and *Pepper Ann*. Other animated series are follow-ups to successful feature films, such as *101 Dalmations: The Series*, *The Lion King's Timon and Pumbaa*, *The New Adventures of Winnie the Pooh*, and *Disney's Hercules*.

Other television programming has been distributed under the Buena Vista and Touchstone labels (although Touchstone was merged into the ABC Entertainment Television Group during 1999). Most notably, prime-time successes (in terms of longevity) have included *Home Improvement*, *Boy Meets World*, *Ellen*, *Blossom*, *Dinosaurs*, *Golden Girls*, and *Empty Nest*. While the company also has an impressive list of failures (*Lenny*, *The Fanelli Boys*, *All American Girl*, *Thunder Alley*, to name only a few), this is no different from other television production companies in a highly volatile, often unpredictable industry. While Buena Vista Television produced the "break-out hit" *Who Wants to Be a Millionaire?* for ABC, it is unclear how long its "phenomenal success" will last.

Of course, the goal is for television series to run long enough to enter the lucrative syndication market. Buena Vista handles Disney's original and off-network syndicated programming, distributing those successful shows listed above, as well as first-run programming, such as *Honey, I Shrunk the Kids: The TV Show*, *The Keenan Ivory Wayans Show*, and daily game shows on cable, including *Debt*, *Make Me Laugh*, and *Win Ben Stein's Money*. Off-network syndication includes *Live! With Regis and Kathie Lee*, *Roger Ebert & the Movies* (formerly, *Siskel & Ebert*), *Disney Presents*, *Bill Nye the Science Guy*, and *Sing Me A Story with Belle*.

Meanwhile, *Mouseworks* – featuring Mickey, Minnie, Donald, Pluto, and Goofy – made its debut in May 1999 on ABC, of course, "bringing Disney's classic characters to a whole new generation."

Theatrical productions   In 1994, Disney arrived at Times Square with the purchase and renovation of the New Amsterdam Theatre on 42nd Street, where a theatrical version of *Beauty and the Beast* was staged. By mid-1999, the show had completed its fifth year on Broadway and was still touring in other countries. A stage version of *The Lion King* opened in November 1997 and won six Tony Awards in 1998, while *The Hunchback of Notre Dame* opened in June 1999. And, early 2000, a Disney version of *Aïda* opened on Broadway.

The company has become an undeniable presence in Manhattan, not only by way of its stage productions at the New Amsterdam Theatre and the massive Disney Store next door, but through extensive real estate holdings, including ABC's headquarters.

Audio products and music publishing   Audio and musical products
offer further opportunities to feature Disney properties and are especially
lucrative for animated features, given the important role of music in these
films. Buena Vista Music Group now coordinates Disney's various recorded
music businesses, which include a wide range of audio and music products.
The company produces and distributes compact discs, audio cassettes, and
records, as well as licensing its music to other companies for printed music,
records, audiovisual devices, and public performances. Disney sells music-
related products through domestic retail sales and direct marketing, including catalogs, coupon packages, and television.

In addition, Hollywood Records, Mammoth Records, and Lyric Street
Records develop, produce, and market a diverse group of musical artists.
The company recently created Hollywood Records Latin, "to focus on the
rapidly growing Latin music market," with Los Lobos as one of their
featured groups. Some of the company's recording ventures have not
always fit with Disney's squeaky clean image. For instance, the company
quickly pulled a controversial album by Insane Clowns in 1997, even
though the release did not directly carry the Disney name.[34]

Consumer products

The company's *1997 Annual Report* states simply: "Licensing of characters
from Disney films remains enormously successful." Talk about an under-
statement! The worldwide proliferation of merchandise is one of the key
features of the Disney empire. Perhaps a better picture is provided by the
following pitch for future employees offered on the Disney website:

> Join Disney Consumer Products and help bring Disney Magic to the world!
> High-fashion apparel! The hottest toys! Award-winning records and books!
> Fine art and collectibles and more!
>
> They're all a part of the hundreds of thousands of Disney licensed
> products featuring Mickey and the gang, Winnie the Pooh, and all the
> characters from Disney motion pictures and television that reach more than
> 90 countries each year. But they don't get out there by themselves.
>
> It takes a team of dedicated professionals to provide and support the
> merchandise that celebrates and preserves the most magical legacy on Earth.
>
> Creativity, quality, and an entrepreneurial culture have helped make
> Disney Consumer Products one of the fastest growing areas within the
> Disney organization.[35]

Disney's merchandising activities are legendary in terms of their historical precedence as well as more recent strategies. As discussed in the previous chapter, merchandising started almost simultaneously with the success of Mickey Mouse's *Steamboat Willie*. Recall that the company was offered $300 to put The Mouse on writing tablets in 1929. And although various histories claim that Walt Disney was not necessarily interested in licensing his characters, these activities still provided needed revenue to continue producing expensive animated films. During the 1930s, the company began to flood the market with Disney products. "Mickey's likeness soon appeared on everything from soap to ice-cream cones to Cartier diamond bracelets for $1,250."[36]

At the height of the Depression, the Disney merchandising bonanza supposedly saved the Lionel Company with the sale of 253,000 Mickey Mouse handcars and the Ingersoll–Waterbury Company with the sale of 2.5 million Mickey Mouse watches. By 1934, annual profits on films and merchandise brought in over $600,000 for the Disney company. Mickey is still claimed to be the most popular licensed character in the world, appearing on more than 7,500 different items, not including publications.[37]

Historically, relatively little merchandising activity took place in Hollywood except for Disney. However, in the 1970s, film companies (as well as toy manufacturers) started to realize the value of movie-related merchandise, especially with the enormous success of *Star Wars* merchandise. Television also joined the bandwagon, with merchandise and tie-ins evolving from children's shows, as well as programs designed around preexisting toys. Media-related merchandise and tie-ins grew dramatically during the 1980s and 1990s, and by 1999, retail sales of licensed merchandise had reached $112.3 billion worldwide.[38]

According to the company's 1997 Form 10-K report: "Although public information is limited, the Company believes it is the largest worldwide licenser of character-based merchandise and producer/distributor of children's audio and film-related products." Despite the inadequate information, trade sources agree that Disney is still the most powerful licensing force in the world. The company reported that an estimated $14 billion in Disney products were sold around the world in 1994. Another source claimed in 1987 that 3,000 companies manufactured over 14,000 Disney-licensed products.[39] While it is unclear what products are included in these figures, it is probable that they do not include those that are manufactured and sold without the company's authorization – in other words, pirated Disney merchandise.

The Walt Disney Company is certainly the foremost merchandising company in Hollywood. Not only has the company been at the merchandising business longer than almost everyone else, but Disney has a reputation for licensing and producing quality products. The company itself manufactures consumer products but also licenses the name "Disney" and Disney characters to other companies that pay royalties based on a fixed percentage of the wholesale or retail selling price of the product. In this, the company is no different from other copyright holders of film and television properties, although the Disney company generally asks for a higher royalty fee than other companies. Consistent with the Disney obsession with control, the company has a demanding process that must be followed by licensees in the development of products, with the Disney company having veto power at every stage.

When Team Disney took over, they emphasized the exploitation of the stable of "standard" characters, such as Mickey, Donald, and Winnie the Pooh, as well as the development of new properties. Not only does Disney continually create new characters for its stable, but the company is able to reinforce these efforts through its extensive business empire. As one of Disney's executives explains, "When you combine the right film with the right products, there's a terrific synergy that takes place."[40] (More about how this synergy works in the next chapter.)

Disney's 1997 10-K report lists the following character merchandise categories: "apparel, watches, toys, gifts, housewares, stationery, sporting goods and domestic items such as sheets and towels." Actually, this short list seems laughable in light of the hundreds of different types of products that have featured Disney characters. Only a few of the product categories will be discussed in the following sections.

Children's products The importance of Disney in the market for children's products cannot be overemphasized. For instance, the company represents well over 10 percent of the $2.2 billion infant products market. In 1988, Disney spent $61 million on Childcraft, a New Jersey company that owned two of biggest mail order lists in the country. By 1990, the company was mailing over 45 million Disney, Childcraft, and Just for Kids! catalogs. Products offered included infant merchandise featuring Disney character brands (the Disney Babies Brand with Baby Mickey, Baby Donald, and friends). The company has ongoing deals with large toy manufacturers, including Mattel and Hasbro, and continues to be a significant player in the toy industry.

Educational products Disney Educational Productions creates audio-visual materials, including films, videos, and film strips for schools, libraries, and other institutions, as well as educational toys, play equipment, and classroom furniture for children, plus posters and teaching aids.[41] In addition, the Disney website offers teachers a range of ideas for lesson plans, plus opportunities to order Disney Educational videos.

In August 1999, the Mouse House acquired a 60 percent share of the on-line educational toy company Toysmart.com for $20 million. Another $25 million was to be devoted to advertising the site on Disney's websites and television outlets. A company spokesman explained that the site was to be used to expand Disney's family.com: "What we've done is build a great parenting site, but what we have not done well is evolve that community site into an e-commerce site. . . . high quality, educational toys represent an exciting business opportunity in a fast-growing market segment."[42]

The company also produces a range of interactive CDs and games, many promoted as educational products. Disney Interactive works with other companies such as Sega and Nintendo to produce games based on film characters, such as Mickey Mouse and Tarzan, as well as television and cable franchises, such as *Who Wants to be a Millionaire* and ESPN.

Art and collectibles The Disney company also sells more expensive items in their art classics line. This includes a wide range of animation cel art and animation-related artwork and collectibles. For instance, porcelain figures of characters from *Snow White and the Seven Dwarfs* are available for around $175 each. As the Disney website explains:

> The Walt Disney Classics Collection captures the hearts and imaginations of collectors through vivid re-creations of Disney's magical movie moments and beloved characters. The images of The Walt Disney Studios transcend the silver screen, lingering in our imaginations and emotions in ways shared and understood around the globe.
>
> Collectors throughout the world cherish Disney fine art. Each remarkable piece of artwork captures a precious moment of film fantasy, humor, or adventure, which can be brought home to enjoy again and again.

Collecting Disney merchandise has become so popular that trade shows, books, and periodicals are devoted to its display and sale. "Disneyana" is defined as "the zealous collecting of the wide variety of Walt Disney character merchandise manufactured from the 1930s right up to the present era of new 'instant' Disney collectibles."[43] The "official" collectors' organization is the Walt Disney Collectors Society, although there are other organizations not formally associated with the company.

Internet and direct marketing

On-line business   In 1993, Eisner stated that the company would not invest directly in new forms of media hardware but would focus on producing software for new multimedia technologies.[44] Since that time, the company's on-line activities have grown substantially.

Disney OnLine was started in 1995 to "develop The Walt Disney Company's presence in the online world." The division creates and distributes content for on-line services, interactive software, interactive television, and Internet websites. The site www.disney.com was launched in February 1996 and has been consistently rated as one of the Web's most popular sites. The Daily Blast was initiated in April 1997 as a subscriber-based website and includes interactive comic strips with sound, on-line coloring books, games, and "digital toys" to download, all featuring Disney characters, plus news and sports provided by ABC and ESPN.

In 1997, the company bought a significant stake in Starwave Corp, a leading producer of Internet media, founded by Paul Allen, as well as the search engine, Infoseek. But, early in 1999, the company moved into cyberspace for real. Infoseek was combined with the company's other on-line activities to form the Go Network (or go.com), claimed to be one of the top five portals on the Internet, as well as providing access to "every form of information and entertainment that Disney offers."[45] The move to fold Infoseek into the Disney empire involved a $2.15 billion deal, approved by stockholders in November 1999. Infoseek stock was converted to new go.com stock, which trades separately from the Disney stock. The Disney company owns 74 percent of the Internet company, which includes Disney.com, Family.com, ABCnews.com, and ESPN.com, as well as Disney's direct mail catalog sales business.[46]

According to one source, the Disney home page itself attracts more than 9.7 million "unique visitors" each month.[47] Meanwhile, Grover estimates that 25 percent of the nearly 80 million Internet users in the USA visit a Disney-related website each month.[48] While there are high hopes for the development of business or e-commerce on the Internet, the profits so far have been minimal. For instance, the Disney company was reported to have spent more than $150 million for on-line development in 1997, whereas the profits estimated for that year amount to around $8 million in product sales and $5 million in subscription fees (for Club

Blast).[49] Although the various Disney Internet sites provide information and entertainment, a major emphasis is product marketing and brand reinforcement.[50]

Consumer product marketing   Disney merchandise is marketed in a multitude of ways. Of course, Disney products are sold at retail outlets around the world, sometimes in special "product corners" which feature only Disney merchandise. Very often, new product lines are introduced with special contests and events. In fact, the wide range of products means that it is often difficult to avoid Disney merchandise. A recent survey of one typical American shopping mall found that over 90 percent of the retail outlets offered at least one Disney-themed product. And this was a shopping mall that included an official Disney Store (see below).

The Disney company also sells its products through its own outlets. The theme parks are jam-packed with gift shops and merchandise kiosks (as will be discussed further in chapter 6), while Disney's on-line sites vigorously promote sales of the merchandise, as noted previously. In addition, millions of copies of the Disney Catalog are mailed monthly, promoting a range of merchandise featuring new and standard characters.

Since 1987, the company has marketed its products directly through its own retail facilities, the Disney Stores. At the end of 1999, 728 stores around the world served as centralized sources for Disney merchandise, (see table 3.8) representing the overriding Disney philosophy. "The core strategy behind The Walt Disney Co.'s retail endeavor, The Disney Store, is to be both entertainer and merchant."[51] The stores often include Disney characters in costume, videos, animation, and other attractions, carefully coordinated with racks of merchandise, as well as promotions for other Disney businesses. By 1991, sales volume had doubled each year since the opening of the first store in 1987. Although overall sales for 1999 were down for the Disney Stores, the company promised renovations, including the installation of computer kiosks allowing consumers to connect to The Disney Store Online for items not available in the store.

Publications   A wide range of printed material is produced by the Disney company, from comic books and children's magazines to adult-oriented magazines and books. At the end of 1998, the company claimed that its print products were published in 37 languages and distributed in more than 100 countries.

By 1988, 120 different Disney magazines and comics were published in 16 different countries, with the addition of new magazines and comic book

Plate 1   The Company Store. The Disney Store in Paris is one of the
company's most successful retail outlets, despite the supposed French
resistance to Disney and American culture.
Photo by Carlos R. Calderon.

Table 3.8   The Disney Stores, 1993–1998

	1993	1994	1995	1996	1997	1998
North America	214	273	337	402	460	478
Europe	19	37	63	82	101	107
Asia-Pacific	6	14	29	46	75	96

Source: The Walt Disney Company, *1998 Fact Book,* p. 12
http://disneyu.go.com/investors/factbook98/creative_content2.htm

titles typically following the release of new Disney films. The company
claims to lead all other publishers in the world in the area of children's
books and magazines. An indication of the proliferation of Disney printed
material are the 500 books and 11 magazines featuring Winnie the Pooh
announced in the company's *1998 Annual Report,* followed by the news
that "even more new titles will appear in 1999."

  In 1999, the company sold the last of the publications inherited with

Table 3.9 Theme Parks and Resorts Division

Year	Revenues (in $ million)	Operating income (in $ million)	Percent of operating income
1995	4,001	859	
1996	4,502	990	
1997	5,014	1,136	26
1998	5,532	1,287	32
1999	6,106	1,446	39

the Capital Cities/ABC takeover. Disney had previously unloaded the newspapers acquired in the deal but had held on to Fairchild Publications, one of the largest fashion news-gathering networks in the world. Finally, the group of 13 trade and consumer magazines was sold to Conde Nast for around $650 million in 1999. However, Disney maintained ownership of *Los Angeles* magazine, as well as retaining the right to use content from a few of the fashion magazines on the Internet. The company also publishes *Family Fun*, *Disney Adventures*, *Disney Magazine*, and *Discover*.

Much of the company's book publishing is organized under the company's trade publishing division, Hyperion, which includes ESPN Books, Talk/Miramax Books, ABC Daytime Press and Hyperion East.

It should be noted that Disney's consumer products are constantly expanding as new businesses are added to the empire. For instance, new products were introduced featuring the franchises acquired in the Capital Cities/ABC takeover. One can now buy products based on ABC's daytime soaps, such as *All My Children* music and *General Hospital* dolls. In addition, ABC Sports watches and sportswear, *Monday Night Football* mugs and blankets and ESPN sportswear, trivia games and publications are all available at ESPN–The Store and ESPN.com. (More on ESPN later in this chapter.)

Theme Parks and Resorts

By late 1998, the Disney Empire included six major theme parks, plus additional parks and tourist attractions. Disney is constantly expanding its theme parks and real estate holdings, which represent a sizable investment and a hefty share of the overall revenues (see table 3.9). This division also includes a cruise line, sports investments, a planned community and the group that designs it all, Imagineering.

Theme Parks   The Disney company states that its theme parks are "the most attended in the world" – a claim that is difficult to challenge. Although attendance figures are difficult to obtain, brief glimpses are sometimes given in company reports. For instance, the *1998 Fact Book* revealed that Walt Disney World received its 600 millionth guest on 24 June 1998.

When Disneyland opened in 1955, it was a departure from typical amusement parks and carnivals, as well as a challenge for the Disney company. Since then, Disney has developed the parks as part of spacious resort areas, including theme parks, hotels and other recreational and entertainment activities. The parks continuously update rides and attractions, as well as adding features and characters, often based on new films. (The parks outside the USA will be discussed later in this chapter, while chapter 6 includes more detailed analysis of the theme parks.)

Disneyland Resort   The first Disney theme park has changed over the years, adding and renovating rides and attractions. The complex includes Disneyland and Pacific Hotels, with additional hotels, shopping, dining, and entertainment venues planned for a new park, Disney's California Adventure, scheduled to open in 2001.

Walt Disney World Resort   As discussed in chapter 2, the Walt Disney World Resort is now located on 30,500 acres of land near Orlando, Florida. The complex is continuously growing, but at the end of 1998 it included the following:

- four theme parks – the Magic Kingdom, EPCOT, Disney-MGM Studios, and Disney's Animal Kingdom;
- 13 hotels and additional villas and suites (totalling more than 16,700 rooms, and not including nine additional hotels located on the company's property, but independently operated);
- Downtown Disney – a 120 acre complex, which includes shopping, dining, and entertainment at Downtown Disney Marketplace, Pleasure Island, and Downtown Disney West Side;
- Disney's Wide World of Sports – a 200 acre complex which includes facilities for a wide range of sporting championships and tournaments;
- Disney's All-Star Movies, All-Star Music, and All-Star Sports resorts;

- a shopping village (Disney Village Marketplace);
- campsites and wilderness homes (Fort Wilderness);
- five golf courses;
- three water parks – Blizzard Beach, River Country, and Typhoon Lagoon;
- other recreational amenities, such as miniature golf, spas, etc.

The company claims that the Magic Kingdom at Walt Disney World has become the best-attended theme park in the world. As the company's 10-K report notes, the park's facilities are "designed to attract visitors for an extended stay." But the resort not only attracts millions of tourists, it represents the second most popular destination for corporate meetings, offering 318,000 square feet of conference meeting space. Meanwhile, "personal enrichment programs" are offered at the Disney Institute.

Almost a theme park: Disney's America   In the fall of 1993, Disney announced plans for another theme park. Disney's America was to be a 3,000 acre theme park located in Virginia, only 35 miles from Washington, D.C., and focusing on key moments in US history. With hotels, shops, golf courses, and residential units, the park was promoted as a boon to development, employment, and the local economy in Virginia. However, despite Disney's usual political strategies (including arrangements for a $163 million bond issue to improve roads in the area), the site was abandoned in September 1994, after a barrage of criticism about the risks to the actual historical sites in the area, as well as the increased urban sprawl, traffic, and air pollution that the project would bring. Still other critics worried about the treatment of American history by the company that has made billions of dollars primarily from the manufacture of fantasy. The company had planned to continue development at another site, but it is now unclear whether or not it will proceed.

Resorts and hotels.   With the expansion of Disney's theme park activity, the company has become heavily involved in real estate and hotel management, as evidenced by the facilities listed above at Walt Disney World. In 1997 the company reported 19,502 hotel rooms at various sites and claimed that it would take 61 years to stay overnight in each room at the Walt Disney World complex alone.

Another real estate project is the Disney Vacation Club, which features ownership of resort facilities at Disney Old Key West Resort and Disney's BoardWalk Resort, both at Disney World, a resort at Vero Beach, Florida, and another at Hilton Head Island, South Carolina. Units at each site are sold under a vacation ownership plan and operated partially as rental property until the units sell. Membership provides "a real estate interest in the Disney Vacation Club Resort of your choice."

The company also owns real estate in Burbank, California, where its studios and executive offices are located, as well as valuable property in Glendale, California, and New York City, as mentioned above.

Regional entertainment   While the Disney theme parks have been immensely profitable over the long run, the initial investment for such enterprises is considerable. In the late 1990s, the company began opening smaller, regional complexes which could draw on the Disney brand names but represented far less financial commitment than the larger parks.

Capitalizing on the popularity of its newly acquired sports properties, the company developed the ESPN Zone, featuring sports-themed dining and entertainment. The first one opened in Baltimore, Maryland, in 1998, followed by sites in New York and Chicago, with several others in the planning stages. The sites often serve as hosts for the company's sports programming, such as ABC's *Monday Night Football* half-time show.

Another form of regional entertainment is DisneyQuest, indoor entertainment venues "combining the magic of Disney with interactive technologies and classic story-telling," as well as retail merchandise and food areas. The first DisneyQuest opened at Walt Disney World in 1998, the second in Chicago, with others to follow.

Cruise Line   The Disney Cruise Line includes two ships (*Disney Magic* and *Disney Wonder*) for voyages designed with stopovers at its Florida complex and its own island in the Bahamas, Castaway Cay. Entertainment on board includes premieres of new Disney films in the Buena Vista Theatre, Disney theatrical productions in the Walt Disney Theatre, and sports action in the ESPN Skybox. Vacation packages, as well as activities on board, are planned for adults and for families. The description:

> The magic and quality of Disney is yours to enjoy on the two magnificent ships that are part of an unforgettable Walt Disney World and Disney Cruise Line vacation. Seven unforgettable days. One incredible vacation, with spectacular entertainment, unique dining experiences, and enchanting adventures that only Disney could create. Here, adults find excitement and romance. Children have the time of their lives. Families unite. And honeymooners sail off into a getaway they'll never forget. It all happens in a world

where fantasy comes to life, aboard the Disney Magic or the Disney Wonder, spectacular ships that float on fun. Join us and Discover Uncharted Magic.[52]

Celebration One of Walt's dreams in the 1960s was a community for about 20,000 residents called the Experimental Prototype Community of Tomorrow. His vision was a futuristic city; however, the project evolved into one of the components of the Walt Disney World Resort – a showcase for corporate development of technology, to be discussed further in chapter 6. In the early 1990s, the idea of a planned community finally emerged, resulting in Celebration – a neo-traditional planned community on 4,900 acres south of Disney World. The population at the end of 1997 was 1,500, with plans for an eventual 20,000 inhabitants.

While Disney's annual report states that "current residents are reveling in the town's combination of leading-edge health, education and technology systems with a comfortable sense of community," other "citizens" were finding the Disney control too stifling. A much closer look at Celebration is presented in chapter 6.

Anaheim Sports Inc In 1992, Disney followed up on its successful film *The Mighty Ducks* by purchasing the rights to a new expansion hockey team in Anaheim, to be called the Mighty Ducks. The company has continued to add sports properties to its empire, with ownership of the Anaheim Angels (formerly the California Angels), as well as an international sports arena in south Florida, which attracts numerous sporting events that receive worldwide coverage.

Walt Disney Imagineering The research and development arm of the Disney company is called "Imagineering." Disney publicity material explains that the division "provides master planning, real estate development, attraction and show design, engineering support, production support, project management and other development services for the company's operations."[53] The more than 2,000 "Imagineers" who work for the division have been involved with everything from designing new theme parks, to renovating Anaheim Stadium, to developing a "visionary community" (Celebration). As well as the continuing additions and updates to the existing parks and hotel complexes, another park is planned for Hong Kong (more in chapter 6), as well as other smaller projects.

The company is not shy about the synergistic potential of its constantly-expanding real estate empire. As noted in its Form 10-K filed with the SEC in 1990: ". . . the Company believes its theme parks and resorts

Table 3.10 Broadcasting Division

Year	Revenues (in $ million)	Operating income (in $ million)	Percent of operating income
1995	414	76	
1996	4,078	782	
1997	6,522	1,294	30
1998	7,142	1,325	33
1999*	7,512	1,611	44

* Segment was renamed Media Networks in 1999.

benefit substantially from the Company's reputation in the entertainment industry for excellent quality and from synergy with activities in other business segments of the Company."

Media networks

Before the Capital Cities/ABC takeover, the company owned a television station, KCAL-TV (formerly KHJ-TV) in Los Angeles and a pay-cable channel (The Disney Channel).[54] With the television, radio and cable properties acquired in 1995, Disney firmly established its role as one of the dominant players in the US media industry. (See table 3.10.)

Television   It had been rumored for years that Disney was shopping for a network. Even though their strength has diminished with the growth of cable and other television outlets, the major television networks still represent important investments in the media business and attract sizable advertising revenues. In many ways, then, Disney's purchase of the ABC network in 1995 was no surprise. The network provides the Mouse House with opportunities to promote Disney-produced programming and other businesses, as well as exploiting ABC's more popular programs throughout the rest of the Disney empire.

Sure enough, more and more Disney programming has appeared on the network, beginning with *The Wonderful World of Disney*. As expected, Disney's children's programming was added to the morning and weekend schedules, most notably *Disney's One Saturday Morning*, the top-rated block of children's programming every Saturday morning on ABC.

Meanwhile, with the acquisition of the ABC network, Disney moved into the news production business. The company's news programs include the nightly network and evening news programs, plus Sunday, Wednesday, and Friday editions of the news magazine, *20/20.* The company claims that "more Americans get their news from ABC – on television, radio and the Internet – than from any other source."[55]

But the Disney company also gained other valuable television properties with the Cap Cities/ABC takeover. At the end of the 1990s, Disney owned 10 television stations reaching around 25 percent of the nation's households. The stations are all affiliated with ABC. Although the company was forced to sell its only previously owned television station (KCAL) because of FCC regulations, the station that it kept in the Los Angeles market (KABC) was obviously the more valuable property.

Radio With the Cap Cities/ABC deal, Disney also added radio to its growing empire. By the end of the 1990s, the company owned 42 stations, reaching 13 million people weekly. Most of the Disney stations are affiliated with the ABC Radio Network, which boasted affiliations on 4,400 radio stations, reaching more than 147 million listeners weekly. ESPN Radio is broadcast 24 hours, with its flagship station ESPN Radio 1000 in Chicago.

In 1997, the company also initiated Radio Disney, featuring special radio programming for children, which was received by 45 stations at the end of 1999. By the end of the 1990s, Radio Disney reached around 50 percent of the USA and was growing rapidly, with hopes of reaching 70 percent of the USA during 2000.

Cable television While Disney's cable enterprises are extensive, the ESPN networks and services are perhaps the most valuable. In fact, ESPN is a widely recognized brand on its own, even without the Disney affiliation. Disney's ownership of ESPN is through ABC, which owns 80 percent of ESPN Inc. in partnership with the Hearst Corporation. As noted in the company's *1998 Annual Report*, the franchise includes four domestic cable networks, regional syndication, 21 international networks, radio, Internet, retail, print, and location-based dining and entertainment.

At the end of 1999, the flagship network reached over 77 million subscribers domestically, while ESPN International has been claimed to reach more than 152 million households in 190 countries internationally. (More on international markets later in this chapter.) ESPN2 claims 67 million domestic subscribers, and ESPNews, a 24-hour sports news cable channel, reaches an additional 14 million. ESPN Classic (purchased in 1997) reaches another 20 million households.

The ESPN franchise has recently diversified its activities even further, adding ESPN Magazine, ESPN Radio, ESPN Zones (the restaurant entertainment centers), ESPN Skybox on Disney Cruise Line ships, and ESPN merchandise. Meanwhile, ESPN.com is claimed to be the most popular sports site on the Internet.

It seems clear that the value of the ESPN enterprise is enormous. In addition to the $600 million annual profit claimed to have been generated by the ESPN franchise, successful sports programming is said to be a key to bringing in audiences for other media offerings.

Disney's other cable holdings are also expanding. The Disney Channel was created as a showcase for mostly Disney products before Team Disney took over in the mid-1980s. Since then, the service has been revamped to feature a wider range of programming, as well as being offered as a pay or expanded basic service instead of only as a pay channel. By the end of 1999, the cable service was received in 59 million households.

Disney's other cable investments include the following:

- 37.5 percent of the A&E Network (reaching 81 million subscribers in the USA)
- 37.5 percent of the History Channel (reaching more than 61 million homes)
- 50 percent of Lifetime Entertainment Services (including Lifetime and the Lifetime Movie Network and reaching 75 million homes)
- 39.6 percent of E! Entertainment Television (including E!, which reaches 52 million in the USA and is seen in more than 120 countries reaching 400 million homes, and "style" – a 24-hour network started in October 1998, devoted to design, fashion, and decorating, reaching 7 million households)
- Toon Disney (started in April 1998 and reaching over 14 million subscribers with recycled Disney programming)
- SoapNet (a 24-hour soap opera channel launched in January 2000)

The discussion thus far has focused mostly on the Disney company's holdings in the USA. We now turn to the international activities of the Disney empire.

International investments and markets

"It's a Small World" is a ride at the Disney theme parks, described as "the happiest cruise that ever sailed around the world. From your boat, watch animated dolls and animals from around the world sing and dance in their native costumes. This heart-warming ride will leave you whistling." The ride was originally sponsored by Bank of America.

While "it's a small world" is a common theme in discussions of globalization, it also represents a core philosophy of the Walt Disney Company in its quest to constantly expand the Disney universe. As noted in a recent annual report, "The company generates revenues from more countries each year as Disney and its brands *continue to be welcomed* around the world" (emphasis added). Indeed, Disney's international activities have grown by leaps and bounds over the last few years, as 1999 revenues from international sources, including US exports, reached almost $5 billion, or 20 percent of the total company revenues. The company's international revenues have grown at a compound annual growth rate of 24 percent over the last five years, aided especially by the takeover of Capital Cities/ABC in 1995. The company claims that it is the world's top-ranked international distributor of motion pictures, not to mention its strengths in home video, television, sports programming, and consumer products.

But even though the company has expanded globally, as outlined in the next several sections, the company expressed concern in its *1999 Annual Report* that revenues from international sources need further development, and that "Disney is underpenetrated overseas." More efforts were promised to position the company "to capitalize on long-term international growth opportunities."[56]

The Disney corporation can be said to represent a typical American-based transnational and is especially representative of USA-based media corporations that have expanded globally during the last few decades. *Fortune* magazine claimed back in 1989 that Disney "has become the archetypal American corporation for the 1990s: a creative company that can move with agility to exploit international opportunities in industries where the US has a competitive advantage."[57] However, the company may represent a special case because of its distinctive brand name and its obsession with control over its entire operation. While the Disney philosophy may be effective and even admired for these qualities within the USA, the company often adjusts its policies and strategies in other countries. For instance, the *1998 Annual Report* notes that there was

Table 3.11 Top selling international video titles, 1997

Title	Industry Rank
The Lion King	1
Snow White and the Seven Dwarfs	2
Aladdin	3
The Jungle Book	4
101 Dalmatians (animated)	5
Beauty and the Beast	6
Toy Story	7
Pocahontas	9
Bambi	10

Rankings as of 30 Sept. 1997.
Source: The Walt Disney Company, *1997 Fact Book,* p. 12
http://www.disney.com/investors/factbook97/index.html. 27 Aug. 1998.

"strategic downsizing" in the company's international activities, especially in Asia.[58]

Creative content   Buena Vista International, which distributes all Disney films outside North America, has been the world's top-ranked international distributor of motion pictures during the 1990s and again crossed the $1 billion box office threshold in 1998 – the first international distribution company in industry history to achieve this feat three years in a row. Although Fox took the lead in international markets for 1998 (mostly due to the success of *Titanic*), Buena Vista was second, with 17.2 percent of the market at $1.17 billion, while Miramax added a 4.7 percent share and $320.5 million. Thus, the Disney company actually represented a 21.9 percent share and over $1.49 billion. In addition, it is involved in distribution partnerships with other studios and coproduces selected movies in Europe and South America.

Buena Vista Home Video label distributes Disney, Touchstone, and Hollywood films to international markets. The company's gross revenues increased fourfold from 1986 to 1990, and there were branches in 64 markets in 1994. Disney claimed to hold up to 60 percent of the family video market in some European countries in 1994. (See table 3.11.) Television production and music products also contribute to Disney's international revenues.

The company reported that 58 percent of the licensing revenues from consumer products were from international markets, where Disney arranges licensing deals with companies that produce and distribute its products. For example, the publishing firm Egmont has licensed the popular Disney comics in Scandinavia since 1949.

As noted previously, the company claims to be the top publisher of children's books and magazines worldwide. Of special interest is the Disney Magic English series, which the company asserts is "the best-selling English language learning program in the world."[59]

Disney products are sold at over 728 Disney Stores around the world, as well as at "product corners" set up in department stores and other key outlets on three continents. Disney's online services are expanding internationally as well, with Disney Online Europe added to Disney's previous on-line activities. In January 1997, Disney Online opened a satellite office in Paris to manage development of original content in European markets. Using the local Disney domains (disney.country domain), these websites are destined to offer European Internet users "the same level of information about Disney products and services."

The Mouse and the Mounties   One of Disney's more controversial merchandising deals illustrates the strength of the Disney brand, as well as pointing to some of the issues involved. In January 1995, the Mounted Police Foundation (affiliated with the Royal Canadian Mounted Police) signed an agreement with Disney to license and control the promotion of Mounties merchandise around the world. The deal was defended as a move to stop the production of tasteless merchandise ("everything from Mountie swizzle sticks to porn flicks") and to raise funds for some of the Mounties' community projects. By mid-1998, Disney had arranged contracts with more than nearly 70 companies to produce everything from Mountie mugs and maple syrup to Mountie diaper bags and pacifiers. Four brands were created by the Disney marketers: RCMP Elite, featuring a traditional dark-haired Mountie in a red coat; RCMP Country, a rugged blond Mountie for outdoor gear; MacLean of the Mounties, a square-jawed cartoon character for teens; and Lil Mountie for infants.[60]

The police group receives 51 percent of the 10 percent royalty charge; Disney receives 49 percent. As of July 1998, the Mounties had received over $300,000. While the agreement prompted strong reactions in a country that has long been sensitive to cultural invasion by US corporations, it also represents the global power of the Disney brand. As an RCMP official explained: "This police force is proud of its reputation and didn't much appreciate things like wrestlers dressed in Mountie uniform using cattle prods and whips. Disney is a world leader of licensing and marketing products of good quality and taste."[61]

Theme parks and resorts

Tokyo Disneyland   Tokyo Disneyland, which opened in April 1983, is built on 600 acres of landfill in Tokyo Bay. The park has been a tremendous success, nearly equaling attendance at the original Disneyland. But the Disney company collects only 10 percent of the admissions, 5 percent of food and merchandise sales, and 10 percent of corporate sponsorships, as the park is owned by the Oriental Land Company. Still, by 1984, the park was generating $40 million annually for Disney. A second park, to be called Tokyo DisneySea, is planned for 2001, together with a "Disney-branded hotel" and monorail system. Yet another Disney hotel is planned for an adjacent complex, the Maihama Station Area. Thus, the Disney company will receive even further income from these new projects.

Disneyland Paris   The European version of Disneyland opened as Euro Disney in April 1992, with more than the usual Disney fanfare (including eggs thrown at Disney executives when the deal was announced in Paris), and has been followed by a good deal of press coverage. As mentioned previously, Disney arranged a lucrative deal from the French government, which offered nearly 5,000 acres of land located approximately 20 miles east of Paris at "rock-bottom price." In addition, the government invested substantial amounts in upgrading and improving the highway system and suburban rail line and offered reduced interest rates on $1 billion in loans. Disney sold securities that provided tax breaks based on accelerated depreciation and held a $1 billion equity offering of 51 percent of the project. Thus, Disney maneuvered a 49 percent interest in Euro Disney for an equity investment of only $250 million, arranging sizable management fees, royalties, and a small share of the profits.[62]

However, the park reported a loss of $87.7 million during its first year, prompting a major debt restructuring, which eventually cost Disney around $750 million and increased the company's financial commitment to the park. Some analysts observed that the source of Euro Disney's financial problems had less to do with public sentiment than with the Disney company's bellicose style during the planning and building of the park.

The company owns a 39 percent equity interest in the company that owns the enterprise.

Despite the problems plaguing the park, which, by 1994, had changed its name to Disneyland Paris, it was claimed to be Europe's most popular tourist attraction, attracting 12.5 million visitors in 1998. The complex includes seven themed hotels, plus shopping, dining, and entertainment.

In 1999, the company announced that a new theme park, "Disney Studios," would be added to the complex. The new park will cost $640 million and will feature television and film production, similar to the MGM–Disney Studios in Florida.

As noted previously, the next major theme park is planned for Hong Kong, with attractions "based on popular rides and shows that debuted at the company's other Disneyland-style parks."[63]

Media networks   The company's media networks include interests in television production and distribution firms in Germany, France, Scandinavia, the UK, and Japan. The company also has a number of programming agreements with television companies in other countries. For instance, Disney has developed a popular live "interactive" program in the UK called "Diggit."

The company has pay television agreements with other companies, such as Sogecable, Telepiu, and KirchGruppe, and owns an equity stake in Latin America's leading pay television entities, HBO Ole and HBO Brasil. The Disney Weekend, a PPV service, is also available in Latin America through Direct TV's Galaxy.

Meanwhile, ABC's radio networks can be heard in more than 90 countries around the world. ABC Radio also produces a prepackaged radio program called "It's a Small World" that is distributed throughout China.

Cable activities include ESPN International, which owns or has equity interest in 20 international networks, and by the end of 1998 was received in 152 million households in 180 countries in at least 21 languages. The company owns 33 percent of Eurosport, a pan-European satellite-delivered cable and direct-to-home sports programming service, 25 percent of Sportsvision Australia and 50 percent of ESPN Brazil. ESPN also owns 50 percent of the ESPN STAR joint venture which delivers sports throughout most of Asia and 32 percent of Net Star, which owns the Sports Network, Les Reseau des Sports, and other media properties in Canada. In addition, ESPN Inc. owns a 20 percent share of Sports-i ESPN, the only cable and direct-to-home all-sports network in Japan.

By the end of 1999, there were ten Disney Channels outside the USA, with plans for several more (including a Disney Channel Latin America) during the next few years.[64] The company states that each channel is tailored to specific markets, and includes locally produced content, although the programming consists "primarily of the company's theatrical film and television programming library."

The Disney Club is another weekly series produced for foreign markets. In 1997 the company's annual report reported that Disney Clubs and Disney animation provided more than 235 hours of programming and 250 million viewers each week. In 1998, the company claimed that Walt Disney Television International (WDTV-1) licensed more than 5,000 hours of programming worldwide and provided more than 400 hours of "Disney-branded" shows weekly.

Mickey Inc.

The Walt Disney Company is similar to other corporations in that it is organized to earn income for its stockholders. The company may add business lines or sell certain holdings over the years, and managers may come and go, depending on their success in contributing to the company's income. However, the underlying motivation – the profit motive – endures.

Today Disney represents a dominant player in the media and entertainment business – a sector that, at least in the USA, has become increasingly more concentrated over the last few decades, as corporations have moved or converged across industry lines to form diversified, multinational conglomerates. Several of these media giants look very much like Disney – The News Corp., Time Warner Inc., and Viacom Inc. Other major corporations hold powerful media outlets, along with other lines of business – General Electric Co., The Seagram Co. Ltd., and Sony Corp. According to a study at the end of 1998, only nine corporations owned the major US broadcast television networks, controlled the production and distribution of theatrical motion pictures, produced, coproduced, or had financial interests in over 95 percent of prime-time television programming, and owned or had financial interests in over 95 percent of the cable channels.[65] Following this study, CBS was taken over by Viacom, thus eliminating one of the nine companies. Consequently, at the end of the 1990s, we are left with eight extremely large corporations forming an unprecedented media and entertainment oligopoly. Although these companies may compete in some ways, they represent an incredible concentration of commercial control over the information and communication resources of the country. The Disney company must be seen and understood within the context of this media oligopoly, which some have called "The National Entertainment State."[66]

In this chapter, we have outlined the Disney empire at the end of the twentieth century. While it is clear that the company has diversified and expanded, one might still wonder how the company actually operates. What strategies and policies are implemented to assure continued stockholder value? The next chapter will provide some examples of specific strategies and policies employed. In other words, we will examine the Disney empire in action.

Corporate Disney in Action

While corporations such as Disney are motivated fundamentally by profit, there are different strategies and policies that are used to achieve this goal. It is not enough merely to describe the extent of a corporation's holdings; it is also necessary to discuss the way that the corporation works and the consequences of its actions. Having described the Disney empire, this chapter will explore some of the ways that this far-flung enterprise operates.

One of Disney's key strategies, synergy, is explored, using a recent animated feature as an example. The chapter also details Disney's efforts to control its empire through copyright enforcement and labor policies. The company's global business is discussed, including political activities, as well as international production and public relations efforts.

Synergy in action

> *Synergy*: combined action or operation. *Synergism*: working together; the cooperative action of discrete agencies such that the total effect is greater than the sum of the two or more effects independently.
>
> *Webster's Ninth New Collegiate Dictionary*

> **Director of Synergy**: Corporate, New York. Coordinate all synergy between Capital Cities/ABC Divisions and also with Division of The Walt Disney Company. Must be able to interact well with all levels of management. Reports to Executive VP. ("Job Listing" from an internal memorandum, Capital Cities/ABC, Inc., 1 April 1996)

The major media/entertainment companies have long been diversified, with business divisions spread across film, broadcasting, print, etc. Yet these companies are increasingly realizing the benefits of promoting their activities across a growing number of outlets, creating a *synergy* between individual units and producing immediately recognizable brands. A recent article in the *Economist* detailed this process as follows:

> The brand is a lump of content – such as News Corp's *The X-Files*, Time Warner's *Batman* or Viacom's *Rugrats* – which can be exploited through film, broadcast and cable television, publishing, theme parks, music, the Internet and merchandising.
>
> Such a strategy is not so much vertical or horizontal integration, but a wheel, with the brand at the hub and each of the spokes a means of exploiting it. Exploitation produces both a stream of revenue and further strengthens the brand. Thus when Viacom licenses *Rugrats* toothpaste and *Rugrats* macaroni cheese, it both makes money and promotes the direct-to-video movie launched last year and the full-blown animation feature due out later this year.[1]

This certainly is nothing new for the Disney company. From its inception, Disney created strong brands and characters that were marketed in various forms (mostly through films and merchandise) throughout the world. However, the company's synergistic strategies accelerated dramatically in the 1950s, when the company opened Disneyland, the theme park that used previously created stories, characters, and images as the basis for its attractions. In addition, the television program *Disneyland* was introduced on ABC, providing further opportunities to promote the theme park as well as Disney's other products. Over the past few decades, the possibilities for synergy have expanded even further, with the addition of cable, home video, and other new media outlets. Indeed, the Disney company has developed the strategy so well that it represents the quintessential example of synergy in the media/entertainment industry. "Disney synergy" is the phrase typically used to describe the ultimate in cross-promotional activities.

While synergy is often a goal of other media corporations, the Disney company claims to be especially suited to such a strategy. As one executive explained:

> It's a unique attribute of the Disney company, the ability to create synergy between divisions, whether it's interactive games, Buena Vista television, or the Disney Channel. We all work together and we do it on a year-round

basis and we do it aggressively. The success of those ongoing roles makes everything in the company work better. We actually have people in every division that are responsible for the synergy relationships of the company and every division has that. We take it very seriously. Disney CEO Michael Eisner takes it very seriously.[2]

The case of Hercules

Pre-release strategies While there are endless examples of Disney synergy, a closer look at the release of one film will provide further insight into how every division of the company becomes involved in the marketing effort. Disney's thirty-fifth animated film, *Hercules*, was released in US theaters on 27 June 1997. However, a wide array of promotional activities and the sale of merchandise started long before that date.[3]

In much of the press and industry coverage, Disney marketing and promotion activities are portrayed as simple – even "natural" – processes. An article in *Children's Business* explains: "For the folks at Disney, the philosophy is simple: The movie is the primary product and serves as the inspiration for the merchandise that flows from it." As one Disney executive put it: "It's important to us that the entertainment comes first. First, the kids will see the movie and fall in love with the characters; then they'll want to bring home a piece of that movie."[4]

But, as noted previously, the film doesn't always come first. For a Disney film, the promotion starts with the initial announcement of the film, usually years before its actual release. Work on the pre-production and production process is covered in entertainment and trade magazines, as well as in Disney-owned media. During the 1996 Christmas season, four-minute trailers for *Hercules* were shown before each theatrical screening of *101 Dalmatians*. *Hercules* trailers were also included on the 21 million shipped copies of the *Toy Story* video and on the 10 million cassettes of *The Hunchback of Notre Dame*.

In February 1997, Disney started its third MegaMall Tour to promote its summer films. The previous mall tours for *Pocahontas* and *Hunchback* had attracted more than 4 million people. But the *Hercules* tour was far more extensive, spanning five months in 20 cities and featuring 11 different attractions. The tour included a live multimedia stage show (presented twice each hour), a "Baby Pegasus Playland" for toddlers, featuring carousels and other play areas, and a 10-minute video workshop called "Learn to be an Animator," where guests were shown how *Hercules* characters were animated. Several carnival-type *Hercules*-themed game booths were offered, with McDonald's providing the prizes. In addition, there were opportunities for guests to take photos, try out the new *Hercules* games introduced by Disney Interactive, and log onto the *Hercules* website at hercules.disney.com. The tour was also sponsored by GM Chevrolet, with one guest in each city winning an all-new Chevy Venture Minivan. While the tour represented collaboration between Walt Disney Imagineering and Feature Animation, other Disney divisions (such as Disney Interactive) were also involved.

At its inaugural stop at an Atlanta area mall, Mayor Bill Campbell welcomed the tour by reading a proclamation from the governor naming 6 February as "Hercules Day" in the state of Georgia. Over the next four days of the engagement, attendance at the mall soared by as much as 30 percent and swelled the parking lot to capacity.

Also in February, Feld Entertainment opened the eighteenth Disney on Ice production, *Hercules on Ice* – the first time an ice show had opened before the release of a film.[5] Previously, such productions opened one year to 15 months *after* a film's opening. By the end of 1997, the show had become one of the top-grossing ice shows. Eventually, it would play in 28 cities, for 310 performances over a five-year tour. Accompanying each show were concession stands selling Hercules dolls, caps, flags, T-shirts, plastic cups, and other gifts.

Ironically, the film itself includes a tongue-in-cheek portrayal of the merchandising and tie-in efforts, featuring "Air Herc" sandals, "Herculade" thirst quencher, and even a "Hercules Store" crammed with figurines.[6] Meanwhile, back in the real world, the licensing process for Hercules merchandise had started much earlier and was reported to include nearly 100 manufacturers and 6,000 to 7,000 products, which began appearing in stores at least three to four weeks before the film's opening.

The Disney company obviously had high hopes for the merchandising potential of the film. "This is classic Disney entertainment with broad appeal for the whole family," said Sean Mitchell, director of Marketing in Filmed Entertainment Licensing. "The film's appeal is truly across-the-board. At its heart and soul it's a comedy – very smart, very witty, very funny. We think that little boys will want to become Hercules, and little girls will want to become Meg. So we try to reflect that in the products we do; the merchandise brings the characters to life."[7]

The Greek theme sent Disney executives into ecstasy: "We've got that whole Greek motif to work with," explained Mitchell. "There are so many icons – Greek flowers and urns, columns and temples, swords and musical instruments. We take these classic icons and, essentially, put them through a 'fun filter' to translate to product in a very entertaining way. From a design standpoint, the scope of mythology provides us with almost limitless opportunities."[8]

As mentioned previously, the Disney company manufactures its own products, as well as licensing specific characters and images to other manufacturers. Disney requires a sizable up-front guarantee and a 16 per cent royalty fee on wholesale orders, although most other movie tie-ins ask about 12 percent.[9]

It is important to point out that the marketing/merchandising effort is not a haphazard or casual affair. Not only are licensees carefully selected, but the Disney company insists on coordinating all aspects of the design and marketing of the products. As one of the licensees explained, "Disney's goal is to have the entire merchandising plan look similar. They want all the products in the store to have the same feel and style. So they'll lead us in their direction. We'll submit artwork, and they may say it should have a slightly different look. They want their property to look uniform; they treat it like a brand."[10] Even the licensees themselves work together, sharing ideas for marketing and participating in joint promotions.

As noted previously, a multitude of products were produced by a wide range of licensees (see table 4.1). While some of these companies arranged one-time only contracts with the Disney company, others were involved in long-term relationships. The Disney deal with Mattel included the production of 10 action figures and seven fashion dolls but also represented the beginning of a three-year alliance with the toy company serving as Disney's "master toy licensee." Not only the Mattel toys, but other products were given a big push at the industry's Toy Fair in New York in February.

Another indication of the range of Hercules products is evident from looking at just one company's product line. Pyramid, a manufacturer of handbags, backpacks, and assorted rainwear, introduced four groups of Hercules products, each featuring a different treatment or look. One group was called "comic book" – bright and vibrant colors, playing up the hero/comic book feel of the movie. Another was the "heroic" group, and another "Meg's Garden," obviously appealing to girls with a "romantic" look. The final group was "Daisy Meg," described as "sixties/seventies retro." The different looks obviously indicate the deliberate attempts to appeal to specific segments of the market.

In addition to the toys, clothes, etc., there were also a myriad of publications associated with the film. A trip to a local bookstore revealed not one or two, but over 15 different Hercules-related publications (see

Table 4.1   Licensees for Disney's *Hercules*

Type of merchandise	Companies
Apparel	AAI, Allison Manufacturing, American Needle, Angel-etts, Fantasia, Freeze, Fruit of the Loom, Giant, H.H. Cutler, Handcraft, Happy Kids, Jem Sportswear, Kahn Lucas Lancaster, Kid Duds, Knitwaves, L.V. Myles, Salant Children's Apparel, Pan Oceanic, PCA Apparel, Pyramid, Stanley DeSantis, Wormser, Wundies
Gifts	Applause, Deco Pac, Gloria Duchin, Golden Harvest, Good Stuff/Fantasma, Imagining3, Kurt S. Adler, Monogram Product, Stylus, Timex
Home Furnishings	Beacon, Dundee Mills, Inc., Franco Manufacturing, Inc., Goody Products, Manual Woodworkers, Priss Prints, Sunworthy Wallcoverings, Town & Country Linens, Tsumura, Wamsutta
Housewares	Alladin, Fun Designs, Thermoserv, Treasure Craft, Inc., Wilton Industries, Zak Designs
Stationery	Anagram, Cleo, Inc., Colorbok, Color Clings, Day Dream, Hallmark, Impact, Mello Smello, National Design, National Latex, Rubber Stampede, Sandylion, Sun Hill, Sunkisses, The Art Group
Toys/Sporting Goods	Disguise, Ero, Hedstrom, Janex, Mattel, Rose Art, Skybox, Tiger Electronics, Tyco/Viewmaster

Source: Danny Biederman, "Disney's 'Hercules' Promises Big Summer Muscle," *Children's Business*, Feb. 1997, p. 24

box 4.1). A survey of the Hercules-themed birthday party products available at a local K-Mart store included balloons, ribbons, colored cord, wrapping paper, blow-outs, two types of paper hats, treat sacks, three types of stickers, three varieties of napkins, a paper tablecloth, two styles of paper plates, cups, three different gift bags, streamers, and many different types of cards and invitations. A Greek Decoder Sweepstakes promotion

Box 4.1   Examples of Disney's *Hercules* Publications

Disney's Hercules: Classic Storybook
Hercules: Illustrated Classic Edition
Hercules, the Hero
Hercules Feel the Power
Hercules: Disney Little Library
Hades: The Truth at Last
Disney's Hercules: Easy Peel Sticker Book
Disney's Hercules: A Party for Baby Hercules
Disney's Hercules: A Race to the Rescue
Disney's Hercules: A Hero's Story Special Edition Color Book
Disney's Hercules: The Helpful Son (Pop-Up Pals)
Disney's Hercules: Growing Up (Super Paint with Water)
Disney's Hercules: The Muses Tell All (Special Edition Color Book)
Happy Birthday, Hercules
Disney's Hercules: Thank Heavens for Pegasus!
Disney's Hercules 3-D Mask Book
Disney's Hercules: The Heart of a Hero
Disney's Hercules: A Budding Romance
Disney's Hercules: A Monster Pop-Up
The Art of Hercules: The Chaos of Creation ($50)

---

was featured on much of the Hercules merchandise and was promoted across many of the Disney divisions.

As the Hercules merchandise started appearing in the Disney Stores, some sites received "visual design and theming in support of the film." Around the same time, Hercules products and promotions were featured by tie-in partners, including McDonald's, Nestlé, Choice Hotels International Inc., Quaker Oats, and General Motors Corp. While each of the tie-ins involved different types of products and activities, the McDonald's promotion, which ran from 20 June to 24 July, was probably the most visible. A PR announcement of the promotion illustrates the extent to which the film and other products were tied together:

A "hero's welcome" awaits McDonald's customers this summer with the launch of a mega Hercules promotion tied to the release of Disney's Hercules film. From specially-designed Happy Meal toys and premiums to Hercules-themed packaging and in-restaurant decor, McDonald's will bring the fun of Disney's Hercules film to life in its restaurants nationwide.

Free Gifts For Kids 12 and Under – As a sneak preview of the promotion, Hercules-themed giveaways will be distributed to kids 12 and under with any food purchase beginning June 13 while supplies last. Gifts include Hercules character decals, mini-movie posters and a 16-page special collectible edition of Disney Adventures magazine.

Happy Meal Toys – Hercules Happy Meals will feature ten state-of-the-art toy character sets from the film. Two different Hercules-themed toys in every Happy Meal will be available each week for five weeks at participating restaurants while supplies last.

Heroic Houseware Plate Collection – Six exclusively designed Hercules-themed plates showcasing characters from the film will be available for $1.99 with the purchase of a Happy Meal or large sandwich while supplies last. Made of durable melamine, the collectible plates are dishwasher safe.

Other products that began to appear included the film's sound track (released by Columbia Records on 20 May), as well as interactive merchandise, including Disney's Animated Storybook, Hercules; Disney's Print Studio, Hercules; Disney's Hercules Action Game.

Meanwhile, *Hercules* hit the Internet. Like other film companies, Disney has taken advantage of this emerging resource as a new way of promoting its products, especially upcoming and newly released films. When the *Hercules* site (http://www.disney.com/Hercules) was launched, it featured details of the 20-city mall tour, summaries of the Hercules story, information about the characters and "stars" of the animated film (each character had a home page explaining his or her personality), plus other activities (a Wheel of Sparta game, testing "general Hercules knowledge") and information. "Guests" to the site could download the film's trailer, as well as get information about purchasing tickets to the film. Yet another example of tongue-in-cheek synergy was represented in the ESPN-inspired page, "OSPN: Olympus Sports Panhellenic Network."

Premiere weekend: *Herc* **hits Manhattan** Closer to the release date, segments of the film were highlighted in the media, especially those channels owned by Disney. However, the hype accelerated dramatically during the weekend of 13–15 June, when Disney seemed to take over the island of Manhattan. "The *Hercules* World Premiere Weekend in New York" included a wide range of events scattered around the city, which were promoted widely and covered extensively by the media.

During the entire weekend, "The Hercules Forum of Fun at Chelsea Piers" (sponsored by Chevrolet) featured live performances, interactive games, and animation demonstrations. Exhibits included "Baby Pegasus Playland," "Titan's Tattoo Parlor," and "Hercules' Arcade," featuring a sneak preview of the *Hercules* video game. As part of the festivities, sweepstakes tickets to win a customized Chevy Venture Minivan themed to *Hercules* had been distributed through New York area newspapers on 6 April. The company reported that "The response was overwhelming. All sweepstakes tickets have been awarded and mailed to excited Forum of Fun goers."

On Saturday, jugglers, dancers, and other entertainers were featured outside the New Amsterdam Theatre (owned by Disney), where the "Heroes from Around the World" ceremony was held. The event featured Disney's chief honcho, Michael Eisner, plus New York Mayor Rudolph W. Giuliani, Robin Roberts of ABC Sports and ESPN, and a group of "world-class athletes known for their Herculean efforts." The world premiere of the film was followed by "The Hercules Electrical Parade," a 1⅞ mile extravaganza which started on 42nd Street and continued up Fifth Avenue to 66th Street. The parade featured the new Hercules edition of Disneyland's "Main Street Electrical Parade," including 103 marchers and 30 floats which had been outfitted with an additional 500,000 new bulbs added for the occasion. The Disney folks had arranged for the city to turn off street lights and had requested businesses along the route to darken their shop windows "to allow parade goers to get a clear view of the leading characters." In addition, 68 speaker towers were installed along the route to provide music for the event. Whereas more than a million people were expected for the parade, only "invited guests" attended an after-parade party at the Forum of Fun at Chelsea Piers.

The festivities continued on Sunday with a "Hercules Breakfast with the Champions" – a news conference hosted by Robin Roberts and held at New York's Essex House Hotel, honoring five US Olympic Gold Medal Decathlon winners (Bob Mathias, Milt Campbell, Bill Toomey, Bruce Jenner, and Dan O'Brien), who received hero proclamation certificates from the City of New York. Dr Frank Zarnowski, claimed to be the world's foremost authority on the Decathlon, also participated in the event. The finale was the kick-off for "The Hercules Summer Spectacular at the New Amsterdam Theatre" – a 12-day exclusive New York engagement of the film before its release, including a live stage show featuring a full orchestra and a cast of Disney characters.

The Manhattan premiere party and parade were covered live on E! and also received extensive coverage by other media outlets. On 20 June, the film began an exclusive seven-day run at the historic Chicago Theater. Before each performance, a live stage production of "Disney's Magical Moments" celebrated Disney animation with singing and dancing performers, a full orchestra, and many of the studio's costumed characters.

Meanwhile, on the other side of the country, the El Capitan Theater in Hollywood was the site of another Forum of Fun, another Chevy Venture give-away, plus live stage shows prior to screenings of the film.

Disney also repeated its sneak preview weekend strategy (used for *Hunchback* and *101 Dalmatians*) to promote the 27 June opening through the Disney Stores, Disney On-Line, and the Disney Catalog. The on-line site allowed "guests" to purchase special preview tickets for the *Hercules* Sneak Preview Weekend (21 and 22 June) and to locate participating theaters closest to them. By ordering tickets, consumers would receive special character collector pins and special offer coupons valued at over $50. Tickets were also available at the Disney Stores, through the Disney Catalog, or through a special hotline. For one penny more, shoppers could also purchase the (already) hit single from the film, "Go the Distance," performed by Grammy Award-winner Michael Bolton; however, the cassette single was available only at the Disney Store.

Not too surprisingly, Disney aired a special prime-time television program introducing the *Hercules* characters and cast – on the ABC network, of course. Media coverage of the film's opening also included two specials on the Disney Channel. *Movie Surfers Go Inside Disney's Hercules* (Sunday at 5:30 p.m. and 8:30 p.m.) explored the movie set and provided facts about the film. *Disney's Hercules Strikes Manhattan* (Sunday at 7:30 p.m. and 10:30 p.m.) featured the "Hercules Electrical Parade" as it moved through the streets of New York. The promotion on Disney's cable channel prompted one reporter to monitor the "around-the-clock promotion, clocking Disney's out-of-control commercialism." He found the following:

- Disney crammed three minutes of "Hercules"-related promotions into a half-hour "Chip 'n' Dale Rescue Rangers" cartoon at 8 a.m. Friday.
- Three 30-second spots, liberally laced with "Hercules" scenes, hyped "Hero to Zero Weekend."

- Two 30-second spots and a 60-second one urged kids to watch a half-hour infomercial, "Movie Surfers Go Inside Disney's 'Hercules.'"[11]

On yet another Disney-owned cable channel, A&E featured Hercules on their Biography series, introducing the program with footage from the Disney film. *The Village Voice*'s comment: "and he's not even a real person!" (15 July, 1997).

Meanwhile, the only movie theater in Celebration, Florida, was showing Disney's *Hercules*, and the Hercules Victory Parade opened at Walt Disney World.

Perhaps one now can understand why one financial analyst recently concluded that "Walt Disney is one of the most efficiently integrated entertainment companies on the planet. All the other entertainment conglomerates talk about 'synergy,' but Disney is the only company that actually does it. They know how to squeeze 'synergy' until it screams for mercy."[12]

The disappointing results?   In its first two weeks of general release, *Hercules* took in about $58 million at the box office – a poor showing compared to previous Disney summer releases, such as *Pocahontas* (1995), which grossed $80 million in its first two weeks, and *The Lion King* (1994), which grossed $119 million.

Numerous explanations were given for the unimpressive showing. Some observers noted that the film failed to capture the whole family and was definitely less appealing to girls. Others thought that the film was dragged down by its subject matter, and still others pointed to the heavy competition from strong action films released around the same time. Another explanation:

> "No one doubted that 'Hercules' would be a biggie," said Arthur Rockwell, an entertainment analyst at the brokerage firm Yaeger Capital Markets. "The reviews were good, the buzz was great. But it may have been hurt by such calculated commercialism. When a movie is made for McDonald's and the retailers, it loses sight of the story and audience. Like 'Batman & Robin,' 'Hercules' is seen less as a movie than as a giant marketing venture."[13]

Although it is possible to surmise that Disney ultimately made a profit on *Hercules*, it is a real challenge to locate reliable data to document such a claim. Researchers are often forced to rely on the whims of company officials and industry trade gossip for the most basic financial data about production costs and actual revenues from films, much less the additional revenues gleaned from home video release, merchandising, tie-ins, etc. Examples: *The Lion King* is claimed to have generated $1 billion in profits from all sources; *Hunchback* is estimated to have added around $500 million to Disney's bottom line. While Disney executives say that animation is more than twice as profitable as all live-action films combined, still, "Calculating exact profits from animation is difficult, because the movies spin off other entertainment like parades at theme parks and TV programming. Some estimates say animation and its ancillary income may account for 70 percent of Disney's profits."[14]

The production cost for *Hercules* was reported to be $70 million (budgets for big animated films are now typically over $100 million). The US box office gross for the film grew to $83,426,924 by 31 July to $90,704,556 by 28 August and $99,111,505 by 3 February 1998. Worldwide box office revenues were reported to be over $245 million in September 1999. *Hercules* was released to video in February 1998 and generated further profits.

Even though the film may not have been the predicted box office or immediate merchandising success, still, the characters from the film were added to Disney's stable of "classic" characters. One clear indication that Hercules had joined the ranks of the classic is the *Encyclopedia of Walt Disney's Animated Characters: From Mickey Mouse to Hercules*, published by Disney's Hyperion Press in 1998.

Several years after the film's release, Disney's marketing outlets continue to promote a wide range of *Hercules* products. Toys, clothes, and gifts are stocked at Disney Stores, and the Disney Store Online features a range of *Hercules* products, including limited edition collectibles (such as a Hercules stained glass at $50). "Hercules fun" is offered on Disney's Blast Online, as well as on the main Disney.com, where on-line guests can hear the Hercules sound track, find out how to arrange "a hero's birthday party" at Club Disney, preview *Hercules* CD-ROMs, and try out computer programs, such as Hercules Print Studio.

The Hercules legacy continues at the theme parks, where *Hercules* characters are featured in parades and other attractions. In September 1998, the television version of Disney's *Hercules* premiered on ABC's *One Saturday Morning* block of children's programs and was also included in Disney's afternoon block of syndicated shows. During the summer of 1999, *Hercules: Zero to Hero* was released directly to video.

Beyond Hercules: *examples of synergistic referencing*

The *Hercules* case demonstrates how all the corporate divisions become involved in promoting a Disney brand, but it doesn't really reveal some of the additional synergies that were created with the ABC merger. The addition of ABC and ESPN dramatically increased the possibilities for cross-promotion or referencing of Disney properties.

Again, there are plenty of examples, and only a few will be mentioned here:

- Shortly after the ABC–Disney merger, *Roseanne* featured several epi-sodes about visits to Walt Disney World and several *Good Morning America* shows were broadcast directly from the theme park.
- The introduction to ABC's *Monday Night Football* during the 1997 season featured an opening sequence in which jets flew across well-known American landmarks, including the EPCOT dome and Cinder-ella's castle at Disney World.
- In 1997, ABC's coverage of the Tour de France included a feature on Disneyland Paris.
- One of the events taking place at Disney World in November 1998 was ABC Super Soaps Weekend.

The merger also allowed for the crossover of talent, especially between ESPN and ABC. For instance, Chris Berman, the popular ESPN sports-caster, now appears regularly on ABC sports programs. Other examples of crossover talent include films, such as *The Waterboy*, a Touchstone produc-tion, which included several sequences with ABC and ESPN sportscasters.

While promotion of products across divisions and crossover talent are probably predictable business strategies, coverage of news and public affairs is another matter. The issue of corporate censorship or influence of news coverage has been addressed over the years by numerous communications scholars.[15] When Disney took over the reins at ABC, and thus ABC News, there was a good deal of attention to The Mouse House's involvement in the news business. While the company claimed that it would institute a hands-off approach to news production, there have nevertheless been instances of corporate meddling.

The most notable example involved the ABC's news magazine program, *20/20*. ABC News was accused of canceling a story about theme park security, which included claims that Disney World does not administer the kind of security checks to potential employees that would identify sex offenders. Apparently, network executives had arranged to use research from the book *Disney: The Mouse Betrayed* but rejected drafts of a script for the story. Of course, company spokesmen claimed that the chairman of ABC News made the decision "on his own without direction from network or Disney executives." This certainly may be true. However, as Leo Bogart points out, the process of influencing news coverage works in subtle and indirect ways. "Few media overlords are so crude as to give direct orders to kill or slant stories. They do not have to do that in order to let it be known what their views are and where their interests lie. Almost imperceptible Pavlovian cues reinforce desired behavior and inhibit what is unwelcome."[16] While claims of direct censorship can often be denied or possibly substantiated in some situations, it is still difficult to separate editorial policies from ownership connections, no matter who makes the decisions.

Controlling the empire, or "keeping the ducks all in a row"

Disney's obsessive control is a theme that runs throughout discussions of the Disney universe, whether in academic studies or in the popular or trade press. We will be returning to issues relating to control when we discuss Classic Disney texts, as well as the theme parks. But, for now, the analysis of Disney as a corporation leads to questions about the company's attempts to control its properties, through copyright, labor relations, and tough tactics.

Copyright control

> **Copyright**: the exclusive right to reproduce literary, dramatic, artistic, or musical work, given by law for a certain period to an author.
>
> **Trademark**: the name or distinctive symbol attached to goods for sale as a warrant of their production by a particular firm.
> *Webster's Ninth New Collegiate Dictionary*

The enforcement of intellectual property rights has become a vital issue for media and entertainment companies, especially in light of the proliferation of branded products, as well as the increased global marketing of products. For instance, American film companies have elicited the assistance of an army of lawyers and the FBI to enforce their property rights in the USA, as well as the State Department and Interpol in foreign markets. Piracy remains a thorn in the side of the Hollywood majors, which claim that billions of dollars are lost each year from unauthorized use and sale of their products.[17]

Disney has long been known for its tough enforcement of intellectual property rights and has a rich history of litigation against and/or harassment of potential copyright violators. When Team Disney took command, the campaign accelerated to the point that the company declared a "war on merchandise pirates" in 1988. "This anti-piracy program continues as one of our top priorities," said Paul Pressler, vice-president of Disney's merchandise licensing. "Our characters are the foundation of our business and project the image of our company, so it's imperative that we control who uses them and how they are used."[18] Between 1986 and 1991, the company filed 28 suits against more than 1,322 defendants. One of the largest actions was in 1991, when Disney filed against 123 California companies and 99 Oregon companies for unauthorized use of characters in various types of merchandise.[19]

While the company regularly pursues a large number of copyright cases, some incidents have received more attention than others. For instance, in 1989, Disney threatened to sue three Florida day-care centers for unauthorized use of their characters in murals. The day-care centers removed the figures and replaced them with characters from Universal and Hanna-Barbera cartoons, which were provided at no expense. The incident was widely reported and is often used as a classic example of Disney's obsession with controlling its characters.

Also in 1989, Disney sued the Academy of Motion Pictures Arts and Sciences when performers dressed as *Snow White* characters were used in the Academy Awards presentation without Disney's permission. The case was withdrawn, but many in Hollywood were amazed at Disney's pettiness.

More recently, the Disney company was able to force a French AIDS association to withdraw a campaign featuring provocative versions of *Snow White* and *Cinderella* characters. While French law allows for parodies of copyrighted cartoon characters, the president of the advertising agency handling the campaign admitted that the campaign was withdrawn because of pressure from the Disney company.

While the corporation may be within its rights in protecting its properties, the company's public responses are often brash and arrogant. To cite an instance, British papers reported early in 1998 that the Disney company was closely watching the development of the Millennium Dome in Greenwich after visits to Orlando, Florida, by British Secretary of State for Trade and Industry Peter Mandelson. One journalist pointed out that the Disney company is "famously protective of its copyright" and cited a Disney executive: "He [Mandelson] may be a minister of the British Government, but we are the Walt Disney Corporation and we don't roll over for anyone."[20]

Yet another case was the refusal of the company to provide free use of Disney characters for US postage stamps celebrating American animation. We have seen Bugs Bunny, Daffy Duck, Tweetie Pie, and Sylvester (Warner Brothers' characters) adorning US mail. As one reporter says:

> But don't expect to see such other cartoon favorites as Mickey Mouse, Donald Duck or Goofy on stamps any time soon. At least not as long as the money-hungry executives at Walt Disney Studios demand that the Postal Service pay royalties for the right to depict their stable of characters on stamps.
>
> Ironically, it was Disney that first suggested a series of stamps depicting the studio's cartoon characters. After securing tentative agreement from Washington, Disney's minions asked how much the quasi-governmental agency would pay for the right to issue a Minnie Mouse or Pluto stamp.
>
> [Postmaster General Marvin] Runyon is reported to have said "not one red cent," and Disney replied "no deal." It was a good ruling on the Postal Service's part.
>
> Warner Brothers immediately stepped in and agreed to allow use of its trademark characters without requiring royalty payments. That's why we saw thousands of bunnies instead of mice on stamps this year.[21]

Copyright Extension Act, 1998 The company's concern witih intellectual property rights became crystal clear when Congress faced the issue of extending copyright protection in 1998. Michael Eisner and the Disney company led a successful lobbying campaign to convince Congress to pass legislation extending copyrights, representing a classic example of how Hollywood clout can influence the legislative process.

The bill, initially introduced by singer/actor turned Congressman Sonny Bono, proposed changes in the copyright law to allow corporations to have exclusive rights over their copyrighted properties for 95 years rather than the 75 years allowed in the existing law. Also, copyrights held by individuals were to be extended to a total of 70 years after death, rather than 50 years.

While proponents argued that the extension was necessary to match the European Union's recent copyright extension, some legal experts pointed out that the bill represented a "wealth transfer" benefiting large entertainment and publishing corporations. While supporters of the bill who held that it was noncontroversial were able to keep it out of public debate, opponents argued that the bill was not in the public's interest. "Making money isn't what copyright law is about," said Adam Eisgrau of the American Libraries Association. "The purpose of the law is to provide a sufficient incentive to authors and inventors to create information, not because there is a constitutional entitlement to compensation but because the information created was regarded as a public good."[22]

Corporate copyright holders, such as Disney, lobbied Congress directly, as well as calling on their pals at the Motion Picture Association of America (MPAA), which used "its own heavyweight lobbyist: its president, Jack Valenti, who called on his own decades-long contacts with legislators to move the bill."[23] But the legislation was apparently too important to rely only on face-to-face lobbying tactics. Disney provided campaign contributions to ten of the 13 initial sponsors of the House bill and eight of the 12 sponsors of the Senate bill.

The significance of the legislation was revealed in press coverage of the eventual success of the campaign, which pointed out that Disney's copyright on Mickey Mouse was scheduled to expire in 2003, on Pluto in 2005, on Goofy in 2007, and on Donald Duck in 2009.[24]

While Disney plays tough when it comes to protecting its own properties, the same treatment is not accorded for those bold enough to offer their ideas to the Mouse House. The Disney website explains that the company's policy prohibits the acceptance of creative ideas or materials, other than those requested. However, if someone does submit such material, the policy is clear:

> the Submissions shall be deemed, and shall remain, the property of DISNEY(sic). . . . DISNEY shall exclusively own all now known or hereafter existing rights to the Submissions of every kind and nature throughout the universe and shall be entitled to unrestricted use of the Submissions for any purpose whatsoever, commercial or otherwise, without compensation to the provider of the Submissions.[25]

Sidebar: the Oregon Duck   The University of Oregon's mascot is a duck: the Oregon Duck, a "fighting" duck − a duck that is a version of Disney's Donald Duck. The University of Oregon is the only university that currently uses a Disney character as a mascot, and the story of the

Plate 2 The Oregon Fighting Duck. The University of Oregon's mascot is a version of Disney's Donald Duck, used with the permission of the Disney company with specific restrictions.
Photo by Carlos R. Calderon.

university's relationship with Disney is an interesting example of the company's thirst for control.

The university has used a duck as its mascot since the 1920s but adopted a version of Donald around 1947, when the Disney company contacted the university about its use. In 1948 Walt Disney agreed to permit the university to use Donald as the model for the Oregon Duck, but evidently no written record was produced. A photo exists of Walt in a University of Oregon jacket posing with university representatives, and that photo has been used for years as the basis for the university's argument that Walt sanctioned the use of Donald's image.

In 1974, the agreement was formalized with a written license arrangement that allowed non-exclusive rights to use the character on a royalty-free basis. The Oregon Fighting Duck (or, as it is referred to around Oregon, The Duck) was distinguished from Donald Duck in various ways, and an "Afro" duck was developed as well.

By 1978, requests from non-university businesses for use of The Duck on merchandise prompted closer scrutiny of the agreement. However, the university's request to add sub-licensing arrangements was denied by the Disney company in 1979.

In 1991, a new and more detailed licensing agreement again authorized the university's "character use" of the Oregon Duck primarily for athletic events but also provided for sub-licensing arrangements. While the university can sub-license The Duck with Disney's trademark to manufacturers, the contract requires a licensing fee of 12 percent, half of which goes to the Disney company. The university would typically charge 7.5 percent on licensed products and thus loses 1.5 percent when The Duck is involved. The amount that the Disney company receives varies from as much as $30,000 to $85,000 each year, depending on how much Duck merchandise is sold. "The money that we send them probably doesn't seem like a lot in the whole scheme of the Disney enterprise," said Matt Dyste, Director of Merchandise Marketing and Licensing at the university. "Walt said that we could use The Duck, and that probably is the only reason that Disney signed the [1991] contract with us. It seemed apparent that they would rather we were not involved in licensing their character."

Another stipulation in the contract is that The Duck be used "in a good manner" and not portrayed in a "negative light." The contract does not provide any further detail but apparently assumes that university officials will be familiar enough with the Disney image to interpret this provision. "They assume that their culture is so seeped into you, that you know what that means," Dyste explains. "Most people have traditionally thought of Disney as wholesome, family, as entertainment of a good quality."

In addition, the contract forbids the university from selling any products with The Duck image outside of the Eugene and Portland (Oregon) areas, which is a real handicap for the University of Oregon, since colleges and universities increasingly sell their merchandise across the country for additional financial revenue that is usually used to support various campus programs. In addition, a more burdensome approval process for new Duck merchandise involves three stages and five production samples to be sent to the Disney company.

So why does the University of Oregon stick with the Donald Duck image? Dyste explains: "We love the character, and the value that The Duck has to the University of Oregon is more than anything that we could generate off licensing revenues if we owned our own character. The history, the character, the alumni. It all fits together. When you think of The Duck, you think of The Oregon Duck."[26] As for the future, Michael Eisner, the current Disney CEO, assured an inquiring stockholder at the 1999 annual meeting that the University of Oregon could count on keeping the Oregon Duck as their mascot indefinitely.

Controlling labor: working for the Mouse House

Another element in Disney's exercise of control is its relationship with its workers. According to the 1998 10-K report, the company employed approximately 117,000 people, including a wide assortment of workers in its diverse businesses. The Disney name is an attraction for potential employees, who may have dreamed all their lives about working at the studio or one of the theme parks. Still, the allure of the Magic Kingdom can be deceptive.

It appears that many Disney employees are quite pleased with their work environment, as reported in a "company snapshot" from Vault-Reports.com, a website that includes information on corporations for prospective employees. Based on interviews and surveys, the report noted that employees feel that working for Disney is a boost to their career, and that the perks offered them are seldom matched by other companies (theme park admission, merchandise discounts, etc.).

Yet, the study also found that salaries are typically below industry standards and that the company's bureaucracy can be discouraging if employee expectations are too high. The report warns prospective workers, "Despite the warm and fuzzy material it produces, at its core Disney is a rigid corporate bureaucracy." As a seasoned Disney worker explained, new employees become "disillusioned because they envision The Walt Disney Company as a Magic Kingdom kind of place which is a fairytale land devoid of bureaucracy, politics, and other unsavory things like financial analysis. No such place exists."[27]

The company promotes itself as a "community," in which employees share in decision making, and promotions are made from within the company. The informal familiarity at Disney is well known, symbolized by everyone being addressed by their first name. However, within different sectors of the company, there are specific ways that employees are controlled. The next two sections discuss workers at the studio and at the theme parks.

Studio workers/animation Historically, the employees who have attracted the most attention at Disney have been those involved with animation. As John Lent explains, American animation was founded on labor exploitation, not only at Disney, but at most of the Hollywood animation companies, where "talented animators worked extremely long hours at grueling, tedious jobs for low wages and with virtually no credit."[28]

As noted in chapter 2, the labor strife in the early 1940s was not at all surprising considering the low pay and lack of recognition at the Disney studio. Salaries were reported to be the lowest in the film industry, with inkers and in-betweeners at Disney receiving between $17 and $26 a week in the 1930s into the 1940s. Long hours and quotas were common, and animators were sometimes forced to take work home. But the loss of control over their work also frustrated Disney employees. Whatever was produced by employees while at the studio belonged to the company, and, as discussed in chapter 2, Walt Disney controlled virtually the entire animation process. Consequently, the Disney style of animation that developed left little room for experimentation and individual creative touches.

During the 1960s, Disney joined other companies in sending work overseas, where it could be done more cheaply. The 1990s renaissance in animation has been due in part to Team Disney's revival of the Classic Disney animated features, but also to new television and cable channels featuring cartoons and animated series. This has meant more work for animators in Hollywood, but also more animation work abroad, especially in the growing offshore animation centers in Japan, Taiwan, South Korea, Canada, and Australia. Typically, pre-production activities are done in the USA, while cel drawing, coloring (by hand), inking, painting, and camera work are done abroad. Post–production is still typically done in the USA.[29]

Although it is claimed that there has been a shortage of animators in the USA during this animation boom, there is ample evidence that producers have looked to offshore animation workers to save money. As one producer explains, "If we had to do animation here, it would cost a million dollars instead of $100,000 to $150,000 to produce a half hour, and nobody could afford to do it except for Disney."[30]

Yet Disney also sends a good deal of its animation work overseas, either to its own companies or as the sole client of other companies. When Disney accelerated its animation production for both film and television in the mid-1980s, it turned to Japanese animation companies. In 1989, Walt Disney Animation Japan was created, where drawing, inking, coloring, and shooting were done. Disney also purchased the Hanna-Barbera Australia studio in 1989, where work on the company's series, specials, and made-for-video movies has been done. Additional work on Disney animated productions is subcontracted to companies in South Korea and China. Closer to home, Disney opened studios in Toronto and Vancouver in 1996, creating about 225 jobs for animators, directors, designers, storyboard and layout artists, as well as a digital ink and paint production team.

While wages at the Asian animation factories are reported to be relatively high for animators and managers, conditions for other workers who perform the "drudge work" of inking, coloring, etc., are less than impressive. As Lent points out, "Of course, that is what attracts the foreign companies in the first place: large numbers of individuals willing to work hard for low wages in a stable setting."[31] How these pools of trained animators contribute to building domestic animation in these countries is still an open question.

Meanwhile, it is also unclear what this offshore activity means for US animators, especially when and if the animation boom slows. Previously, American animators have protested runaway production, specifically in 1979, when the Motion Picture Screen Cartoonists IATSE Local 839 walked out and demanded a restriction on the export of work from Los Angeles studios unless qualified union members were hired first. Nevertheless, the studios continue to use foreign labor, even when high unemployment rates are experienced by union workers. Consequently, it seems likely that the historical tension between animators and management may continue.

Theme park workers The "happiest places on earth" are renowned for their happy and helpful employees. But this doesn't happen automatically, and, by some accounts, working at the Magic Kingdom is not always magical.[32] After a two-year study of Walt Disney World, Kuenz concluded that "Disney's control of its labor force is apparently near total; the workers themselves certainly perceive it as such." Despite the company policy requiring employees to waive their right to write about their work experiences, Kuenz found employees who were more than anxious to talk about their jobs at the Magic Kingdom.

As noted above, the chance of working at one of the Disney parks is an alluring fantasy for some people. Thus, the Disney company seems to have no problem in finding plenty of interested workers for its parks and resorts. It's a question of whether these potential employees fit (or are willing to fit) the Disney mold.

One of the ways that Disney actively recruits young, eager workers is through the Walt Disney World College Program, which attracts over 3,000 students from the USA and other countries each year. The program includes seminars that encompass work and classroom experiences. While a job at the park may not necessarily follow, students who complete the program are awarded mock degrees, a Mousters or a Ductorate.

Employee training is a common practice for many American corporations, but Disney's training of theme park employees is legendary. With the opening of Disneyland in the 1950s, the company created its own training program called "The Disney University," which now operates "campuses" at each of the theme parks and at the Disney studio in Burbank. The training program includes teaching future employees ("cast members") the company history and philosophy in a two-day course called "Traditions," which has been cited by management experts as one of the "best indoctrination programs" in the world.[33] It is here that new employees learn to accept the control of the company. Zibart explains it as "a mix of company legend, behavioral guidelines, and psycho-social bonding. 'You come out totally believing in "The Disney Way",' said a five-year veteran. 'It's almost like Walt is alive and well. . . . We call it getting doused with pixie dust. It lasts about a year – and of course some people have to go through it again.'"[34]

During the course, new employees learn about "The Disney Culture" – defined in company literature as "the values, myths, heroes and symbols that have a significant meaning to the employees . . . Ours is a culture that is so strong it has withstood the test of time and is recognized all over the world."

Most importantly, park workers learn about the Disney approach to serving the public and "preserving the integrity of the show." Employees are required to smile, to make eye contact, to display appropriate body language, and to seek out guests. Some analysts have referred to this as "emotional labor," defined as "expressing socially desired emotions during service transactions."[35] There is also a long list of taboos, including: never embarrass a guest, never be out of character, never improvise with scripts,

Box 4.2   Guidelines for a Guest Service Fanatic

Service
- Always makes eye contact and smiles
- Exceeds guest expectations and seeks out guest contact
- Always gives outstanding quality service
- Greets and welcomes each and every guest
- Maintains a high personal standard of quality in their work

Teamwork
- Goes "beyond the call of duty"
- Demonstrates strong team initiative
- Communicates aggressively with guests and fellow Cast Members
- Preserves the "magical" guest experience

Attitude
- 100% Performance
- Extremely courteous and friendly
- Displays appropriate body language at all times
- Exemplifies the Disney Look
- Says "Thank You" to each and every guest

Recovery
- Provides immediate service recovery
- Aggressively seeks opportunities to fully satisfy our guests
- Solves guest problems before they become dissatisfied
- Demonstrates patience and honesty in handling complaints
- Always preserves the integrity of our show

Emphasizes safety, courtesy, show quality, and efficiency!

Source: Material distributed by the Walt Disney Company

never fraternize with other workers, never wear costumes anywhere but in the assigned area, etc. Those employees who learn well and exhibit exemplary service are called Guest Service Fanatics, as outlined in box 4.2.

Training also includes specific guidelines on what to do in emergency situations, as the Disney company is notorious for keeping these situations under their control. For instance, safety guidelines instruct workers never to use "panic words" – fire, car accident, ambulance, and evacuation – but to use "Disney terminology" – Signal 25, Signal 4, Alpha Unit, and Exiting. Employees are carefully instructed on how to deal with these situations to avoid upsetting guests, as well as to control the potentially damaging publicity that may follow.[36]

After the Disney indoctrination, all "cast members" are on probationary status for a specific period of time, while their "leader" (or just "lead") monitors their performance. Seasonal cast members are on continuous probationary status and are thus advised by the company to "pay particular attention to our policies and procedures."[37]

In addition to wearing specific "costumes," "cast members" must also adhere to a strict grooming code. In other words, the uniform, "squeaky-clean" look of employees at the parks is not automatic or natural, but the result of strict enforcement of "The Disney Look." Some of the specifications of the code, drawn from a company brochure entitled "The Disney Look," include the following:

> For hosts – neat, natural haircuts "tapered so that it does not extend beyond or cover any part of your ears." [Illustrations in the "Disney Look" manual provide examples of acceptable and unacceptable haircuts.] No mustaches or beards are allowed, however, deodorant is required.
>
> For hostesses – no "extremes" in hair styles; confinement of long hair by acceptable accessories, . . . a plain barrette, comb or headband in gold, silver, or tortoise shell without ornamentation of any kind including bows. No more than two barrettes or combs; only natural makeup is permitted, and only clear or flesh toned fingernail polish. Polishes that are dark red, frosted, gold or silver toned are not considered part of the "Disney Look." Finger nails should not exceed one-fourth of an inch beyond the fingertip.

More recently, the restrictions have been expanded to include no shaved heads, no visible tattoos, no nose or other piercing, except the ear lobe, where two are allowed for women only. The Disney Look is serious business. According to the employee (or "cast member") handbook, "continued violation" of the appearance policy is grounds for dismissal.

There are lots of other reasons why theme park employees may be "fired on the spot" – especially those workers who wear the famed Disney character costumes around the park and hotels and for special appearances. Most importantly, they are never, ever, ever allowed to remove their character's head in front of park guests, even if they are ill or unconscious, which apparently is quite often. With no peripheral vision, navigating in the awkward and sometimes dangerous outfits can be tricky, although the workers inside them must always stay in character. The costumes are so hot and heavy that those inside them often become sick to their stomachs or pass out.[38] It seems obvious that preserving the "magical" guest experience is more important than workers' welfare. (More on the theme park experience in chapter 6.)

In addition to staying in character, maintaining the show, and serving guests, park employees must also be aware that they are being watched or monitored. Employees report an obsession with getting people through the rides as quickly as possible, with time-motion experts monitoring the "hourly operational ride capacity." A former employee explains, "At Big Thunder Mountain, I'm supposed to handle 2,000 visitors an hour. It's just like a factory with assembly-line production, only this is a fun factory."[39]

Furthermore, the workers who Kuenz interviewed suggested that everyone is spying on everyone else at the theme parks. "Foxes" are disguised employees (dressed as tourists with cameras) who spy on guests, attempting to prevent various kinds of mischief, including shoplifting and theft in the park. Meanwhile, "shoppers" – also disguised as tourists – monitor and test employees to make sure they are adhering to the Disney rules of behavior. Kuenz concludes:

> The collective paranoia inculcated in Disney workers from the get go – manifested in the suspicion that there is always another rule one can be found breaking – and which results in their feeling that they are always expected to perform the frequently irritating role of "Disney cast member," is a function of both the tight control that the company exercises over its dominions and a segmented and hierarchical system of relations between management and labor and within labor itself.[40]

The rewards: salaries, promotions, perks Although the workers at the parks are subject to a particular kind of control, other policies apply to all employees of the company. The VaultReport cited earlier notes that "The Disney pay scale, unfortunately, doesn't match the high sheen of the Disney name." Prospective employees are warned that the company's pay scale is 10–15 percent below the market, and raises are slow and erratic. Another employee explains that "in a way, you're paid just with the Disney name." The report concludes that "This works to Disney's advantage, but can be a trap [for employees].[41]

Moreover, Disney workers are certainly well aware of the "exorbitant executive salaries" discussed in chapter 3. Recall that the Chief Mouse, Michael Eisner, receives a $750,000 salary with stock options that regularly

Table 4.2   Salary compensation comparisons

	Annual	Weekly	Daily	Hourly	Per minute
Eisner	$204,236,801	$3,927,631	$785,526	$98,191	$1,637
Minimum wage					
earner	$9,880	$190	$38	$4.75	$0.08
Average Worker	$24,700	$475	$95	$11.88	$0.20
President of the USA	$200,000	$3,846	$769	$96	$1.60

Source: "Paywatch Fact Sheet," NABET-CWA website,
http://pw2.netcom.com/-nabet16/page24.html (using 1997 AFL-CIO data)

place him in the top brackets of executive compensation. Meanwhile, the lowliest of Worker Mice at the Disney theme parks typically work for minimum wage.[42] A comparison of these different salaries is presented in table 4.2. As a union representative explains:

> The fact of the matter is that real wages and benefits for most rank-and-file workers at Disney have gone down significantly since Eisner and his top crew came aboard. And, to be sure, this sacrifice on their part is a major reason why corporate profit and executive salaries have gone up at Disney. But what about the sacrifice on the part of Eisner and his senior executives. Where is it? I guess leadership by example doesn't count for much these days.[43]

The company also appears to be inflexible in negotiations with prospective employees. The VaultReport quotes an employee who explains that "Disney is an 800-pound gorilla in the marketplace. They know it and aren't afraid to use it, which can be frustrating."

Despite the rhetoric of equal opportunity and promotion from within, employees claim that "to move into a higher position, they had to be favored by someone above them, which usually requires them to be obsequious, not make problems, not complain."[44] For instance, promotions at the theme parks are often made to the position of "lead" – a sub-management job that is not actually considered that of a supervisor or a manager. However, leads are still the "first line of supervision," although they have little power and, contrary to company rhetoric, do not often move subsequently into actual supervisory positions.[45] The hierarchical system at the parks divides the work force into specialized units with separate managers, who are "all working earnestly at their one task, the left hand oblivious to the right." As Kuenz notes, it's the model for work in the new world order: "This is a world in which all social planning has been replaced – as every attraction at EPCOT's Future World predicts and hopes it will be – by corporate planning, every advance in social coordination conforming to and confirming the logic of the company's needs."[46]

Contributing to this Brave New World scenario, many employees are exceptionally devoted to the Disney company, which is claimed to have an unusually low employee turnover rate (although there are contradictory claims of a relatively high worker turnover).[47] One explanation is that the company "fosters both a sense of responsibility and a sense of fun."[48] It's a company where the lowliest worker calls the CEO "Michael," where "cast members" make people from all over the world happy, where employees receive free passes to the parks, where apparently there is an endless supply of pixie dust.

Mickey as Teamster   Disney deals with a number of trade union organizations, as do other Hollywood corporations.[49] Generally, union representation for the film and entertainment industries has become increasingly more diversified, as the different types of businesses incorporated by Hollywood companies have involved further differentiation of labor, making it difficult for workers to form a united front against one corporation. For instance, workers employed by Disney include animators at the Disney Studio, hockey players on the Mighty Ducks hockey team, and Jungle Cruise operators at Disneyland.

The differentiation of labor is especially apparent at the theme parks, where workers are represented by a wide array of labor organizations, many unrelated to those active in the film industry. For instance, over a dozen labor organizations have contracts with Disney World, where unions have formed trade councils to negotiate contracts.[50] Over 30 unions have been represented by eight contracts, with 14 unions negotiating under two trade council agreements.[51] Meanwhile, at Disneyland, five unions usually negotiate a master agreement for about 3,000 employees. The trade unions include the United Food and Commercial Workers; Service Employees International Union; Hotel Employees and Restaurant Employees; Bakery, Tobacco and Confectionery Workers; and the International Brotherhood of Teamsters (who represent workers who wear the Disney character costumes at the park). Although the notion of Mickey Mouse and Donald Duck as Teamsters may be jolting to many Disney aficionados, at least they are represented by an employee association, which is sometimes not the case at other theme parks.

Generally, the trend towards diversification has contributed to a weakening of trade unions' power as well as to a lack of unity among workers. As *Los Angeles Times* labor reporter Harry Bernstein has observed, "These days, corporate tycoons own conglomerates that include businesses other than studios and networks. They may enjoy movie-making, but money seems to be their primary goal. So if production is stopped by a film industry strike, their income may be slowed, but money can still roll in from other sources."[52]

Thus, the Disney company attempts in various ways to maintain control over its workers throughout its diverse business endeavors. And, despite the techniques that some employees use to find their own pleasures and satisfaction in their work, the company usually gets what it wants. As a Disney insider quoted in the VaultReport advises those considering working for The Mouse, "It's important not to lose sight of the fact that Disney is a huge company which is in business for the sake of our stockholders – owners who want to make money by growing the company's value."[53]

Control through tough tactics

The 800-pound gorilla analogy used above is fitting for Disney's tactics beyond the labor market, for the company has become notorious for its tough and sometimes unscrupulous style of dealing with other companies, as well as its employees.

Since Team Disney took over, the company's "formula for success" has been "talk tough, talk cheap, and keep total control."[54] In addition to the cost-cutting measures discussed in chapter 3, the company has stepped on numerous toes in the industry to get what it wants. Examples abound, but one of the most often cited is the lucrative licensing arrangement for the Disney–MGM Studios, which Disney was able to negotiate for a pittance with MGM's lawyers and refused to reconsider. The park's construction also became controversial when Disney's supporters helped convince the Florida legislature not to support a similar plan by MCA/Universal. To add to the drama, the very idea of a studio theme park in Florida was claimed to have been lifted by Eisner, while he was at Paramount, during a meeting with the head of Universal.[55]

Disney's tactics have led to a plethora of lawsuits, not only over copyright issues, as discussed previously, but over a wide range of other business deals. One lawyer observed that tangling with the Disney company was "like suing God in the Vatican."[56] The company is known for not paying bills, withholding royalty payments, insisting on its own terms with theater owners, etc. Lewis notes that in 1987 Disney was involved in 17 major lawsuits involving 700 defendants in the USA and 78 others overseas.[57] As one industry observer noted, "Disney's critics say doing business with the company means facing teams of lawyers who will stake out extreme positions on virtually every negotiating point and often return to try to reargue issues later if Disney isn't pleased. Mickey Mouse may be the soul of this company, but you'll find the heart somewhere over in the legal department."[58] It is no wonder, then, that the Disney studio is known around Hollywood as Mousewitz, and Team Disney as the Rat Pack.

Disney's globalization

Nevertheless, Team Disney has succeeded in rebuilding and expanding the company's holdings, not only in the USA, but also internationally. In 1989, *Fortune* magazine claimed that "the company has become the archetypal American corporation for the 1990s: a creative company that can *move with agility to exploit international opportunities* in industries where the US has a competitive advantage" (emphasis added).[59] Of course, the company's success in foreign markets does not happen automatically, or necessarily because Disney's products are universally demanded. The next two sections of this chapter will discuss a few ways in which the company clears the way for its products in foreign markets, as well as takes advantage of global opportunities made possible through the exploitation of international labor.

Global agility: political persuasion

The Disney company, like many other USA-based multinationals, "move[s] with agility" in foreign markets not only because of its own activities, but with assistance from the US government. The company's activities are supported, whenever and wherever necessary, by the State Department's efforts to enforce copyright claims and break down national policies that inhibit USA companies' "agile moves."[60] For instance, the company joins with other US-based media corporations in insisting on copyright protection for their products in foreign markets and relies on the US government to enforce these rights using whatever means are necessary.[61]

Just as the Disney company waged a campaign to support the copyright extension bill discussed earlier, US entertainment companies continuously make financial contributions to election campaigns, so that politicians and government officials will feel favorably disposed to supporting their interests in foreign markets. For instance, the Washington-based Center for Responsive Politics, in a study based on reports to the US Federal Election Commission, included major contributions to the Democrats from entertainment and communications companies in 1995. Among them: $125,000 from the Walt Disney Co. and $373,000 from Miramax Films Corp. In light of these contributions, it is not surprising to find that President Clinton's trade negotiators have challenged policies that limit the sale of American films and television programs in international markets.[62]

Though the Disney company is similar to other multinational companies, it is also notable for eliciting assistance from foreign governments on its own, especially in the construction of its parks and resorts, in ways that other companies probably only dream about. While there are numerous examples that could be cited, a relatively recent *coup d'état* was the support received from the French government in the construction of Disneyland Paris. To attract the Disney company and the estimated 30,000 jobs that would be provided by the park, the French government assisted in various ways, including cut-rate land deals, low-interest loans, tax breaks, infrastructure improvements, and other investments.[63]

Meanwhile, in late 1999, the following announcement was made:

> The Hong Kong government may lend Walt Disney Co. as much as $1 billion and take a majority stake in a new theme park that the world's second-largest media company may build in the city, a source familiar with the plan said. Such an agreement . . . would be the first such government investment in a private enterprise.[64]

While the Disney company doesn't always get its way with governments around the world, or even in the USA, its ability to do so in many situations provides it with important advantages in foreign markets, and thus the Disney brand continues to cross international borders, and Disney products continue to be interpreted as "universal."

Global opportunities: exploiting labor

Not only is Disney generally able to move with agility in global settings, but the company also succeeds by "exploiting international opportunities." Like other multinational companies, Disney takes advantage of chances to make its products outside the USA, where labor is cheaper and operational costs are lower.

Film and television production are arranged where labor is cheap or tax advantages are lucrative, which often means countries outside the USA. As discussed above, animation production is often cheaper in other countries, so some of Disney's work is done in Asia, Australia, and Canada.

But Disney's extensive merchandising activities also benefit from the globalization of labor that has accelerated over the last few decades.[65] Like many other American companies, Disney often designs its own products, then licenses the actual manufacture to independent subcontractors, mostly in Third World countries. The company obviously benefits from controlling the design of products, which can then be produced at lower costs and sold at higher profit margins. But the company also benefits from a global division of labor that perpetuates the deskilling and devaluation of labor in the process.[66]

The company licenses the rights to its intellectual property to contractors at relatively high rates, thus subcontractors seek to manufacture products at the lowest possible cost. For products that depend on manual labor (clothing and toys, for instance), this often means that products are manufactured where labor costs are low, meaning American sweatshops or factories located in developing countries.

One source claims that Disney-licensed products are manufactured at an estimated 3,000 factories worldwide, often in Third World countries where workers are paid poverty-level wages and often work in inhumane conditions. For instance, in December 1998, the minimum wage for workers in Haiti was 30¢ an hour, which equals $2.40 a day, or $624 a year. If a worker is paid on a piece-rate system, it is possible to receive around 42¢ an hour, which is still not enough to pay for a family's food for one day. Human rights groups have organized efforts to call attention to these conditions, calling for a living wage of 60¢ for Haitian workers.[67]

Licensed products are also produced in China, Macau, and Vietnam, where workers are sometimes paid late (or less than promised) to work in factories where they are exposed to toxic chemicals. Other products are made in Hong Kong, Taiwan, Dominican Republic, Mexico, St Lucia, Malaysia, Brazil, Thailand, Columbia, El Salvador, the Philippines, Indonesia, Sri Lanka, Honduras, India, and Bangladesh.

James Tracy argues that products manufactured in these countries are sold at prices set as if they were manufactured in industrialized countries, making it difficult for workers to purchase the products they make. The average GNP per capita for the previously listed countries in 1997 was $3,296. At the same time, the per capita GNP for the US was $25,860, and $34,360 for Japan. Tracy argues:

While the labor of developing countries produces these articles, the laborers are excluded from consuming their products. Further, surplus value created by underpayment is embodied in the products. When Disney prices the product as if it were manufactured in an industrialized country, Disney profits from that surplus value.[68]

In a study of Disney merchandise available in one American city, Tracy compared different types of Disney products and where they were produced. He found that a majority (80 percent) of the toys, jewelry, and ceramics (which require manual labor) were manufactured in dependent countries, while media products (which benefit from automated production) were overwhelmingly (92 percent) produced in industrialized nations.[69]

Though Disney is not the only multinational company to take advantage of globalization trends, the international prominence of the Disney brand, as well as the emphasis on products for children, should draw special attention to these business practices.

Promoting and marketing The Mouse

Disney's popularity or universality is not automatic, but a result of deliberate, coordinated marketing, advertising, and promotional activities. The company has developed its own expertise in marketing its products, both nationally and globally. In the USA, the coordinated efforts involve advertising and promotion by the company's own outlets, as well as carefully planned tie-ins with other companies and public relations campaigns, as exemplified by the *Hercules* case described earlier in this chapter.

The company spends a substantial amount each year on advertising its various businesses. In fact, Disney was the seventh largest US advertiser in 1997, ranking behind General Motors, Proctor & Gamble, Philip Morris, Chrysler, Ford, and Sears. Disney spent $1,249.7 million in 1997, which was actually down 1.1 percent from 1996, when it ranked fifth overall among US advertisers.[70] Table 4.3 indicates where Disney advertises in the USA and how much is allocated to Disney product lines. But it is also important to note that the company ranked thirty-fifth for its advertising expenditures outside the USA, where it spent $293.7 million in 1997. This represented a 40 percent increase over 1996, but was primarily directed at 18 countries, mostly in Europe ($236.5 million), but also in Asia ($32

Table 4.3 The Walt Disney Company's advertising expenditures, 1996–1997 (in $ thousands)

	1996	1997
Magazine	75,704	82,100
Sunday magazine	8,755	9,177
Newspaper	112,599	109,342
National newspaper	3,440	7,501
Outdoor	7,407	11,620
Network TV	267,209	263,920
Spot TV	176,044	137,986
Syndicated TV	37,361	55,937
Cable TV networks	44,205	55,224
Network radio	1,100	1,872
National spot radio	23,426	15,069
Internet	847	3,504
Measured media total	758,096	749,801
Unmeasured media total*	503,397	499,867
TOTAL	1,263,493	1,249,668
By brand:		
Buena Vista Pictures	465,700	406,500
Disney entertainment	97,503	106,063
ABC TV network	47,037	54,681
ESPN cable	21,416	17,010

* Unmeasured media figures are *Advertising Age* estimates and include direct mail, promotion, co-op, and special events.
Source: "100 Leading National Advertisers," *Advertising Age*, 28 Sept. 1998, pp. s3–50.

million) and Canada ($23.6 million). Relatively little was spent on advertising in Latin American ($1.7 million), and none in either the Middle East or Africa.[71]

As with many other corporations, the company uses a variety of promotional strategies in addition to advertising. However, Disney seems to be particularly adept at creating its own promotional opportunities. A wide range of events are organized and promoted, such as children's festivals, teacher awards, etc. Specific examples include the Children's

Summit at Disneyland Paris and Mickey for Kids International Rapid Chess Tournament.

A highly promoted program sponsored by the company is the Disney Learning Partnership – a "philanthropic initiative designed to draw on the strengths of The Walt Disney Company in support of creative, innovative teaching strategies." The program includes teacher recognition and professional development, collaborative school-wide learning initiatives, and strengthening parent-teacher connections. The American Teacher Awards have been presented since 1989, honoring hundreds of extraordinary teachers across the country.

A more recent promotional campaign is called the Millennium Dreamers Award, and is described as follows on the Disney website:

Are You a Millennium Dreamer?
As we welcome the new millennium, Disney and McDonald's, in association with the UNESCO (United Nations Educational, Scientific, and Cultural Organization), have created the Millennium Dreamers Awards. This global children's recognition awards program celebrates the remarkable achievements of young people around the globe by recognizing their ability to make our world a better place today.

Millennium Dreamers demonstrates the ongoing commitment that The Walt Disney Company and the McDonald's Corporation have to young people around the world. Incorporating a search from more than 100 countries around the world, Millennium Dreamers is the most far-reaching program of its kind ever.

A total of 2,000 "Millennium Dreamers" ages 8–15 will be selected and receive a trip to the WALT DISNEY WORLD® Resort, May 8–10, 2000, where they will participate in an awards celebration and children's summit.

Yet another example is described in the company's *1997 Annual Report*:

Winnie and his friends plan a host of special events and an array of new merchandise. On August 2, Pooh will again be the huggable ambassador of Friendship Day. In Europe and throughout the rest of the world, he will appear on new lines of products for children and on video games from Disney Interactive.[72]

Moreover, Disney never misses a chance to celebrate an anniversary, whether for one of its characters or parks or films. Coverage of these events by the press is not left to chance, as the company is well known for "schmoozing" journalists, treating them to expense paid trips to the theme parks and showering them with gifts. The results are often glowing "news" reports about the company's activities. Hiassen discusses these junkets, as well as echoing the emphasis on celebrations, in his book *Team Rodent*:

> The company is gung-ho on anniversaries, these being splendid occasions for inviting battalions of reporters to Orlando for weekends of high-end gluttony and mooching. Depending upon how cheap your newspaper or broadcast station happens to be, Disney is prepared to pay for just about everything, from air travel to lodging to entertainment.[73]

As Hiassen notes, the press becomes part of the Disney team, most often reporting positively on whatever event or product the company introduces.

A similar kind of partnership is fostered with travel agencies. It is no coincidence that travel agents help to promote the Disney theme parks as ideal family vacation destinations. The company has organized its own training program for travel agents, awarding degrees for successful completion of the program. It is impossible not to see how these efforts contribute to attendance at the parks, although it is more difficult to assess exactly how much.

The Disney company also makes every attempt to promote and sell its products in foreign markets, often tailoring its efforts to local markets. The company also prepares its products with foreign markets in mind. One recent example was the music prepared for the company's animated feature *Tarzan*, which was dubbed for over 35 different markets. This required Phil Collins to record the film's music in German, Italian, French, and two dialects of Spanish, and the film was also dubbed by local talent in other languages, such as Bahay Malay for Malaysia. Previously, Disney's films have been subtitled; however, the company is increasingly dubbing music lyrics, as well as dialogue, to make the films "more accessible" to young children and adults who don't like to read subtitles. A Buena Vista executive explained: "This gives us a tremendous promotional and publicity tool, and it's another step in localizing our product. It means we can take our movies around the world and make them sound like local movies."[74]

The company often receives help in its international marketing efforts from its local representatives. For instance, Buena Vista Distribution/ Denmark helps to distribute Disney films in Denmark, as one of their employees explains: "We are just an auxiliary arm of the film producers,

Plate 3   Global Mickey. The Disney characters appear in sites all over the world, as indicated by a mural outside a party shop in Fabens, Texas (near the Mexican border) and a tourist store in the seaside town of Piran, Slovenia.
Photos by Carlos R. Calderon and Andrew Jakubowicz.

and our purpose is to present the spirit of each work to the Danish audience. It is the enthusiasm and inventiveness of the Disney employees in each country which is the motive power of the launching of a film."[75] An example of how such inventiveness works is the promotion that took place in Denmark several months before the film *Pocahontas* was released in 1994. The company arranged a tour called Pocahontas Interactive that explained the story of Pocahontas through a live stage show, interactive displays, and other exhibits. Danish representatives helped to arrange the show at one of the large shopping centers outside Copenhagen (Lyngby), where children and their families could hear about the story and its animation. At the same time, *Pocahontas* merchandise was available in many of the shops at the center. Of course, the Pocahontas Interactive exhibit also traveled to other countries, preparing other audiences unfamiliar with the story for the arrival of the Disney film.

Many, many other examples could be cited. However, the point to be made here is that the Disney company does not merely advertise its products; it publicizes and promotes the Disney brand through a multitude of calculated and highly coordinated strategies and schemes, both in the USA and in foreign markets.

The bottom line, after all The activities and policies of the Disney company – as any corporation – are difficult to summarize in complete detail. However, one of the aims of the last two chapters has been to emphasize that Disney operates *as a corporation* with the same goals as any profit-motivated company. Some corporate policies and strategies may differ; for instance, the Disney company may be more emphatic about control over its properties than other companies. Nevertheless, the goal ultimately is to accumulate profits for the company's shareholders. But, although the company has been enormously successful in these efforts over the years, to the point that company representatives have been guaranteeing annual growth and specific returns on investment, the Disney company is not infallible or exempt from the usual business trends. Despite the image of Disney as a special, magical domain, business exigencies still apply to the Disney empire.

Now that we have explored the Disney empire and understand a bit more about how the corporation works, we turn to the messages and meanings of the Disney products. Chapter 5 will focus mostly on Disney's animated films, while chapter 6 looks more closely at the theme parks.

5 Analyzing the World According to Disney

We make the pictures and then let the professors tell us what they mean.

Walt Disney

The unique characteristics often attributed to the Disney company make it especially important to look carefully at what is actually produced and what meanings may be associated with these cultural artifacts. The previous chapters have discussed the evolution of the Disney company and some of the strategies that the company uses to pursue its primary objective of creating shareholder value. In this chapter and the next, we will look more closely at some of the Disney products, especially those identified as Classic Disney, what they mean, and how the company's primary objective influences them. The next chapter will consider similar interpretations of Disney theme parks and real estate projects.

Approaches to interpreting media content

Popular culture continues to be analyzed in many different ways, including those that consider form as well as those that focus on content. As prominent examples of popular culture, the products distributed by the Disney company have been interpreted in these various ways, as well. Since the first Mickey Mouse cartoons were released, Disney films have been analyzed in the popular press by film critics and analysts, who have mostly employed an assortment of aesthetic and art criticism and literary analysis.[1]

The next two chapters, however, will present an overview of the academic discussions of Disney products that have emerged from a wide range of disciplines, from film and television studies, to geography, anthropology, history, and architecture. In general, the analysis of content, or texts, has been a technique or method of studying media and popular culture from within a variety of interpretive paradigms. In communications studies, media content has often been studied utilizing quantitative methods of analysis from a positivist perspective; but rarely have these techniques been used to study Disney products.[2] More often, studies of Disney content have employed qualitative or interpretive forms of textual analysis, often drawing on literary and film studies, but also on cultural studies and feminist perspectives.[3]

In general, film theory and criticism have reflected many of these theoretical and methodological approaches to textual analysis. Thus, a review of the styles of film criticism over the years is a helpful beginning in trying to situate the various approaches that have been used to interpret Disney products. Braudy and Cohen discuss four periods in over 100 years of film theory and criticism.[4] The first period was basically formalist, and considered the artistic merits of film. The second period evolved during the 1960s and 1970s, as the academic study of film gained momentum, and critiqued earlier film theories, posing questions related to race, class, gender, and language. The third period introduced a variety of new interpretive approaches from linguistics and a wide range of semiotic and structuralist models, including cultural anthropology, Marxism, and Freudian psychoanalysis. Most recently, Braudy and Cohen note that film analysis has become more eclectic, with attempts to merge various approaches from history, psychology, and linguistics and to draw upon feminism, neo-formalism, cognitive psychology, empiricism, and phenomenology.

This chapter will present examples of the most prevalent forms of analysis that have been used to study Disney content, including aesthetic, feminist, psychoanalytical, and Marxist analysis, and will consider specific issues or areas that have been repeatedly analyzed: specifically, the reinterpretation of children's literature, the character of Mickey Mouse, and the representation of women, race, and nature. The next chapter will consider the themes that have been identified in the analysis of the Disney theme park, including postmodern approaches. Most of these studies have focused on Disney products that have a common set of characteristics. So, before going into the various interpretations of Disney content, the Classic Disney model will be outlined.

Classic Disney

Film scholars have studied American film studios and identified unique attributes during particular time periods or for specific film genres. Although the Disney company has produced a wide range of entertainment products and even a variety of motion pictures, the company is still known for products based mostly on a specific formula that was established at the studio while Walt Disney was in charge and has changed little over the years.[5]

It is possible, therefore, to identify something called "Classic Disney," which refers to the company's animated films, cartoons, and some live-action films, plus the stable of characters which emerge from these productions, as well as the consistent set of themes and values that generally represent "Disney" to the general public and critical analysts.

Such live-action productions include such films as *20,000 Leagues Under the Sea*, *The Absent-Minded Professor*, and *The Love Bug*, as well as some television programs, such as *Davy Crockett* and *Zorro*. However, the company now also distributes live-action films oriented to nonfamily audiences that certainly do not have the Disney look or feel, or even the Disney name (as discussed in chapter 3), and thus would not be considered "Classic Disney." (Examples include *Pulp Fiction, Armageddon, Scream, Jackie Brown*.)

There are other Disney-produced or distributed products that may not immediately come to mind as "Disney," but nevertheless include many of the Classic Disney characteristics. Examples might include some of Disney's television productions, such as, more recently, *Home Improvement*. It may also be necessary to distinguish Disney comic books from the animated features, although the comics still retain some of the Classic Disney characteristics.

Generally, though, it is the animated features and cartoons that constitute Classic Disney. It is also possible to refer to these products and characters collectively because they generally include a specific style, a standard formula of story and characters, as well as a set of common themes and values. It is interesting to note, too, that it is typically the Classic Disney films and characters that are featured in merchandise, as well as at the company's theme parks. The characteristics that define Classic Disney will be explored in the rest of this chapter through examples of analyses and critiques that have not only focused on the content of Disney's products or texts, but also contributed to defining Classic Disney. First, though, we need to discover how Classic Disney developed and evolved.

Evolution of Classic Disney   Robert Sklar has observed that Disney's first cartoons were imaginative, magical, and open-ended, without obvious points and with no fixed, logical order.[6] However, after 1932, there were more closed fantasies with distinct beginnings and usually happy endings. The more structured story lines became moral tales with overt values represented. The changes became especially obvious in some of the Silly Symphonies, which helped to develop the Classic Disney model as well as serve as experiments in technology (sound/color) and aesthetics (animation techniques, movement, etc.). The Classic Disney style came to be typified by light entertainment, punctuated with a good deal of music and humor which revolved mostly around physical gags and slapstick, relying heavily on anthropomorphized (human-like), neotenized (childlike) animal characters. Indeed, animators were told to "keep it cute" when it came to creating characters, as the description of each Disney character reveals. Perhaps not so coincidentally, this also helped sell merchandise, as well as films.

The first Silly Symphony, *The Skeleton Dance* (1928–9), is an example of the very early period, in which Disney produced imaginative and open-ended animation. The film was relatively unstructured and even a bit grotesque. Set in a cemetery at night, several skeletons rise from graves and perform various dances set to appropriate music, finally returning to their graves at dawn.

By contrast, only a few years later, *Flowers and Trees* (1932) presented a moralistic story with a distinct beginning and a distinct ending, anthropomorphized characters, and good triumphing over evil. The story involves a male and a female tree falling in love, fighting the dark, evil tree (with the help of other forest friends), and ultimately marrying.

Another good example of emerging Classic Disney was *The Three Little Pigs* (1933). The cartoon based on the Grimms' tale became the most famous of the Silly Symphony series and was extremely popular in the USA and elsewhere. Its theme song ("Who's Afraid of the Big Bad Wolf?") became a "national anthem" that was said to provide optimism in the midst of one of the worst depressions in US history. Numerous critics have offered interpretations of the film's appeal, emphasizing the historical context of its release and claiming that the pigs' story had a strong impact on a Depression-weary American public, encouraging citizens to work hard and maintain an optimistic attitude. Schickel observed that "philosophically the message is Hooverian, stressing self-reliance, the old virtues of solid, conservative building and of keeping one's house in order."[7]

Despite Disney's reported astonishment at these interpretations, *The Three Little Pigs* clearly revealed some of the values and ideals that contributed to establishing the Classic Disney model that characterized future films. The popularity of *The Pigs* also meant that it was enormously profitable, grossing $125,000 during its first year of release and "twice that before its run was finished."[8] In addition, a major merchandising campaign accompanied the film, with numerous items featuring the Big Bad Wolf and the pigs, including a wide variety of toys, dolls, school supplies, and games, as well as everything from wrist watches to Christmas tree lights.[9]

Characteristics of Classic Disney   There is no doubt that the Disney style of animation was influenced in its early years by Walt Disney, but others at the studio also contributed to this unique, identifiable style.[10] Classic Disney developed as a specific type of story with a predictable plot featuring a collection of formulaic characters. In addition, the themes emphasized in Disney productions came to represent specific values and a fairly well-defined ideology.

Many writers have attempted to capture the essence of the Disney style or model, with references to the common traits and characteristics of Disney products. As noted in the first chapter, Real has identified the Disney universe,[11] while Jackson refers to the "Disney vision," including the way that Disney markets its products.[12] Other writers sometimes refer to "Disney culture," while other analysts refer to typical characteristics of Disney products, without using a specific label.[13]

To get a better sense of Classic Disney, it is sometimes helpful to contrast it with other examples of animation. The most common comparison is that between Disney and Warner Brothers' products.[14]

One of the most compelling assessments of the Disney style is that of Steven Watts, who argues that Disney drew from modernism modified by realism, or an aesthetic hybrid that he calls "sentimental modernism." His description is worth quoting in detail, as it incorporates many of the commonly ascribed characteristics of Classic Disney.

> First, it blended the real and unreal, naturalism and fantasy, and manipulated each in an attempt to illuminate the other.

Second, it secured nonlinear, irrational, quasi-abstract modernist explorations comfortably on the cultural map by utilizing certain tropes from the Victorian past – an exaggerated sentimentality, clearly defined moralism, disarming cuteness – as familiar artistic signposts.

Third, it willingly dug down through layers of consciousness to engage the fluidity of experience and action, but always returned to embrace rationality.

Fourth, it animated the world – literally – by ascribing intention, consciousness, and emotion to living and inanimate objects alike, but did so in such a way as to downplay the presence of evil and tragedy.

Fifth and finally, it good-naturedly satirized the pretensions of high culture and sought to invigorate it with the vitality of popular cultural expression.[15]

Watts considers *Fantasia* the best example of Disney's sentimental modernism, although his formulation fits most of Classic Disney and touches on many of the themes that other critics and analysts have identified over the years. However, Watts's delineation of the Disney style can be expanded by looking at the types of stories, characters, themes, and values that are continuously represented in Classic Disney. Without a doubt, there are exceptions and variations, as not all of the characteristics have been included in every product or text. (See box 5.1.) These characteristics will be discussed further in the case studies that follow.

Classic Disney stories

Reinventing folk tales   Disney often used, and still relies quite heavily on, classic folk and fairy tales as the basis for feature films and even shorter cartoons. Indeed, Disney's versions of some of these stories are sometimes better known than the originals, especially in the USA. As many critics have noted, stories and characters typically go through a process of Disneyfication, which involves sanitization and Americanization. These critiques will be discussed further later in this chapter.

Narrative style   Classic Disney films represent commercial, Hollywood cinema and thus have employed familiar narrative elements. In fact, Disney seems to fit rather nicely into Bordwell, Staiger, and Thompson's well-known model of "Classic Hollywood Cinema," which is described as follows:

Box 5.1 The Classic Disney

Style
- light entertainment
- music
- humor (usually physical gags and slapstick)

Story
- often revised fairy tales or folklore
- classic Hollywood cinema model

Characters
- anthropomorphized, neotenized animal characters
- formulaic heroines, heroes, villains, sidekicks
- stereotypical representations of gender and ethnicity

Themes/Values
- mainstream American
- individualism
- work ethic
- optimism
- escape, fantasy, magic, imagination
- innocence
- romance, happiness
- good over evil

1. Though occasional memories, fantasies, dreams or other mental states may be rendered, the narrative is mainly set in a present, external world.
2. Individual (not group) characters with clear motives cause the narrative's actions and consequences.
3. The main characters have a goal.
4. The main characters must confront various antagonists or problems to reach the goal.
5. The main characters succeed in reaching the goal (happy endings), and the film has closure, not unresolved plot lines.
6. The emphasis is on clear causes and effects of actions.
7. Continuity editing and other filmmaking techniques assure clear, linear development.[16]

It is interesting that the Disney formula has adhered so closely to this model, especially in that animation provided the potential for illimitable innovative and creative possibilities. While other animators were known for anarchistic and inventive styles, Disney played it safe and followed the traditional narrative style.[17]

In addition, Disney films have almost always revolved around a love story, in one way or another and most often feature music. In fact, more recent Disney animated features have drawn on Broadway talent for music and lyrics and thus have been converted rather easily into actual Broadway musicals, as in the case of *Beauty and the Beast* and *The Lion King*. As Hahn explains in his "behind-the-scenes look" at Disney animation, "Songs are important because they express the major turning points in the story. In the development of an animated film, the songwriters are an essential part of the storytelling team."[18]

Classic Disney characters

Classic Disney includes characters who are usually quite predictable. The Disney animators followed careful formulas in creating characters and stories, which typically revolved around heroes or heroines who are strikingly handsome/beautiful, with an upper-class or aristocratic background. There is always a villain, who is typically the opposite of the hero/heroine, often ugly, extremely fat or extremely thin, with exaggerated facial features. In addition, humorous sidekicks are usually provided for the main characters.

Identifying the Disney formula for stock characters in its animated features is not just an academic exercise – these characteristics can be perceived without any deep readings or semiotic analyses. Early in 1998, *Entertainment Weekly* rated recent Disney characters according to how well they fulfilled the standard "job description" in the Disney formula. Their job descriptions and the top ratings were as follows:

> Hero/Heroine: Embody nascent all-American sex appeal, mope around, sing at scenic viewpoints, heed call of duty, leave home. Top rating: Belle, in *Beauty and the Beast*.
> Love Interest: Incite villain's lust, have great hair, start as perceived enemy of hero/heroine, be an individual (females only). Top rating: Esmeralda, in *Hunchback*.
> Sidekick: Behave like hero/heroine's naughty younger sibling, eat anything in sight, provide comic relief. Top rating: Cogsworth, Lumiere and Mrs. Potts in *Beauty and the Beast*.
> Mentor: Be reluctantly pressed into service by hero/heroine's worthiness,

come across as ethnic, pour tea (Mrs. Potts only). Top rating: Genie, in
Aladdin.

Villain: Crave control of universe, keep nose in air, be either huge or
emaciated, collect mortal souls, perish by falling. Top rating: Frollo, in
Hunchback.

Henchman: Get clonked on the head, spar with sidekick, furnish ineffectual
support that sinks villain's plan, escape scot-free. Top rating: Flotsam and
Jetsam, in *The Little Mermaid*.[19]

These predictable characters also say quite a bit about the Disney world
view, which seems to have changed little over the years. For instance,
some may argue that female characters in Disney films have been narrowly
construed and remain so even in the newer Disney films. The Classic
Disney heroine is represented especially well by the first one, Snow White,
who was innocent, naive, passive, beautiful, domestic, and submissive.
And, while they may display far more intelligence and independence than
Snow White, Cinderella, or Sleeping Beauty, the more modern Disney
heroines (Ariel in *The Little Mermaid*, Jasmine in *Aladdin*, and Belle in
Beauty and the Beast), still live in male-dominated worlds, and ultimately
find fulfillment through their romantic relationships with Prince Charm-
ings.[20] Disney heroines are *always* beautiful, shapely, and often sexually
attractive, while female villains are typically ugly and either extremely thin
(Cruella) or grossly fat (Ursula), thus perpetuating norms of physical beauty
prevalent in mainstream American culture.

Disney women also seem to be alienated from other female characters,
as represented, for instance, by the absence of any interaction between
Ariel and her sisters. Another recurring theme is the absence of mothers
(and sometimes parents in general) in Classic Disney stories. Dorfman and
Mattelart present an intriguing analysis of the "asexual, sexuated world" in
Disney comics. But the animated features have also perpetuated this
tradition. For instance, Ariel, Jasmine, and Belle have fathers but no
mothers. While "the sanctity of the family" is said to be a dominant theme
in Disney features, ironically, few complete families are represented.

Classic Disney themes and values

It is often assumed that the values represented in early Disney products
were influenced initially by Walt Disney's own Midwest conservatism. But
it might also be argued that Classic Disney evolved from what Walt Disney
and others at the studio perceived an audience would accept and enjoy, or,

in other words, how they could entertain and amuse audiences through their animated productions.

From the mid-1930s, Disney films were increasingly interpreted (usually positively) by critics, despite Disney's reluctance to acknowledge anything other than their entertainment value. This sentiment is represented in the epigraph of the beginning of this chapter, which Disney apparently repeated often in various ways. As Schickel notes, "If an idea did not stem from his conscious mind or receive acknowledgment from it, it simply did not exist for him."[21]

Nevertheless, the products manufactured by the Disney company are laden with meaning and values, some deliberately encoded and others that may not have been intended. A reading of the themes and ideas presented in all of the products manufactured by Disney is certainly not possible here or perhaps anywhere else. But it is possible to suggest some of the dominant themes and values that have been continuously represented in Classic Disney.

Individualism and optimism   Taxel describes the Disney value system as consistent with the Basic American package: "individualism, advancement through self-help, strict adherence to the work ethic, and the supreme optimism in the possibility of the ultimate improvement of society through the progressive improvement in humankind."[22] Historically, certain Disney cartoons have strongly reinforced these values. *The Three Little Pigs* immediately comes to mind, as well scenes from *Snow White*, as the dwarfs dutifully sing and whistle as they work. Not only hard work, but individual solutions are consistently represented as Mickey Mouse and other characters confront evil characters and difficult situations. Similar sentiments are expressed in more recent Disney fare: Ariel takes matters into her own hands so that she can become a human.

While Disney may not have been alone in reinforcing these values in the popular cultural sphere, the characters and stories represented in Classic Disney provide unmistakable models for a dominant all-American ideology.

Escape, fantasy, magic, imagination   Many Disney plots revolve around characters wishing to escape from their current setting or situation. The examples are plentiful, from Snow White (her theme song, "I'm Wishing") and Gioppetto (his wish for Pinocchio to be a real boy), to Ariel (who yearns to be human) and Aladdin (his theme song, "A Whole New World"). And, of course, the wish is most often granted or made possible by a fairy or magical being, not necessarily by the actions of the character. Certainly, this is an attractive fantasy – to be able to escape without any effort from one's current life or world to another more appealing one. The fantasy and escapist themes are stressed in the emphasis on *magic*, for example, the *magic* kingdom. But this is not a world of fantasy or magic run amok. Fantasy is carefully controlled, and little is left to the imagination, as will be discussed further in the next chapter on theme parks.

Innocence   The worlds created in Classic Disney represent a wholesomeness and innocence that somehow seem foreign to the world in which we actually live. And while many argue that this quality is healthy for children, the Disney world is not geared only at children. Walt once explained: "I do not make films primarily for children. Call the child innocence. The worst of us is not without innocence, although buried deeply it might be. In my work, I try to reach and speak to that innocence."[23] Another view is that Disney's productions were actually aimed at adults and utilized "obvious symbols of the adult world." Meanwhile, yet another critic explains that "everything is so sweet, so saccharine, so without any conflict except the obvious one of violence."[24] And Henry Giroux calls the Disney universe a "pedagogy of innocence," teaching children specific lessons through beguiling and pleasurable entertainment.[25]

Another theme that is related to innocence is the coming of age of the typical Disney hero or heroine, which often ties together the themes of individualism and absent parents, as noted by Hahn:

> Have you ever noticed how many heroes come from nontraditional families? Belle, Jasmine, Pocahontas, and Ariel have no mother. Snow White, Dumbo, and Cinderella have no father. Aurora in Sleeping Beauty is separated from her parents. Mowgli, Aladdin, Quasimodo, and the Beast have no parents at all. Part of the subtext of a fairy tale is the journey from childhood and being dependent on parents to adulthood and relying on yourself.[26]

Romance and happiness   Leading characters most often fall in love at first sight, and stories revolve around their quest for love. While Disney is not alone in stressing romantic aspects of life, the films often concentrate on them to the extreme. Most of the "problems" which preoccupy Disney characters are of a personal, very often, romantic variety. And, of course, there are always happy endings.

Good triumphing over evil   The moralism is clear and overt. Good is rewarded, evil is punished. Characters are clearly either good or evil, with little ambiguity or complexity. And good always triumphs; dealing with defeat, failure, or injustice is typically not explored in the Disney world. Everything always works out for the good guys. Always.

Of course, many of these themes are not unique to Disney, and not all of Disney's products include all of these characteristics or values. However, it might still be argued that Classic Disney has consistently represented this package of mainstream American values over the years, reinforcing dominant themes of the political and cultural context in which they were created. In addition, there is strong and effective reinforcement of this package through the successful synergistic activities of the company.

The remainder of this chapter will discuss examples of Classic Disney, examining how specific films fit the model and how the pattern may have changed over the years, as well as exemplifying various approaches that have been used to analyze Disney products.

Aesthetic analysis

One way in which cultural products have often been discussed is in terms of aesthetics, or as objects of art. Aesthetic approaches typically examine the design and assess the beauty of art objects, with little regard to the context in which the object was produced.[27] A wide range of problems have been raised over aesthetic analysis, including the attempt to transcend historical context and a propensity towards subjectivity, as well as tendencies that perpetuate a hierarchy of high/low culture. However, it is necessary to discuss this type of analysis, because an enormous amount of material considers Walt Disney as an artist and Disney animation as art. Most often these discussions focus on Classic Disney films, as discussed above.

Walt Disney, the artist, the auteur   As noted in chapter 2, Walt Disney is often praised as an artistic genius. Throughout the 1930s and 1940s, a host of art critics sang the praises of "Disney, the Artist," comparing him to da Vinci, Michelangelo, Brueghel, Rembrandt, and Picasso, among other famous artists.[28] The academic world joined the art world, with exhibitions and awards of honorary degrees to Walt Disney by Harvard, Yale, and the University of Southern California.

While praise of individual filmmakers is not uncommon, Langer notes that animation producers have been treated as individual artists more often than other filmmakers: "Until recent years, there has been a tradition of analyzing animated cartoons by attributing their characteristic features to the particular achievements of an individual, paralleling *auteur* methodology in the study of live action film."[29] *Auteur* theory, an approach that credits one person (usually a director) with the creative inspiration behind a film, has been a popular form of film analysis over the years. However, the attention that Walt Disney has attracted goes far beyond that of any other animation producer and many film directors. Finch, for instance, praises Disney as "one of the most vigorous and innovative filmmakers in the entire history of the cinema."[30]

This attention may not be so surprising, as Disney typically grabbed most of the glory for himself, not even giving credit to animators in early productions, as discussed in chapter 2. It also helped that the Walt Disney story fit so well the American dream of individual success.

However, it is a mistake to focus attention only on Walt as the creative genius behind the Disney phenomenon. As noted previously, Walt may have been a major force in the studio's development, but he was not the only one responsible for the success of the company's films. Commercial filmmaking in general, and especially animation, is a collective art form. As simply explained in a "behind-the-scenes" book published (perhaps ironically) by Disney, "Animation is a team sport. Yes, there are leaders and followers, but for the most part, an animated film is created by a team of very creative people."[31]

Walt Disney's actual contribution to "Disney art" is difficult to assess, as the rhetoric of his artistic genius is so pervasive and deeply enmeshed within these discussions. Most of his biographers have qualified their discussions of Disney's talents, pointing out that he was not a great artist, didn't contribute a single drawing to any of his cartoons after 1926, and even had difficulty duplicating his famed signature. He was much more of a producer, story editor, and designer, with a strong sense of story line, timing, and character. While Walt was the guiding force at the studio in the early years, Roy Disney also contributed greatly to the company's success, as did many others at the studio. In other words, Walt relied on other artists and managers to do the studio's work and to create "Disney art." It might also be noted that while Walt Disney's interests in the later part of his life turned to other projects, the Disney style of animation continued to develop long past his direct involvement, refined by key animators at the studio and reinvigorated with the New Disney.

Disney as art   After Walt's death, more attention was focused on the animation process itself and on some of "the real animators." The Disney style of animation has been thoroughly documented and dissected in countless books and articles which discuss the rationalized production process and the control and training of artists, as well as the technology the studio used in attempting to create realistic animation (examples include the development of the multi-plane camera, the use of the rotoscope, and live models).[32] A number of works have focused on Disney animators, who have recently obtained some kind of fame of their own.[33]

Walt Disney usually avoided discussing his work as art, at one point explaining, "we are not artists but only moving picture producers trying to offer entertainment."[34] Further, he noted, "I've never called my work an 'art.' It's show business, the business of building entertainment."[35] Nevertheless, the notion of Disney as art has been common in much of the discussion of Disney films since the 1930s. Indeed, art and film critics were enamored by the Disney studio's work in the 1930s, praising the stylistic innovations and the populist themes represented in the animated films. Many filmmakers expressed their awe of Disney, including the Russian filmmaker Sergei Eisenstein, who was especially fond of the studio's cartoons and *Snow White*.[36]

Although Jackson claims that it was not until the release of *Snow White* in 1937 that Disney's work was taken seriously as an art form, Watts cites countless examples from the early 1930s, pointing to major debates about whether or not Disney represented art.[37] As early as 1933, work by Disney began to appear in art galleries, and to become the focus of articles comparing Disney animation to ballet, etc. While some debated whether or not Disney products actually represented art, others had no doubt, as evidenced by the numerous books and articles entitled "The Art of Walt Disney."[38] In 1942, Feild exclaimed that Disney animation was "perhaps the most potent form of artistic expression ever devised."[39]

While Disney attracted attention from art and film critics during the 1930s and 1940s, the theoretical analysis of animation in general was relatively neglected by the emerging field of film studies in the 1950s and 1960s.[40] As Pilling explains:

> Few film critics or theorists seem to feel equipped to deal with an aesthetic that often relates more to the graphic and plastic arts than to conventional film fiction narrative grounded in photo-realism and psychologism. When writing about live action, reference to genre, shooting style, performance modes, lighting or editing can be used as shortcut descriptions or points of

comparison, so that even if the reader hasn't seen the film under discussion, they can follow the writer's argument. Such descriptive analysis is more difficult with animation.[41]

Although animation became more of a focus for at least some film scholars in the 1960s, their attention was mostly directed at independent, experimental, or "high art" animation. It was not until the 1970s that Hollywood or commercial (or "low art") animation, represented by Disney, the Warner Bros, and others, became a legitimate focus of intellectual discussion. Langer argues that "the growing acceptance of animation by the institutions of high culture coincided with its acceptance by more broadly-based social institutions. Certain areas of animation have been validated by mainstream culture as something other than simple-minded entertainment directed toward a juvenile audience."[42] Indeed, some have argued that commercial animation, and especially Disney, often dominate discussions of animation.[43] As Philip Kelly Denslow notes:

> In Hollywood, marketing and thinking about a film as animation automatically throws it into the sphere of influence of the Walt Disney Company. Disney, and now perhaps Turner's cartoon channel on cable, control how most audiences define animation. It is this perceived definition of audiences that studios gravitate toward or avoid when they choose whether or not to use the word animation to describe their product. Obviously Disney and now Turner have a vested interest in controlling the public's idea about what animation is and who the public should look to as a source of it.[44]

It has also been argued that the academic and public discussions of animation generally, but Disney animation in particular, still adhere to the "great man/great artist" model. As Langer notes, "with the growing acceptance of popular animation as art and of commercial Hollywood figures like Disney and [Tex] Avery as artists, the boundary between high and low has shifted."[45]

While the aesthetic analysis of Disney products continues, other forms of analysis have also emerged. The next sections move beyond the aesthetics of Disney art to look at specific case studies that exemplify other approaches to studying Classic Disney.

Mickey Mouse

"Remember, this all started with a mouse"

One obvious place to begin our interpretation of Disney is with the character who has come to represent the Disney empire. Mickey Mouse has evolved to mean something far beyond the role that an animated mouse plays in cartoons produced by the Walt Disney company. The Mouse is an immediately recognizable, and possibly the most widely recognized, cultural icon in the world.

The Mouse (as he is referred to around the Disney studio) represents a fascinating interweaving of culture, politics, and economics: a symbol of just about everything *American*, as is the Disney company. He is part of the American popular culture package: Cadillacs, Elvis Presley, Marilyn Monroe, and Mickey Mouse.[46] Indeed, the term "Mickey Mouse" has developed its own "dictionary" meaning: lightweight, unimportant, cheap, and foolish. But The Mouse also represents fantasy, pleasure, and escape for audiences around the world.

Mickey has been the subject of much analysis over the years.[47] For instance, Walter Benjamin used the "globe-orbiting" Mouse as an example of "a figure of the collective dream." Others have interpreted Mickey in Jungian terms, as a circular symbol representing ultimate wholeness; he has also been identified as the "archetypal mouse." Meanwhile, Erich Fromm thought that audiences identified with Mickey because he was close to their own lives as individuals pitted against the larger society.[48]

Mickey was claimed to be first cartoon character with a distinct personality. While this may or may not be true, it is clear that The Mouse has changed over the years – from definitely a rodent (long nose, small eyes, skinny limbs) to something more cuddly, with big eyes and round features. It has been noted that there was some economy in redesigning the character thus, as circles facilitated faster drawing.[49]

As noted previously, many of Disney's characters emphasize two processes: anthropomorphization and neotenization. Brockway has discussed the neotenization process with Mickey, arguing that the character represents a state of constant youth and incomplete development (represented by four fingers, rather than five).[50] In fact, Lawrence argues that Mickey's youthful characteristics serve to take people back to their childhood.[51]

Schickel and others have contrasted Mickey's development with Walt's personality and the role he played in the company. Not only was Walt's

Plate 4 Hidden Mickey in the Stones. Disney fans enjoy finding "hidden Mickeys" at the theme parks and in other locations. Artist Peter Wood has created original pieces that feature the hidden Mickey theme, such as "Hidden Mickey in the Stones"
Courtesy of Peter Wood.

voice used for Mickey, but both seemed to advance through several similar stages: (1) cruel but playful character, (2) straight man, (3) supporting player, (4) corporate symbol. While Walt's biographies reveal these various stages in his life, Mickey's evolution is represented by specific cartoon examples: (1) the youthful, playful Mickey: *Mickey's Orphans* (1931); (2) Mickey, the hero and straight man: *The Mail Pilot* (1933); (3) the more mature Mickey: *The Band Concert* (1935) and *The Brave Little Tailor* (1938).

And though Mickey may retain some of the meanings associated with these various stages, his primary role today is as the corporate logo of the company. The Mouse has appeared in only a few films over the last few decades but serves primarily as a signifier of the entire Disney universe. Thus, it is not surprising to read Eisner's interpretation of the symbolic nature of the character in Disney's *1993 Annual Report*:

> Mickey, like the rest of the classic Disney characters, does not live in the temporal world of mortals. Instead, he and his Disney counterparts live in the hearts, memories and minds of people everywhere. He is renewed with each generation, which means that Mickey at 65 . . . or 165 . . . will remain eternally young, eternally optimistic, eternally plucky.

Critique of Disney's interpretation of children's literature

As noted previously, critics during the 1930s and 1940s were mostly positive about, and typically gushed over, Walt Disney's products, praising his artistic development. However, after World War II, more harsh criticism emerged. Some argued that in the quest for realism, Disney had become conventional, static, and less exciting than other studios' animated productions. But the criticism also went beyond aesthetics and sometimes focused on Disney's interpretation of classic children's literature and folklore, which were the sources of many cartoons and most of the animated features.

Disney's manipulation of children's stories typically entailed profound changes in the original theme and characters, as well as the cultural and geographic settings.[52] The Disneyfication of fairy tales and children's stories prompted harsh criticism from folklorists, children's literature experts, and educators, who argued that the changes tended to sanitize the original and deny the essence and motivation of the original tales. Furthermore, critics claimed that the narrative structure and balance in the Disney versions overemphasized some parts of a story or certain characters for entertainment purposes and thus distorted the original intent of the tales.

One particularly damning assault was launched in 1965 by a well-known children's literature expert and librarian, Frances Clarke Sayers. Her initial comments were in response to Max Rafferty, Superintendent of Public Instruction in California, who claimed that Disney's films were "lone sanctuaries of decency and health in the jungle of sex, sadism and pornography created by the Hollywood producers." Sayers responded by saying that Disney falsifies life. "He misplaces the sweetness and misplaces the violence, and the result is like soap opera, not really related to the great truths of life."[53]

Sayers called on Walt Disney personally "to account for his debasement of the traditional literature of childhood, in films and in the books he publishes." Further, Sayers argued that Disney manipulated and vulgarized everything "for his own ends. His treatment of folklore is without regard for its anthropological, spiritual, or psychological truths. Every story is sacrificed to the 'gimmick' of animation."

Sayers echoed other critics when she observed:

> Disney takes a great masterpiece and telescopes it. He reduces it to ridiculous lengths, and in order to do this he has to make everything very obvious. It all happens very quickly and is expressed in very ordinary language. There is nothing to make a child think or feel or imagine. . . . I think Mr. Disney is basically interested in the market. He sees this all as a means of reaching a wider audience.[54]

Other commentaries also tied Disney's reworking of classic children's literature to the marketplace. May points to Disney's "total merchandising" concept, noting that the Americanization of classic (mostly) European literature was tied to the marketing of a wide range of products.[55] Folklorist Jack Zipes goes further, arguing that Disney "violated" the literary versions of fairy tales and packaged his name through merchandising. "Instead of using technology to enhance the communal aspects of narrative and bring about major changes in viewing stories to stir and animate viewers, he employed animators and technology to stop thinking about change, to return to his films, and to long nostalgically for neatly ordered patriarchal realms."[56]

Meanwhile, using a slightly different approach, Colin Sparks has looked more carefully at the Disneyfication of Winnie the Pooh, arguing that changes were made for overtly economic reasons.[57] His analysis contrasts the Milne version (the Classic Pooh) with the Disney Pooh, identifying changes in appearance, sound, location, language, narrative, and character. Sparks argues that the Classic Pooh was transformed to fit American expectations, even though the character was to be packaged and sold internationally: "Disney transforms the products it acquires, not into global products, but into American products. It is American products that it sells around the world." Thus, Sparks's Pooh analysis and discussion are as much about the nature of globalization as they are about Disney's transformation of children's literature.

Other critics have commented on the changes in meaning and values represented by Disney versions. Rather than Disney's tales providing children with positive, constructive values, Dorfman and Mattelart observed that the messages are much more problematic. "Beneath all the charm of the sweet little creatures of Disney . . . lurks the law of the jungle: envy, ruthlessness, cruelty, terror, blackmail, exploitation of the weak. Lacking vehicles for their natural affection, children learn through Disney fear and hatred."[58]

More recently, Zipes has asserted that Disney has achieved a kind of "spell" over fairy tales, revolutionizing them through animation. However, Zipes (as well as others) doesn't feel that the revolution is much of an improvement: "The great 'magic' of the Disney spell is that he animated the fairy tale only to transfix audiences and divert their potential utopian dreams and hopes through the false promises of the images he cast upon the screen."[59] While other early animators produced versions of fairy tales, Zipes argues that Disney may have been obsessed by the fairy-tale genre because it reflected his own life struggles.[60]

More compelling, however, is Zipes's discussion of Disney's adaptations within the context of the evolution of the fairy tales themselves. Tracing the oral tradition of storytelling through literary versions at the end of the seventeenth century, Zipes reminds us that by the end of the nineteenth century, fairy tales were often "read by a parent in a nursery, school, or bedroom to soothe a child's anxieties, for the fairy tales for children were optimistic and were constructed with the closure of the happy end." The transition to print also influenced the reception of fairy tales in other ways. As Zipes relates: "In printed form the fairy tale was property and could be taken by its owners and read by its owner at his or her leisure for escape, consolation, or inspiration." Furthermore, the illustrations in fairy-tale books were usually anonymous and served to enrich and deepen the story; in other words, they were subservient to the text.

The changes that ensued when fairy tales were interpreted cinematically, however, were even more profound. "With film, the images imposed themselves on the text and formed their own text in violation of print but also with the help of print culture." Zipes concludes that Disney's adaptation of the literary fairy tale to the screen has led to the following specific changes in the genre:

1. Technique has precedence over story; story is used to celebrate the technician and his means.
2. The images narrate through seduction and imposition of the animator's hand and the camera.
3. Images and sequences engender a sense of wholeness, seamless totality, and harmony.
4. Characters are one-dimensional and serve functions of the film. There is no character development because the characters are stereotypes, arranged according to a credo of domestication of the imagination.
5. The "American" fairy tale colonizes other national audiences, as the ideas and types are portrayed as models of behavior to be emulated.
6. There is a thematic emphasis on cleanliness, control, and organized industry, which reinforces the technics of the film itself.
7. Private reading pleasure is replaced by pleasurable viewing in an impersonal cinema.
8. The diversion of the Disney fairy tale is geared toward non-reflective viewing. Everything is on the surface, one-dimensional, and we are to delight in one-dimensional portrayal and thinking, for it is adorable, easy, and comforting in its simplicity.[61]

With these changes, the cultural industry in general, and Disney in particular, have erased much of the potential empowerment once offered by fairy tales in particular and fantasy in general. In other words, fantasy *à la* Disney has been thoroughly commodified and instrumentalized, much the way the Frankfurt School analysts observed in the 1930s. Whether or not there is room for alternative or subversive readings, however, is another question, which will be posed in chapter 7, when Disney audiences are discussed.

The critique of Disney's films by folklorists and other literary analysts is likely to continue as long as the company continues to adapt and rework classic stories and folk tales according to the Disney recipe.[62] Examples of the Disney versions of two fairy tales – *Snow White* and *The Little Mermaid* – provide further insights into this process.

Snow White and the Seven Dwarfs

Zipes and other critics cite *Snow White* as the film that established the model for Disney's reinterpretation of children's literature. The film has attracted a good deal of critical attention from different perspectives, but, most importantly, it represents a prime example of Classic Disney.

Snow White and the Seven Dwarfs premiered in December 1937 and was Disney's first animated feature. It is claimed as the first American animated feature and the first Technicolor feature and received special Academy Awards in 1939. Before its release, however, it was also known as "Disney's Folly," as many in the film industry were not convinced that audiences would sit through a feature-length cartoon. Nevertheless, by some accounts, Disney persevered primarily because he was convinced that the introduction of the double bill would eventually squeeze out short cartoons, and that the only profitable future for animation was in features that would attract more revenues.

Snow White was started in 1934 and took more than three years to complete. By the time it was finished, the cost was reported to be $1.5 million, although Schickel claims it was $1.7 million. The film earned $8 million on its first release and had been reissued six times by 1983, with revenues increasing to $47 million. With its fiftieth anniversary release in 1987, the film attracted $40 million in less than eight weeks.

Even though the story had already been produced as an animated film (Betty Boop was featured as Snow White by Max Fleischer in 1933), Disney considered Snow White to be the perfect narrative, replete with humor, romance, and pathos. According to Zipes, "it was in *Snow White and the Seven Dwarfs* that Disney fully appropriated the literary fairy tale and made his signature into a trademark for the most acceptable type of fairy tale in the twentieth century . . . *Snow White* became the first definitive animated fairy-tale film – definitive in the sense that it was to define the way other animated films in the genre of the fairy tale were to be made."[63]

Most analysts agree that Disney adapted the story of Snow White to suit an American audience, incorporating numerous changes from the printed Grimm brothers' tale. The following is a summary of these changes, following Zipes:

Grimms' version	*Disney's version*
• mother dies/father is alive	• no parents
• Snow White does not work	• Snow White works as a maid, cleans the castle

- Prince: "negligible role"
- Queen: –
- Animals: –

- Dwarfs: anonymous, play humble roles
- Queen visits three times
- Queen is punished by dancing in hot iron shoes at Snow White's wedding
- Snow White returns to life when dwarf stumbles while carrying coffin

- Prince featured at beginning of film
- Queen: jealous of Snow White
- Animals: Snow White's friends/ protectors
- Dwarfs: have names, personalities, starring roles
- Queen visits only once
- Queen is killed while trying to kill dwarfs
- Snow White returns to life when kissed by prince

While some analysts have found these changes problematic, Stone reminds us that the Grimms' version was also a revision of the original oral versions of the Snow White tale, which were altered and adapted according to who was telling the story.[64] Stone notes that textual and contextual sacrifices are inevitable when shifting from oral to printed to filmic forms, but concludes that the film version represents the most rigid and manipulative interpretation of the story. The Disney film "isolates creators and receivers, and offers them even less possibility of interaction since it furnishes sights, sounds, and motivations. The filmed text thus provides the narrowest bridge of all, with the most closed text and context. There is only one *Snow White and the Seven Dwarfs*."[65]

While it is clear that the Grimms' and Disney versions share similar approaches to the domestication of women, Zipes argues that Disney went much further in making the tale the "triumph of the banished and the underdogs" and again relates the film to Disney's own life. The Prince is ultimately the champion of the film, just as Disney is the one who controlled the production process. In other words, for Zipes, the overriding sign is "the signature of Disney's self-glorification in the name of justice," as well as (once again) the quest for control:

Disney wants the world cleaned up, and the pastel colors with their sharply drawn ink lines create images of cleanliness, just as each sequence reflects a clearly conceived and preordained destiny for all the characters in the film. For Disney, the Grimms' tale is not a vehicle to explore the deeper implications of the narrative and its history. Rather it is a vehicle to display what he can do as an animator with the latest technological and artistic developments in the industry. The story is secondary . . .

The manner in which he copied the musical plays and films of his time, and his close adaptation of fairy tales with patriarchal codes, indicate that all the technical experiments would not be used to foster social change in America but to keep power in the hands of individuals like himself, who felt empowered to design and create new worlds.

Disney always wanted to do something new and unique just as long as he had absolute control.[66]

There have been many other discussions of Disney's version of Snow White, focusing on how Disney used romantic elements to emulate love, sentiment, and romance,[67] and examining themes of beauty.[68] However, we turn now to how *Snow White* combined these various elements, and exemplified Classic Disney, as outlined above.

Classic Disney and Snow White   The Disney version presented an Americanized Snow White and might be said to have fully established the Classic Disney formula. Above all, the film was entertaining, with emphasis on the dwarfs and their comic escapades. One technical reason for this change had to do with the limitations of animation at the time, since humans didn't animate especially well. The more cartoonish dwarfs thus provided comic relief by way of gags, mostly physical and slapstick, and thus actually dominated much of the film.

The film also features music throughout, a characteristic shared by most Classic Disney films. The characters are revealed and developed through the music; themes are set up and developed by it. Again, Disney adds anthropomorphized animal characters, although the animals do not play as large a role as in other Disney productions. Childlike behavior is featured, as cute characters abound, including Snow White herself, the animals, and the dwarfs.

The work ethic is emphasized in the Disney version of the story, as the dwarfs sing and whistle as they dutifully go off to work ("Whistle while you work" and "Heigh ho, heigh ho, it's off to work we go"). Snow White is industrious and hard-working, as evidenced in the first scene in which she is seen cleaning at the palace, as well as cleaning sequences at the dwarfs' cottage.

Snow White's theme song ("I'm Wishing") sets the stage for the theme of escape and fantasy. Other scenes include the magic wishing apple (dreams *will* come true) and especially Snow White praying for her dreams to come true.

Innocence is represented overtly through Snow White's name, but also by her character. She trusts the dwarfs, but also trusts the witch. There is an emphasis on cleanliness. Snow White seems always to be cleaning, and the dwarfs' washing song also stresses cleanliness and purity.

Classic Disney is emphatic in its depiction of good triumphing over evil. The Queen/witch is obviously evil and therefore is punished eventually with death. Snow White is innocent and good and is therefore rewarded. Ultimately, she finds fulfillment through a romantic relationship with a prince. Optimism and happiness prevail, "With a smile and a song." The essence of the story is romance, and, as usual, it's love at first sight. "Someday my prince will come." And he does. And there is the happy ending – in this case, a very quick ending, as the Prince appears and they exit to the castle. Snow White's dream comes true, so we must assume that happiness followed. Anyway, we are told so: "They lived happily ever after."

Feminist analysis of Disney products

Introducing feminist textual analysis

A feminist critique of popular culture has evolved with the growth of feminist theory over the past few decades. Early approaches to media from a feminist perspective focused on the absence, marginalization, or trivialization of women in media products, or what Tuchman has referred to as a process of "symbolic annihilation."[69] Feminists have also drawn attention to the relatively few women in cultural production, as well as the disregard of women audience members. Feminists argue that it is not surprising that media stereotypes reflect dominant social values, in that media producers are influenced by these stereotypes.[70]

More recently, feminists have argued that, while media images of women may be more prevalent, they still reflect sexist conceptualizations of women and their roles in society.[71] Further discussion has revolved around the representation of patriarchy, as well as issues dealing with ideology. In addition, feminists have called attention to the relative exclusion of gender issues in the academic study of popular culture.

Consequently, it is not surprising to find that a good deal of recent textual analysis of Disney films focuses on gender issues, for the portrayal of women, in particular, in Classic Disney provides a rich text for feminist analysis.[72] Some link the Disney portrayal directly to Walt, who once was reported to have said, reflecting on his youth, "Girls bored me. They still do." But, again, we should be cautious about giving one person full credit for the attributes and characteristics of popular cultural products. Indeed, the representation of women in Classic Disney may not differ very much from other popular cultural depictions. However, the enduring Disney stereotypes, as well as their popularity with children, demand that we take a closer look at the patterns of representation in Classic Disney products.

While a feminist analysis of Disney products would seem to be elemental, there were relatively few examples before the last decade or so. Drawing on feminism, as well as the critique of the Disneyfication of children's literature, Stone reviewed the heroines in stories by the Grimm brothers and the Disney versions. She observes that while the Grimms' heroines are relatively uninspiring, "those of Walt Disney seem barely alive. In fact, two of them hardly manage to stay awake." Stone criticizes Disney's portrayal of women as stereotypically bad or good and contrasts Disney's heroines with his heroes. She concludes that the heroes succeed, not because of how they look or what they wish for, but because of what they do. "The only tests of most heroines require nothing beyond what they are born with: a beautiful face, tiny feet, or a pleasing temperament. At least that is what we learn from the translations of the Grimm tales, and especially from Walt Disney."[73]

More recently, Hoerrner reviewed Disney films from *Snow White* to *The Lion King* and found that women are portrayed as weak, pristine, and incapable of independent action. On the basis of content analysis, the study found that males account for 57 percent of Disney characters, while females represent only 21 percent. In addition male characters are far more aggressive, with 47 percent of their actions comprising of physical aggression.[74]

A closer look at one of the more recent Disney features will provide an example of how feminist perspectives have been used to interpret The Classic Disney.

The Little Mermaid

While *The Little Mermaid* prompted a flurry of feminist analyses of Disney products, the interpretations have been conflicting. Released in 1989, *The Little Mermaid* was the first "classic" animated feature since Disney's death. Roy Disney explained that it was "The kind of movie Walt would have made." The film was three years in production, with a $23 million budget, and brought in $84 million at the box office during its first release. The film and its heroine proved to be especially popular with young girls and has been developed as a television series, as well as released in video and rereleased in theaters. During the first video release, 9 million cassettes of *The Little Mermaid* were sold. Merchandising efforts included 40 licensees and attracted $25 million during the first year alone.

More Disneyfication   The Hans Christian Andersen tale *Lille Havfrue*, was molded into the Classic Disney formula with numerous changes in both the story and the characters. In the original tale, the mermaid wants an immortal soul, not necessarily to be human or to marry a prince. To prove herself, she is given human form and must win the prince's love, but her primary aim is immortality. The transition from mermaid to human is quite painful, and eventually she fails and dies, although subsequently she finds that she can acquire a soul by performing good deeds. Meanwhile, the prince marries another woman, who receives the sympathy of the mermaid.

In the Disney version, the mermaid first longs to be human because of "all of the neat things" that humans produce. But, after saving Prince Eric, she becomes fixated on becoming human and marrying him. She succeeds, of course, but only with the assistance of other characters added to the story, especially Sebastian and Flounder.

The changes in the story and the characters in *The Little Mermaid* are consistent with Classic Disney, as established in the 1930s. The film displays Disney's ability to produce technically impressive animation, especially in many of the underwater sequences. Colors have been carefully coordinated, with luscious settings and attractive, seductive characters. Above all, the film is entertaining. Humor and music are emphasized throughout. Indeed, the characters are again revealed through music, as are the main themes of the story. While anthropomorphized animal characters are common, it is of interest that there are also animals (such as a shark) that are not given human attributes.

Some analysts have argued that the more recent Disney animated films have been updated and modernized, especially as reflected in the "new" female heroines. Ariel is a sensual, aggressive, mischievous, adventurous, savvy, independent teenager, in contrast to Snow White, who is shy, obedient, hesitant, naive, innocent, and motherly. However, both are surrounded by male characters, are dissatisfied with their current lives, and wish to marry a prince. Some things obviously have not changed. In fact, Zipes points out that once Disney established the formula for feature-length filmed fairy tales, it continued and still continues with the New Disney. "There is nothing but the 'eternal return of the same' . . . that makes for enjoyable viewing and delight in techniques of these films as commodities, but nothing new in the exploration of narration, animation, and signification."[75]

The Little Mermaid provides a fertile text for different kinds of feminist analysis. Many authors begin by examining the representation of the female characters in the film. Ariel has been viewed as a more positive role model than other Disney heroines, such as Snow White. She is intelligent, inquisitive, and rebellious; but, of course, she exemplifies the beauty that characterizes all Disney heroines, with an extremely trim, shapely, even sensual figure. One author has compared her to a slightly anorexic Barbie Doll;[76] another image that comes to mind is the silhouette of a woman sometimes seen on the mud flaps of semi-trucks in the USA.

On the other hand, the female villain, Ursula, is ugly, fat, and, most definitely, evil. Roberta Trites draws attention to these differences, noting that Disney started to represent the cultural preoccupation with weight in the 1970s. She argues that "the movie's portrayal of good as fairer and thinner than evil presents a bigoted distortion of the human body."[77]

Meanwhile, Ariel resembles most of Disney's other heroines, in that she represents royalty, lives in a male-dominated world, and ultimately finds fulfillment through marriage to a prince. In Disney's version, Ariel is alienated from other female characters, especially her sisters. She receives advice from her male companions, whereas the original mermaid in Andersen's tale looked to her grandmother for advice and was assisted by her sisters. As Trites notes, "The grandmother, the enchantress [Ursula, in the Disney version], the princess, the sisters, and the daughters of the air are all strong, beautiful, supportive, and feminine. But by changing their gender, by making their motivations anti-feminine, or by editing their functions from the story, Disney destroys all of these characters."[78] Again, there is no mother, unless Ursula is to be considered a mother figure.

Access and identities   Meanwhile, Laura Sells considers the film in the context of the feminist debate over the definition of "woman":

> *The Little Mermaid* reflects some of the tensions in American feminism between reformist demands for access, which leave in place the fixed and complementary definitions of masculine and feminine gender identities, and radical refigurings of gender that assert symbolic change as preliminary to social change. In this context, then, the mermaid figure becomes both an icon of bourgeois feminism and the sign of the stakes in reinventing the category of "woman," or reimagining women as speaking subjects.[79]

Sells discusses the challenges of autonomy and independence and the costs of entering the "white male system," but also notes that Disney obscures these issues through "sanitizing maneuvers," such as shifting Ariel's "fascination with the human world" to love for Prince Eric, "easing the pain of access by sanitizing the physical, bodily pain of Ariel's self mutilation when she trades her fins for feet," and sacrificing Ariel's connection to the feminine in the "matricide of Ursula, the only other strong female character in the film." Sells admits that the film is difficult to subject to a "feminist resistant reading." Although Ariel eventually gets her voice back, the film still "teaches us that we can achieve access and mobility in the white male system if we remain silent, and if we sacrifice our connection to 'the feminine.' "[80]

Matriarchy versus patriarchy   Some feminist critiques include an assessment of where power ultimately lies in society, and unquestionably it is with the males in these stories. Both of the worlds represented in Disney's version of *The Little Mermaid* are patriarchies, in which society is dominated by men. But the film also presents "male power as positive and female power as negative."[81] Not only does Prince Eric kill Ursula, but Triton is ultimately responsible for Ariel becoming human and marrying Prince Eric. While Andersen's tale presented a society that was close to being matriarchical, Disney eliminates many of the female characters and undermines feminine power. As the Ingwersens conclude:

> Andersen's sea was nearly a matriarchy (there was a queen mother, a king, and many princesses) – but Disney's shows only the negative side of feminine rule and the positive side of masculine rule. . . . Disney's neat folktale ending is satisfying; but its change in emphasis from the strength of good to the strength of evil in female power is troubling, even though the substitution of mortal love, eros, for spiritual love, agape, is familiar from profane ideas of happiness, both ancient and modern. The public seems to prefer lovers to saints – and Disney assumes it prefers a definite patriarchy to the ambiguities of a matriarchy.[82]

It is likely that Disney films will continue to receive attention from feminists, for as long as the Classic Disney model persists, it is inevitable that there will be issues involving gender representation.

Psychoanalytic analysis of Disney's world

Another form of textual analysis has evolved from psychoanalytic theory, based on the original formulations by Sigmund Freud on the internal psychic structures and complex relations between them. Freud's theoretical framework evolved from the treatment of neuroses, initially prompted by the realization that many of his patients' physical complaints did not in fact have any physiological bases but instead stemmed from psychological origins. More recently, a form of psychoanalysis has been popular within cultural studies, based mostly on the work of Jacques Lacan, who focuses on linguistic structures and the unconscious. Meanwhile, feminists have also drawn on psychoanalysis to analyze sexuality and sexism.[83]

While there are few cases of recent forms of psychoanalytic theory being applied to Disney texts, psychological analysis and Freudian concepts have been used to interpret a few films. Consistent with some other approaches, psychological interpretations often attribute specific elements of Disney texts directly to Walt Disney, noting his obsessive personality and other psychological traits.

Since Brody argued that *Pinocchio* was Disney's "psychologically greatest movie," a closer look at this film will be used to highlight some of the psychological themes that have been identified in Classic Disney.[84]

Pinocchio

Pinocchio was Disney's second feature-length animated film, released in February 1940, with a budget of close to $3 million. The film was critically successful, but because of World War II and the loss of the European market, it was not initially as successful financially as *Snow White*'s first release. However, with reissues in the USA and Canada, *Pinocchio* brought in over $13 million through 1973. With the 1984 rerelease, the total rose to $26 million.

Pinocchio is one of the most visually innovative and technically brilliant of Disney's classic films, considered by some to be Disney's best feature. For instance, the studio used the multi-plane camera more than in *Snow White*, with one of the opening shots of Pinocchio's village employing 12 different planes at a cost of $25,000.

Again, Disney modified the original story, which was first published in serial form by Carlo Collodi (Carlo Lorenzini), "Le Avventure di Pinocchio," in 1913. In the original story, the cricket character remained nameless and was killed by Pinocchio rather early in the story; whereas in the revised story, he has a much expanded role and is given the name Jiminy Cricket. He was one of the first characters to be used by Disney to lighten up a story or as a narrative device. In addition, Disney's Pinocchio was far more good-natured than the original, who was a mean-spirited, playful prankster and somewhat of a delinquent. Disney represents the puppet/boy as innocent, naive, and a victim of other characters. While *Pinocchio* still exemplifies the Disney style, it is also characterized by more action, excitement, and terror, and less music and romance, than many other Classic Disney films.[85]

Psychoanalysis and Pinocchio   Brody observes that anal images and incorporation themes have been common in Disney tales, citing examples from *The Three Little Pigs* and *Peter Pan*. Anal images, especially featuring the "often-kick-in-the butt" Jiminy Cricket, are as rampant in *Pinocchio* as images of erection (Pinocchio's nose, the donkey ears), and incorporation is apparent in the scenes of Pinocchio and Gepetto in the whale's stomach. However, there are other character and narrative elements that lend themselves to Freudian interpretation.

Pinocchio has no mother, nor are there any sexual references, both common for Disney stories. Indeed, Pinocchio is "born" in a rather unusual way – he is given "birth" by his father, thus evoking the Freudian concept of male pregnancy fantasy. Role representation is obvious, with Jiminy Cricket as superego; however, there is also a common Disney device when Pinocchio saves his father, representing role reversal. Brody argues that this technique pleases "the child" in the adults, who bring the children to the films. He notes that "Going to the movies or watching TV is more acceptable if you as well as your children are entertained."[86] Disney's version of the Pinocchio story also features certain childhood fears. The concept of humans as pleasure seeking is clearly represented in the depiction of "Pleasure Island," which presents Pinocchio with a wide range of taboos, resulting in the terrifying sequence in which boys are turned into donkeys.

Berland argues that Disney's reworking of the story sanitizes the violence and inhibits the fantasizing that is necessary for children to mature, as the Disney stories typically encourage children "not to grow up or to grow up too suddenly." Berland further observes that Disney "cleaned up" some of the classic children's stories; thus they "lost their psychological value, but not their box-office appeal."[87] Meanwhile, Bettelheim has observed that when fantasies are mass-produced, children's own fantasies then become either right or wrong, and thus the conflict that helps the maturing process is avoided.

While some have difficulty accepting psychological, especially Freudian, interpretations of Disney's films, it is almost inevitable that this type of analysis will become even more prominent, given the persistence of psychoanalytic theory in cultural studies and feminist analysis.

Disney's representation of race

While the representation of race has been an ever-present issue in popular entertainment, during the last few decades increasing attention has been focused on racial stereotypes in general, as well as on Disney's portrayals of race in particular. As Wilson and Gutierrez observe, stereotyping (a formulaic and usually oversimplified concept, opinion, or belief) has been used as a device since the beginning of literature and drama. While stereotypes can provide shortcuts to character development, they become problematic when used with prejudice and within historically specific contexts.[88]

The visual arts are particularly challenging, for instance. As one reviewer has noted, "given the highly visual nature of film, it may be impossible to strip away the potential for problems," while animated characters can be even more difficult.[89] In certain cases, representatives of the Disney company have responded to criticism by explaining that they did not intend to misrepresent minorities. The problem is that even though creators of popular cultural products may have admirable, nonracist goals, nevertheless, we are left with their creations, not their intentions. And those creations, when they are accompanied by the Disney name, become even more significant because of their prominence as well as their special appeal to young audiences. As Russell Means, a Native American activist who participated in the production of Disney's *Pocahontas*, explained: "Because it's Disney, millions of children forever are going to see this in their most formative years, and it's going to affect how they see my people and our culture all the way through their lives."[90]

One of the earliest cases of problematic racial representation in Disney films was the caricature of the wolf in *The Three Little Pigs*. One of the disguises adopted by the villain was that of a Jewish peddler, which Schickel linked to Disney's apparent anti-Semitism. "Disney appears to have shared . . . the anti-Semitism that was common to his generation and place of origin. His studio was notably lacking in Jewish employees, and at least once he presented a fairly vicious caricature of the Jew on screen."[91] However, St John argues that the cartoon was far more complex, and brought "brilliantly to life an entire range of Indian, black, and Jewish stereotypes."[92] Even though most interpretations pointed to the symbolism of the Big Bad Wolf as the Depression and the Practical Pig as the hard-working American public (as discussed briefly in chapter 2), St John argues that the right-wing message of the cartoon was actually the "specter of impending racial rebellion" that haunted the country.

Another example that attracted attention was the depiction of a group of crows in *Dumbo*, which were reminiscent of Amos and Andy characters. While these stereotypical representations and others were included in some of Disney's early films, the issue became much more critical in the 1940s, with the interpretation of the Uncle Remus tales in *Song of the South* (1946). Created by Joel Chandler Harris, Uncle Remus stories were significantly distorted in the Disney version, which was highly selective in recreating only a few of the more than 100 original stories. Some of the scenes were found to be "sickening both in [their] patronizing racial sentiment and its sentimentality."[93] Whereas the original character of Uncle Remus was a storyteller of dignity, many claimed that Disney turned him into a racist stereotype or another Uncle Tom.[94] Apparently, someone at the company agreed, as the film was withdrawn from circulation in the late 1950s; however, it has since been rereleased on video.

During the 1950s and 1960s, there were further problematic represen-tations in Disney features, especially featuring Native Americans. Even studio representatives admit that "all the Indians were caricatures" in *Peter Pan* (1953), while depictions of Native Americans in *Davy Crockett* have been (mostly) overlooked.[95]

More recently, the New Disney's introduction of animated features during an era of multiculturalism has prompted a renewed round of criticism over racial representation. For instance, Disney's version of *Aladdin* attracted immediate attention from Arab-American groups, who denounced some of the images and musical lyrics. The protests led to a change in the lyrics of one of the songs for the video version, but the offensive images of certain Arab characters remained.[96] For many, further reading of the film revealed "a bigoted and quite traditional European reading/writing of the medieval Persian story."[97] Addison argues that the film revolves around "naive" individualism, represented by the main characters' goals of freedom. Princess Jasmine's role is key to the film's racial and gender ideology, which are complementary. Jasmine's "freedom" takes the form of an American-style romance, which frees her from restrictive Islamic gender codes, as well as providing "moral justification for changing Islamic culture." Addison further argues that:

> *Aladdin* offers up, in the character of Jasmine, a pseudo-feminist image in service of a deeply racist film, a film which animatedly reinscribes at least two American cultural strategies. The first is a domestic strategy which shapes gender conceptions: the mystification of power through romantic love, and the packaging of romantic love as freedom for women. The second is foreign policy: Aladdin's political strategy protracts the complex American metaphor of a "free marketplace, pure of political intent or impact," where wealth and opportunity are the birthrights of "free" individuals. In that ideological marketplace, Muslin women are prizes to be won.[98]

The Disney version was certainly not the first film interpretation of the Aladdin story; Sharman explains that other feature and cartoon versions have displayed similar visual elements and ideological leanings.[99] However, the Disney company was breaking new ground with *The Lion King*, which one might have thought to be unproblematic in terms of racial representation. Problems were revealed, however, with the portrayal of three "hooligan hyenas," definitely recognizable as Black and Hispanic characters lurking about in a jungle version of a ghetto.[100] In addition, cultural analysts have found that the film reveals homophobic, racist, and sexist ideologies, reinforcing hierarchical and conservative values.[101]

Meanwhile, the filmmakers responsible for *Pocahontas* (1995) explained that they consciously intended to respond to the criticism that other Disney films had attracted because of racial stereotypes — an admirable idea, especially since the film was to be based on actual historical figures. As with most Disney features, the creators did extensive research before writing the screenplay and designing the characters. In this case, they visited the site of the original Jamestown colony, as well as talking with historians, academics, and descendants of Pocahontas. They also hired Native Americans as consultants, to make sure that they "got it right."[102] Despite the careful research, the visually stunning film is still historically inaccurate, resorting to many of the elements of Classic Disney. As Edgerton and Jackson note, "The filmmakers at Disney never really intended *Pocahontas* to be historically accurate, despite all the sentimental rhetoric; they were producing yet another animated film after all."[103]

To begin with, there is the image of Pocahontas herself. Rather than a 12-year-old girl, which she actually was during her first encounter with John Smith, she is portrayed as a much more mature "Native American

Barbie." The film's supervising animator was said to have looked at paintings of Pocahontas and decided to "improve" on her looks, adding Asian eyes, a thin waist, and incredibly long legs – "less American Indian than fashionably exotic." More than one male (including Mel Gibson, the voice of John Smith) has proclaimed that, "She's a babe."[104]

The story exaggerates some episodes of Pocahontas's life and fabricates others, while passing over some of the more unpleasant aspects of the original story. As in most Classic Disney stories, the story revolves around a romantic love affair, although in actuality Pocahontas and John Smith were never lovers. The Disneyfied story excludes Pocahontas's kidnapping by the English, her conversion to Christianity, her marriage to an English aristocrat, and her death from tuberculosis when she was 21. Finally, the typical "happily ever after" ending is dodged in an attempt to avoid offending anyone. Nevertheless, Edgerton and Jackson argue that the final scene ultimately reinforces yet another stereotype, casting Pocahontas in the role of mediator. "The film's final impression, therefore, is that, with Ratcliffe bound, gagged, and headed back to England, American Indians and Euro- peans are now free to coexist peacefully. Race is a dramatic or stylistic device, but the more profound consequences of institutional racism are never allowed even momentarily to invade the audience's comfort zone."[105]

The film has also been interpreted as exemplifying neocolonialism, or in other words, legitimating colonialism and racism by its representation of Jamestown as a land of savages.[106] Kilpatrick argues that the depiction of Native American culture and the colonial English is one-dimensional.[107] (For the most part, the British press adamantly agreed with the latter point.)

In the end, *Pocahontas* attracted mixed responses from critics as well as from audiences.[108] Some reviewers praised the film, noting that is was a "sharp revision of the classic Disney fairy tale formula" and calling Pocahontas Disney's "most subversive heroine." Some of the Native American participants also applauded the film (for instance, Means called it "the single finest work ever done on American Indians by Hollywood"), while others were distressed by the rewriting of history. Edgerton and Jackson conclude:

> Whether 'subversive' or sexist, 'daring' or reactionary, *Pocahontas* is a deeply conflicted text. . . . Inherently fraught with contradictions, Disney's *Pocahon- tas* sends an abundance of mixed messages, which probably underscores the limits of reconstructing the native American image at Disney or, perhaps any other major Hollywood studio that operates first and foremost as a marketer of conventional dreams and a seller of related consumer products.[109]

Marxist analysis/the imperialist Disney

Some of the interpretive approaches referred to already have drawn in some ways on what might be called a Marxist approach to analyzing culture. While a thorough discussion of Marxist cultural analysis in all its variations is not possible here, an overview offered by Donald Lazere may be helpful:

> Applied to any aspect of culture, Marxist method seeks to explicate the manifest and latent or coded reflections of modes of material production, ideological values, class relations and structures of social power – racial or sexual as well as politico-economic – or the state of consciousness of people in a precise historical or socio-economic situation.[110]

Probably the best-known example of this approach as applied to Disney is the short study called *How to Read Donald Duck*. Ariel Dorfman and Armand Mattelart presented their critique of Disney comics in 1971, while the democratically elected Popular Unity government was attempting to build a socialist society in Chile. However, as David Kunzle explained in his introduction to the English edition, "it proved easier to nationalize copper than to free the mass media from US influence."[111] Even after the Allende government was in place, much of Chile's television programming and 80 percent of the films shown in cinemas were from the USA, as well as there being many US-owned newspapers and magazines. Thus, Dorfman and Mattelart's critique was originally written to encourage the Chilean people to resist these foreign cultural products. It is not surprising, therefore, that after the US-backed counterrevolution in Chile in September 1973, the book was banned there. In addition, the US Customs Bureau initially seized shipments of the book coming into the USA, citing "infringement" of Disney's copyrights.[112] The book has since emerged in countries all over the world.

As Kunzle observes, *How to Read Donald Duck* is "an enraged, satirical and politically impassioned book."[113] But it also encompasses a combination of approaches, basically drawing on a Marxist critique of "Disney ideology" which incorporates class analysis, as well as semiotic and psychoanalytic approaches. The analysis draws upon a sample of 100 Disney comic books that were distributed in Chile in the 1970s. The comic books feature mostly the Disney ducks – Donald and his nephews, Huey, Dewey, and Louie, and Uncle Scrooge – but also a few other characters, including

Mickey, Minnie, and Pluto. The authors dissect the comic books texts, directing attention to some of the common characteristics of Disney ideology, but also highlighting the notion of cultural imperialism – a concept that was actively discussed and hotly debated in the 1970s and 1980s. While there are a number of analysts who have looked into Disney's representation of foreign cultures,[114] Mattelart and Dorfman's study had the most dramatic impact on this debate.

One of the primary themes identified in the Disney comics by Dorfman and Mattelart is the portrayal of people of the Third World as "the noble savage[s]." Specific nationalities are stereotypically represented, especially of Third World countries where people are presented as backwards, primitive, savage, and/or ignorant. "Disney did not, of course, invent the inhabitants of these lands; he merely forced them into the proper mold . . . According to Disney, underdeveloped peoples are like children, to be treated as such. . . ."[115]

Typically, the Duck stories featured a quest for fortune, which is revealed and produced magically, there being little evidence of work or production in the lands portrayed in the comics. "In the world of Disney, no one has to work in order to produce. There is a constant round of buying, selling and consuming, but to all appearances, none of the products involved has required any effort whatsoever to make. All employment is a means of consumption rather than production."[116] The emphasis on consumption is evidenced by the Disney characters' constant quest for money. It is "a carousel of consumerism. Money is the goal everyone strives for because it manages to embody all the qualities of their world."[117]

Many Americans may not find the ideological messages presented in Disney at all problematic or troubling, as they may indeed share those values. However, these same messages become far more problematic when imported to other countries. As David Kunzle has observed,

> If important sectors of the intelligentsia in the US have been lulled into silent complicity with Disney, it can only be because they share his basic values and see the broad public as enjoying the same cultural privileges; but this complicity becomes positively criminal when their common ideology is imposed upon non-capitalist, underdeveloped countries, ignoring the grotesque disparity between the Disney dream of wealth and leisure, and the *real* needs in the Third World.[118]

A note on Disney comics   Generally, there have been fewer studies of Disney's comics than of Classic Disney films, and this is one reason why they have been somewhat neglected in this discussion. Apparently, Walt Disney was not very interested in the company's line of comic books, not least because they were not perceived to be as profitable as other products. Thus, the artists who were responsible for the comics were said to have been able to work outside of Walt's control, which may explain why the Disney comics sometimes represent something of a departure from Classic Disney.

However, the comics are still tremendously popular in many international markets, even though they generate less interest in the USA these days, as noted in chapter 3.[119] Whereas Dorfman and Mattelart dissected some of the themes in the Disney comics distributed in Chile during a specific time period, other analysts have considered the Disney comics from other vantage points.[120] Obviously, much more attention to these products is needed.

Disney's representation of the natural world

It was inevitable that Disney's representation of nature would be a theme identified by critics, for the depiction of animals has been an important part of the Disney legacy over the years. While animation allows the opportunity to use animals as characters, the extent of Disney's anthropomorphization of animals in cartoons and feature films has been an issue for some critics.[121] But the company went even further in the 1950s, in its production of documentary films with more explicit depictions of the natural world.

According to Walt Disney, the studio's foray into documentary nature films started with the production of *Bambi* (1942), when real animals were brought into the studio to help artists with their depictions of animated animals. However, Disney apparently wanted even more realism and arranged for footage of animals in natural settings to be shot and saved for possible future use. The result was several documentary series, beginning in 1949 – *True-Life Adventures, People and Places*, and *True-Life Fantasy* – which moved the studio more deliberately into the realm of educational media.

Schickel reports that, from 1952, Buena Vista rented 16 mm versions of Disney theatrical releases to schools and other organizations. However, the studio had also developed its nonfiction prowess during World War II with the production of government films, as discussed in chapter 2. After the war, the company continued producing educational films for schools, churches, and civic clubs, including over 15 filmstrips for the *Encyclopaedia Britannica*. During the sixties, Disney offered schools more than 200 short films (1–4 minutes), accompanied by a simple, portable projector. Often these filmstrips were taken directly from previous Disney releases, especially the nature films, and prominently featured the Disney name. As Schickel observed in 1968, "the studio reaps promotional benefits as well as more conventional profits and the advantages of a foothold in the growth industry of educational technology."[122]

There might have been even more involvement in educational media, but it was reported that the studio encountered too many restrictions from educators (yet another example of the Disney pursuit of control). Nevertheless, many of the nature documentaries, plus a few other educational shorts, became "staples on the school circuit" and are still used in schools and educational settings in the USA and other countries. Disney's educational films and documentaries of this period deserve more attention than they have received from textual analysts. The next section will look more closely at the *True-Life Adventures* series, drawing on the few studies of these films.

True-Life Adventures

On the surface, the company's nature films do not necessarily reflect Classic Disney, which typically applies to Disney's works of fiction. However, it is instructive to see how these "documentaries" actually do fit the Disney formula in many ways.

Sometime in the late 1940s, Disney arranged for amateur photographers Al and Elma Milotte to gather documentary footage in Alaska, resulting in the *True-Life Adventure* series, beginning with *Seal Island* in 1949. Although at first the film was difficult to book in theaters, it became a box office success after receiving an Academy Award for best short subject.

And that success translated into some tidy profits for the Disney company. Although the company's best equipment and supplies were used in production, the costs for the nature films were far lower than for animated features. For instance, *The Living Desert* was released in 1953 for $400,000 – almost half the cost of a typical Hollywood feature at the time – and earned ten times that amount. While *Seal Island's* budget was reported to be $300,000, and *Beaver Valley* was budgeted at $400,000, the two films brought in nearly $9 million. Thirteen *True-Life Adventures* were produced between 1948 and 1960, six of which were feature films and became the studio's "cash cows" during that time.[123]

The films not only received the approval of the film industry through numerous Academy Awards, but also built Walt Disney's reputation as a documentarian and educator, as evidenced by the following awards:

- a citation from the Photographers Association of America "for his documentary moving pictures of nature," in 1955;
- the Audubon Society Medal for"distinguished service to conservation," awarded in 1955;
- appointment to the President's Committee on Higher Education, in 1956;
- commendation of Disney as "a superb teacher of natural history, geography and history" by the National Geographic Society, in 1963.

Despite the praise and adulation, Disney himself denied the educational significance of the company's productions, explaining at one point, "I'm not an educator. My primary purpose is to entertain – though if people want to read education into my work, that's fine with me."[124]

The *True-Life* films were praised for introducing nature and nonfiction films to a wide audience, for high-quality cinematography, for "presenting forbidding and physically repulsive forms of wildlife," and for innovative story treatment and cinematic technique applied to the documentary form.[125] As King notes,

> This is nature, but a very special kind: not an ecosystem, but an ego-system – one viewed through a self-referential human lens: anthropomorphized, sentimentalized, and moralized. Critics of this approach called it sensational-izing and patronizing. Those who saw in this new breed of documentary an innovative and positive appreciation of nature called it subjective, approach-able, and humanizing.[126]

Schickel acknowledged that critiquing the nature films was exceedingly challenging, noting that the unique productions were certainly of high quality, bringing unseen scenes from the natural world to the screen for the first time. However, the Disneyfication of the natural world was still disturbing.

One can get a sense of some of the problems with the films by contrasting the studio's own descriptions of the films. On the one hand, the promotional material from the company explained:

> Factual honesty in essence as well as in detail is the distinguishing hallmark of the *True-Life Adventure* films. The theme of a Disney factual is usually

elemental – often it is the fight for survival. The tempo of the telling must be leisurely. The tone must be respectful – no ridicule. No condescension, particularly when dealing the wisdom of the ages and the tales of the master story-teller.[127]

On the other hand, Walt Disney himself explained the aim of the films thus:

Anything carrying the Disney name was going to mean entertainment – this I insisted upon. We'd have authenticity, of course, but we'd also have drama and laughs and music. Our intent is not formal education in natural science. Our main purpose is to bring interesting and delightful entertainment to the theater.[128]

To begin with, the films were sometimes not factual or authentic, for inaccurate depictions and staged scenes were often included. Even some of Disney's strong supporters have acknowledged these difficulties: "Although Disney's purpose in the *True-Life Adventures* was to share with audiences his own awe and enthusiasm for nature, his commitment to a story tradition invariably results in some fanciful elements and inaccuracies in the explanation of natural phenomena."[129] There are numerous examples, but the best-known incident involves a scene from *White Wilderness* in which lemmings throw themselves into the ocean, "a staged mass suicide that contradicts what scientists claim happens in real life."[130] As an expert in photofakery notes, "thanks to Disney, several generations of Americans believe that lemmings do [commit suicide]."[131]

Moreover, nature is inevitably distorted through the filmic process, especially through the use of time-lapse photography and telephoto lenses, but also through the editing process that reduces the natural world to a tabloid version of nature featuring only the most dramatic shots. Of course, as King points out, Disney's films are not the only ones to display these effects, even though for many Americans, the Disney version of "tabloid nature" may have been their first exposure to the natural world.

Above all, the Disney nature films emphasized entertainment, as Walt insisted, and it is perhaps not surprising to find that the films incorporated many of the same techniques and values that were used for fictional films in the Classic Disney model. For instance, music and humor are used throughout the *True-Life Adventures*. In addition to the emotional interpretation and humanization provided by the continuous music, the narrator deliberately guides the viewer with explanations and judgments of the animals' behavior and even their thoughts, as well as instructing the viewer on how to respond.

In general, the nature films relied heavily on anthropomorphism, as have many of Disney's other films. While possibly more acceptable in fiction films, the extent to which Disney "humanized" animals was far more problematic in the nature films and sometimes even went beyond accurate representations of the "true" nature of some animals. Names were often given to specific creatures, emphasizing their characters and establishing whether they were to be considered heroes or villains.

Throughout the films, animal behavior was interpreted in human or homocentric terms. In other words, a moral hierarchy was established, with explicit human attributes, values, and morals ascribed to animals. We are introduced to "heartless mothers," devoted mothers," and "kindly nature." As Schickel concludes, "The tone of a Disney nature film is nearly always patronizing."

Critics further point out how Disney represented animals not only in human form, but primarily to serve human needs. The ultimate value of animals, according to the Disney perspective, is similar to the attitudes some people have towards pets, which are thought of as for personal gratification or for basically entertainment purposes. In other words, the meanings and values in Disney's depiction of the animal world come directly from the human world. Rather than providing understanding, Schickel argues that this reductionism ultimately demonstrates Disney's immaturity:

> confronted with things that were inexplicable to him, he either turned away in disgust or willfully falsified them by reshaping them in terms that he understood and approved. Much the same thing had happened in his animated films in which all material was reshaped to suit the limited artistic style he insisted upon, however incongruous that style might be to the subject matter.[132]

So, rather than "true-life," nature was subjected to the Classic Disney version of entertainment. As film critic Bosley Crowther observed, there is a "playful disposition to edit and arrange . . . so that it appears the wild life . . . is behaving in human and civilized ways . . . all very humorous and beguiling. But it isn't true to life."[133]

The Living Desert   A closer look at one of the *True-Life Adventures* better illustrates these critical comments. *The Living Desert* was the first feature-length *True-Life* film and won an academy award in the documentary category in 1953. The film has been cited as an example of Disney's innovative cinemagraphic techniques, as well as the bold step of personalizing relatively inaccessible and unfamiliar animals.

At the beginning of the film, we are introduced to the desert – a strange, unusual, and mysterious world where "Life is on the grim side." However, the film focuses on the "drama" and "mysteries" of the land. And, true to Disney style, we are treated to music and humor throughout the film, to interpret the "mysteries" of the desert.

In addition to the many inaccuracies (a flash flood and many other scenes were staged), there are numerous examples of anthropomorphization and condescension towards the desert creatures. The most frequently-cited scene involves a number of scorpions who appear to be square dancing, thanks to the accompanying music and the narrator's calls at "the sting-eree." In other scenes, we encounter a roadrunner who is described as "odd," "nosey," and a "joker"; a "bashful" tortoise; and "Skinny, the squirrel," who later becomes the film's hero. Meanwhile, a Gila monster, tarantulas, and various kinds of snakes are identified as villains.

In other scenes, the narrator introduces us to Mrs Tarantula (a "lethal lady" who tends to swoon), Mrs Rat ("Mother's work is never done"), and the "chivalrous" tortoises, who fight over a female tortoise, who is called "the lady fair" and "gives the males the run-around." It doesn't take much to see that stereotypical gender roles are also ascribed to the animal world.

What also seems striking throughout the film is the use of human (mostly American) clichés. For instance, the notion of "home sweet home" is accompanied by the music, "There's No Place Like Home."

Disney and nature   Many claim that the Disney nature films had a great affect on subsequent animal films, and that techniques still used in contemporary nature programs, such as plot structure, anthropomorphism, animal biography, species hierarchy, and stock technical effects, are all "offshoots" of the Disney formula.[134] It has also been argued that Disney's influence on the public's attitudes towards the natural world has been profound, especially because of the increasing distance from nature experienced by most Americans who live in urban and suburban locations. As King points out:

Our reliance for nature's image and context shifted from first-hand experience to the novel, western-school painting, and nature photography, culminating with the film and television versions that were shaped, and continue to be influenced by, the Walt Disney Company's animated films and its live-action *True-Life Adventures* series of the late 1940s.[135]

Disney's nature films are credited with drawing attention to the relationship between humans and nature far more successfully than other sources and thus were "humanistically correct" in providing the groundwork for the growth of environmentalism. As King further observes:

> The implications of film drama featuring animal rather than human stars hold the key to understanding not only the human/nature face-off as a cultural problem, but the power of film to temper, guide, and shape that relationship. Disney films, which reached millions of children and their parents in theaters and on television, as well as in the classroom, exerted a cultural influence far wider than Rachel Carson's *Silent Spring* or the Sierra Club. They taught Americans to think of nature in terms of "courageous" ants, "playboy" fiddler crabs, "industrious" bees, and even "successful" wild oats.[136]

It is also important to bear in mind how profitable the films were, as well as how they were integrated into the company's other businesses. The distribution of these films to educational institutions has already been mentioned. But the nature films were also recycled for the *Disneyland* television series on ABC during the 1950s and 1960s, as well as providing themes for Disneyland attractions, which, in return, reinforced the popularity of the nature films.

Nature and animals continue to be featured as themes in Disney products, as evidenced most recently by the new Disney Animal Kingdom, which prompts us to consider Disney's worlds – or the theme parks – which will be the topic of the next chapter.

Reading the whole Disney This chapter has considered a variety of approaches to interpreting Disney's animated films and cartoons. As noted at the beginning of the chapter, it is important to study the images and ideas that are represented in Disney products, and we have looked at an assortment of these textual readings. While there are variations in approaches to Disney texts, there is still a good deal of consistency in the interpretations, similar to what we will find in the analysis of Disney theme parks in the next chapter.

It might be argued that this agreement has to do with the company's careful adherence to its brand, or what we have called Classic Disney. In other words, Disney products are carefully constructed and manufactured to be recognized as *Disney* products. While this point may seem obvious and redundant, it is often either neglected or underplayed by textual analysts. Unless the corporate context in which Disney operates is taken into consideration, we are left with readings of individual Disney texts that mostly just apply the latest method of textual analysis to a wider range of products.[137]

Furthermore, if we are to fully understand the Disney phenomenon, the reception or consumption of Disney products also needs to be taken into account. Though recently some analysts have attempted to integrate audience responses and reception with textual readings (more discussion of this trend follows in chapter 7), most of the analyses of Disney texts merely reinforce the subjective nature of these readings.

Furthermore, by focusing only on individual texts, the overall output or ideological position represented by Disney is neglected. Herb Schiller expressed this idea many years ago:

> Just as the Disney management finds it profitable to use a systems approach to sell its products, the best way to understand the message it is selling is to adopt a systems analysis approach to the product – that is, to take the Disney machine as an entity, and to examine its many outputs as *elements in a totality* with some common features.[138]

Schiller's call for a "systems approach" echoes the aim of this book, which is to present an integrated approach to understanding Disney. In other words, the analysis of production and consumption of Disney texts is necessary to understand their significance.

An integrated approach is especially relevant in considering the Disney theme parks, which present the Classic Disney ideology in material form, providing sites of pleasure, fun and family entertainment, but also serving as highly successful businesses. The next chapter focuses on the wide range of perspectives that have been used to study the Disney theme parks.

6 Dissecting Disney's Worlds

> To all who come to this happy place: Welcome. Disneyland is your land. Here age relives fond memories of the past . . . and here youth may savor the challenge and promise of the future.
>
> – dedication plaque at Disneyland

"I'm going to Disneyland."[1]

In 1967, Schickel observed that the "aesthetic content of Disneyland has been endlessly debated by intellectuals."[2] That was more than 30 years ago. Since then, a deluge of studies have attempted to interpret not only the aesthetics of the Disney theme parks, but their meanings and significance as sites of contemporary American culture. As Wilson observes, "Among Walt Disney's many contributions to American popular culture, his theme parks call for special attention, because they form the landscape against which Disney's visions met the historical and political realities of America."[3]

While many would agree with Wilson's sentiments, the company and its supporters are typically defensive about any kind of interpretations of the park other than the obvious one of family entertainment. However, in spite of official intent, the *result* of Disney's efforts is a value-laden environment, which extends and expands Classic Disney into a material or physical existence, as well as providing a strong dose of all-American ideology.

As noted previously, much recent Disney scholarship has focused on the theme parks, which have been interpreted in a myriad of ways. This chapter will not offer yet another guided tour of the parks, but will present an overview of the approaches that have been used to understand how Disney's worlds have contributed to the Disney phenomenon, as well as to American culture in general. First, it will discuss briefly the historical development of the Disney parks, followed by a summary of the major themes identified by park analysts. It will conclude with a look at the Disney community of Celebration, as an extension of the Disney theme park concept into at least some people's everyday lives.

History of Disney's worlds

The creation of the first Disney world – Disneyland – is often identified as the beginning of the concept of theme parks. But, as many commentators have pointed out, the historical precedents can be seen in popular amusement parks or urban resorts, such as Coney Island in the USA and Tivoli Gardens in Europe. In the early years of the twentieth century, such amusement sites provided recreation and pleasure for throngs of workers, immigrants, and young people. Adams reports that there were between 1,500 and 2,000 amusement parks in the USA by 1919. Following a decline during the Depression, amusement parks again became popular in the post-World War II period, when American families with higher incomes discovered leisure-time activities.[4]

Disneyland was also especially reminiscent of world fairs, which combined a celebration of the past with visions of the future. Bryman describes the Disney parks' uniqueness as "the combination of the transformation of themed attractions into one of themed environments with the transformation of the world's fair/exposition concept into a permanent site."[5] Davis argues that Disney's important contribution was the concept of a fully designed themed environment, or "land," with all services provided in-house.[6]

The popular story of Disneyland's conception is part of the constructed Disney history and connected closely with the image of Walt Disney as a creative genius, as well as a loving and devoted parent. Most often the story involves Walt's dream of building for his daughters a clean and safe amusement park that adults also would enjoy. However, it appears that plans for a back-lot tour of the Disney studio, featuring a train ride and specific themed areas, were discussed at the company as early as the 1930s and especially during the 1940s. Furthermore, in the early 1950s Walt worked on a project that included miniaturized scenes or tableaus with automated characters that extolled America's past and was called Disney-landia.[7] At the time, he was involved much less in the studio's filmmaking and more with his own projects, especially his railroading hobby.[8] In fact, Marling presents an interesting account of how Walt Disney's plans for Disneyland were influenced specifically by the 1948 Chicago Railroad Fair, which featured dramatizations of the past and future of railroading, themed restaurants, etc.[9]

Thus, Disney's motivations for building Disneyland were undoubtedly much more complex than the simple paternal urges implied in the official story. As Mills speculates:

> Disney recognized a novel opportunity to create not just a profitable enterprise but an heroic agency to promote US values far beyond the limitations inherent in the movies. He saw a window of opportunity to create not a sterile monument to American values but a dynamic agency by which he could promote them, helping to resolve what he saw as a crisis in US society. Whereas the Depression had been resolved by the collectivist activities of mass mobilization, Disney sought to write both the cure and the disease out of the public memory by re-establishing popular faith in both the individualist myths of the past and the technological possibilities of the future.[10]

Thus, the parks also gave Disney the opportunity to expand upon Classic Disney themes and to emphasize and promote American values, or at least those that Disney believed in. Furthermore, Disneyland was designed to recycle existing Disney stories and characters in another commodified form. While the company embellished its later parks with a multitude of vacation and resort attractions (especially at Walt Disney World), Disneyland, as the first Disney park, exemplified the essential philosophy, as well as establishing most of the specific themes for the Disney worlds that followed.

The parks and resorts have been introduced in chapter 3 and are described in great detail in many other studies.[11] (See table 6.1.) Since visits to the Disney worlds are commonplace, the following discussion assumes some familiarity with the parks by readers, while offering apologies to others who may have escaped or avoided the experience. (Reference to these types of individuals is included in the next chapter.) Further, the discussion will be directed mostly to Disney's theme parks, not more recent resort facilities, as most of the analytical commentary has focused on the parks.[12]

Table 6.1   Disney theme parks

Park	Opening date	Admissions, 1998
Disneyland Anaheim, Calif.	July 1955	13.7 million
Walt Disney World, Orlando, Florida		
The Magic Kingdom	October 1971	15.6 million
EPCOT	October 1982	10.6 million
Disney–MGM Studios	May 1989	9.5 million
Disney's Animal Kingdom	April 1998	6.0 million
Disneyland Paris	April 1992	(unavailable)
Tokyo Disneyland	April 1983	(unavailable)

Source: Mark Albright, "Theme Park Attendance Nationwide Drops," *St. Petersburgh Times*, 23 Dec. 1998.

Analyzing Disney worlds

Over the years the Disney worlds have attracted criticism as well as praise from the intellectual world. One of the first critiques, by novelist Julian Halévy in 1958, is often cited as an example of the condescending tone of Disney critics.[13] Halévy compared Disneyland with Las Vegas, concluding that Disneyland offered "cheap formulas packaged to sell," and that even Las Vegas was a more reasonable source of satisfaction.[14] Of course, Schickel's well-known study of Disney in the late 1960s included commentary on Disneyland, and especially strong objections to the Audio-Animatronic version of Abraham Lincoln.[15]

In 1973, Schiller and Real both focused on Disneyland in their broader investigations of mass media's role in society.[16] A few other pieces appeared during the 1980s, including an entire issue of the *Journal of Popular Culture* devoted to the parks, plus brief commentaries by Eco and Baudrillard, setting the pattern for further postmodern musings during the 1990s.[17]

The company's theme park expansion during the Disney Decade was met with a deluge of academic studies from a variety of disciplines, including anthropology, art, architecture, business, ethnic studies, film and media studies, cultural studies, gender studies, geography, history, market-ing, political science, popular culture, rhetoric, and urban planning.[18] It is not possible here to explore all the issues presented in these wide-ranging studies; however, some of the common themes should be helpful in understanding the Disney phenomenon.

Bryman presents a commendable discussion of the many textually based studies of the Disney worlds, noting that the approaches range from Marxist analysis to postmodern critiques. Despite the diversity, he points out that analysts seem to agree on what the parks represent, as noted in the introductory comments to his study:

> although quite a wide range of themes have been extracted in the analysis to be presented here, writers have often contributed to each theme indepen-dently of their theoretical positions or of their individual projects when examining the parks. This commonality is interesting in itself since it means that writers working within frameworks as diverse as Marxism and semiotics can generate conclusions which are consistent, if not almost identical. Perhaps the power of 'theming' exerts greater influence over writers than they or we as readers are aware.[19]

The discussion that follows draws on Bryman's organization, but especially emphasizes themes that express the interaction of economic and ideological characteristics represented by the parks. While there are a variety of textually oriented studies, it is essential to understand the parks within the context of their role as key components of the Disney empire. In other words, the theme parks represent a profitable and lucrative business for the Disney company, as well as supporting conservative, corporate, and consumerist ideologies. To appreciate more fully this interweaving of the economic and the ideological, it is helpful to first recall how the theme parks actually work within the Disney empire and why they are so important to the primary corporate mission. Therefore, the discussion will begin with the themes or motifs that seem most closely related to the economic dimensions of the parks and then move on to other prevalent themes identified by theme park analysts.

Themes from a theme park

Synergy

In the mid-1950s, the combination of Disneyland–the theme park and *Disneyland*–the television program was a model of media cross-promotion.[20]

As noted in chapter 2, ABC bought stock in Disneyland, Inc., and Disney agreed to produce a weekly television program on the network. The park was featured prominently on the one-hour program, which also included episodes corresponding to the various lands (Frontierland, Tomorrowland, etc.), thus further promoting the theme park.

As noted previously, these arrangements have been called a systems approach. By the 1990s, however, the same concept was called synergy, and theme parks had come to represent the ultimate synergy, bringing together media products and merchandising at one site. Davis explains that theme parks are major vehicles for merchandising, and "the potential of the theme park industry to sell and support licensed products is central to synergy."[21]

For Disney, theme parks and resort activities contribute significantly to overall corporate goals, providing ongoing revenues and promotion for other parts of the corporate empire, as noted in chapter 3 and demonstrated in chapter 4. Indeed, it is difficult to think about the Disney brand without reference to the theme parks.

Commodification/consumption

The Disney parks can be described as a careful integration of entertainment and fun with commodification and consumption. For Fjellman, this is the fundamental description of Disney's overall business: "The Company – especially at its theme parks – produces, packages and sells experiences and memories as commodities."[22]

The "experiences" and "memories" of visits to the Disney worlds are ultimately wrapped up with consumption. First of all, the parks are commodities themselves, amassing sizable revenues just from entrance fees. While it is difficult to obtain accurate figures on revenues from admissions, Davis estimates that 50 percent of theme park revenues generally are from admission fees.[23] Overall revenues from the Disney Theme Parks and Resorts Division were $6.1 billion in 1998.

Visitors are encouraged to stay longer at the parks because of entrance fee pricing, thus boosting revenues from hotel and other resort activities, as well as from additional food and merchandise purchases. Further consumption beyond the admission price is difficult to avoid because of the basic design of the parks, which are skillfully arranged to constantly lead visitors to gift shops and kiosks featuring a wide range of appropriately themed Disney merchandise. Schickel observes that "The park's general design further enhances one's willingness to contribute to its economic well-

Table 6.2 Number of shops at Walt Disney World, 1991

Park	No. of shops
Magic Kingdom (including Main Street USA 16)	55
EPCOT Center	65
Disney–MGM Studios	22
Hotels	29
Disney Village Marketplace	20
Typhoon Lagoon & Pleasure Island	13
TOTAL	204

Source: Fjellman, *Vinyl Leaves*, pp. 178–83.

being. The layout encourages a sense of discovery that, in turn, encourages impulse buying."[24]

In his 1992 study, Fjellman prepared "The Mall Register" – a list of the 204 stores at Walt Disney World, not including restaurants or other food concessions. (See table 6.2.) Not only do the theme parks provide opportunities to sell merchandise based on continuing and new characters and stories, but the parks themselves generate merchandise, such as T-shirts, hats, and publications, identified with specific areas of the park or the park as a whole. As Willis notes, there are even shops that feature Disney villains, for those who want to avoid the typical Disney consumerism. However, in the end, Scar plush figures and Ursula dolls still contribute to the company's proceeds.[25]

Indeed, some observers have pointed out that certain attractions at the parks are *mostly* about consuming. For instance, the World Showcase might better be renamed the World Shopping Mall, with 52 stores included in the 11 international pavilions.[26] Main Street USA is also a sort of mall, with all of the individual shops connected. As Bryman notes, "consumption is presented as an aspect of the fun and fantasy. To become a full participant, the visitor needs to consume."[27]

Many of the theme park commentators have discussed this interweaving of consumption and entertainment, sometimes "called dedifferentiation," or "a tendency for shopping, eating, hotel accommodation and theme park visiting to become inextricably interwoven."[28] Wilson calls it: "An Architecture of Merchandising . . . the fullest representation of commodified space we have in North America. . . . [It] organizes public space according to the market; it understands private space as an architectural adjunct of individual consumption."[29]

Commercialization/corporatism

Long before the notion of "strategic alliances" came into vogue, Disney enlisted other corporations as its partners. The original Disneyland involved 32 companies that sponsored exhibits or restaurants at the park, including Carnation, General Electric, and Monsanto. And, of course, visitors' impressions were better remembered if captured at the designated Kodak memory spots around the park.

Corporate involvement continues throughout the parks, especially at EPCOT, where attractions are sponsored by AT&T, General Motors, Kraft, and Eastman Kodak, and the World Showcase pavilions feature national companies, such as Japan Airlines, Labatt Beer, etc. The involvement of outside corporations lessens the risk for the Disney company and also promotes and reinforces corporate ideals and values. Indeed, the very essence of EPCOT is to promote these values. In the company literature, EPCOT is described as "a community of ideas and nations and a testing ground where free enterprise can explore and demonstrate and showcase new ideas that relate to man's hopes and dreams." As Fjellman concludes, "WDW is the teaching shrine for the corporate world of commodities."[30]

Beyond EPCOT are numerous examples of corporatism that have been referred to by park analysts, but a favorite one is the Carousel of Progress sponsored by General Electric. The original Carousel debuted at the 1964 New York World's Fair, moved to Disneyland with General Electric as the sponsor, and then to Walt Disney World (with some updating) in 1975. The exhibit portrays the "improvements in American life that have resulted from the use of electricity" and depicts four scenes featuring a "middle-class robot family" from around 1900, the 1920s, the 1940s, and the present. The family members celebrate the various labor-saving devices in each scene, looking forward to even further improvements, thanks to "those research people at General Electric." The exhibit is not simply a commercial for General Electric but, as Wallace points out, a "paean to Progress – defined as the availability of emancipatory consumer goods."[31] As with many of the EPCOT attractions, the Carousel blatantly promotes corporate ideals but also links them strongly to other park themes, especially those relating to representations of the past (which will be discussed later). It is no wonder that the sponsors are pleased with the results of these efforts. As a GE representative remarked, "the Disney organization is

Table 6.3   Top ten US theme park attendance, 1998

Park	Attendance
Magic Kingdom (WDW)	15.6 million
Disneyland	13.7 million
EPCOT (WDW)	10.6 million
Disney–MGM Studios (WDW)	9.5 million
Universal Studios, Florida	8.9 million
Disney's Animal Kingdom (WDW)	6.0 million
Universal Studios, Hollywood	5.1 million
Sea World Florida, Orlando	4.9 million
Busch Gardens, Tampa Bay	4.2 million
Sea World California, San Diego	3.7 million

Source: Amusement Business, Dec. 1998.

absolutely superb in interpreting our company dramatically, memorably and favorably to the public."[32]

So not only are the Disney worlds cultural products in themselves, they actively promote and legitimize the capitalist system as a whole. Fjellman explains:

> As the commodity form becomes a central part of culture, so culture becomes available for use in the interest of commodification as particular cultural items, as a source of commercial arguments, and as symbolic legitimation for the entire system. Culture and the commodity form become dialectically intertwined.[33]

"I'm going to Disneyland."

Who goes to the Disney theme parks and why? Although the Disney company does not release attendance figures, trade sources reported that the Disney parks attracted 55.4 million visitors in 1998. Total attendance for the top 50 parks in the USA was 165 million in 1998, representing a 1 percent decline from 1997. As indicated in table 6.3, not only do Disney parks lead all other US theme and amusement parks in terms of attendance, but the Walt Disney World Resort as a whole is claimed to be the biggest tourist attraction in the world.

As Adams points out, Disneyland's initial success was possible to some

Table 6.4   Prices at Disney theme parks, 2000

Park	Price of pass
Disneyland	
1-day pass/adult	$41
/child (3–9)	$31
3-day flex passport/adult	$99
/child	$75
Walt Disney World	
1-day/1-park pass/adult	$48
/child	$39
4-day park hopper/adult	$196
/child	$158

Prices above represent only a few of the wide variety of passes sold by the parks.

extent because of the baby boom after World War II, which became the "children boom" of the 1950s. The popularity of theme parks also grew with the increase in disposable income for leisure activities and the growth of tourism, as well as advances in transportation. By 1997, the average American household was spending $1,813 each year on entertainment.[34]

By 1989, it was claimed that 70 percent of all Americans had visited either Walt Disney World or Disneyland.[35] Even when the number of children decreased, adults became more prevalent than children at the parks by a ratio of four to one.[36] Moreover, Team Disney continued to add features specifically aimed at adults to the parks and resorts, including Pleasure Island, a profusion of recreational and spectator sports activities, and the Disney Institute (offering educational workshops for elderly tourists).

Nonetheless, the Disney parks still revolve around the theme of families. Promotional and advertising material features families, and they are depicted in various ways throughout the parks (for instance, the robot families mentioned above in the Carousel of Progress). More specifically, middle-class families are portrayed, for, as most analysts point out, the ideals and values depicted in the parks are decidedly middle class.

With entrance fees (see table 6.4) and transportation expenses as barriers for some families, it has been reported that three-quarters of WDW adult visitors are professionals, technical personnel, or managers, with only 2 percent representing laborers. And despite their frequent representation in Disney's advertising campaigns, only 3 percent of WDW visitors are Black, and only 2 percent are Hispanic. As Fjellman states, Walt Disney World "is the major middle-class pilgrimage center in the United States."[37] The idea of visits to Disney worlds as family pilgrimages is a major theme for other park analysts as well and has been discussed both in the sense that the parks have become "sacred centers" that people feel compelled to visit and as rituals in which pilgrims encounter liminal states in unfamiliar and unstructured settings.[38] Although Moore and others contend that a pilgrimage to one of the Disney worlds has become a pseudo-religious experience, Bryman suggests that the pilgrimage metaphor is limited by the controlled nature of the park experience. He contends that park visitors return home not with a new sense of reality, but with "a renewed sense of their roots."[39] (Disney's presentation of the past will be further discussed later.) Meanwhile, Adams uses the pilgrimage metaphor to emphasize some of the key themes discussed previously:

> Just as a journey to Mecca, Canterbury, Lourdes, or Rome represents a rite of passage that sanctifies a pilgrim as a member of a holy community, a visit to Walt Disney World ratifies the values of corporate culture and allows the 20th-century pilgrim to reaffirm faith in capitalist scriptures of progress through technology, control through managerial hierarchy, and consumerism.[40]

"Backstage magic"

For some visitors, the appeal of the Disney parks is experiencing the amazing creations that have been designed by those crafty Imagineers and trying to figure out how it all works. Other visitors appreciate the parks' cleanliness, efficiency, and organization.[41]

Numerous writers have commented on the meticulous planning that contributes to this distinct aesthetic appearance, including carefully concealed utilities and service entrances, as well as a complete underground complex at Disney World that includes power facilities, employee transportation, storage, etc. The underground system is called the Utilidor (or utility corridor) and includes a mile of tunnels, which provide easy access for employees, as well as concealing the "non-magical" aspects of the park, including garbage collection, wiring, utilities, vents, fiber-optic lines, and computer operations.[42]

Park operations are impressive, state-of-the-art technology. For instance, trash is collected on the surface and transported via pneumatic tubes directly to garbage trucks in the basement. The park is operated with the assistance of computers, which monitor and control energy consumption, refrigeration, reservations at the park and resorts, and sound' systems. Maintenance is a nightly activity, and involves not simply sweeping the streets and tidying up the grounds, but repainting and refurbishing countless features around the parks. For example, Birnbaum's guidebook to WDW introduces Main Street USA as follows:

> Inside and outside, maintenance and housekeeping are superb. White-suited sanitation workers patrol the street to pick up litter and quickly shovel up any droppings from the horses who pull the trolley cars from Town Square to the Hub. The pavement, like all in the Magic Kingdom, is washed down every night with fire hoses. There's one crew of maintenance workers whose sole job is to change the little white lights around the roofs; another crew devotes itself to keeping the woodwork painted. As soon as these people have worked their way as far as the Hub, they start all over again at Town Square. The greenish, horse-shaped cast-iron hitching posts are repainted 20 times a year on the average – and totally scraped down each time. . . . Some visitors find all these details so fascinating that it takes them a good deal longer than the 40 minutes spent by the average guest to get from one end of Main Street to the other.[43]

The overall management and operation of the park have been acclaimed by experts over the years. In fact, the Disney company is so well known for its managerial strategies (as mentioned in chapter 3) that the company now offers its own brand of business and management programs at the Disney Institute, including courses focusing on people management, leadership, customer loyalty, quality service, creativity and innovation, and human relations management. Walt Disney World serves as a model, or "living laboratory," for the courses, as well as an enticement for potential students. (Theme park admission is included in the program fees.)[44]

The strict management of the parks is consistent with a number of themes identified by park analysts and represents an especially obvious example of the control themes that will be explored in much more depth below. As a Disney representative once explained: "The cleanliness of the park, the safety of the park is far more a search for excellence and quality on our part in entertaining people than some ivory-tower, ideological exercise." [45] Nevertheless, the obsession with cleanliness just happens to be one of those Classic Disney themes that is represented in the look of the park, as well as the appeal to visitors. As Hunt and Frankenberg conclude, linking this issue to the type of guests at the parks, "Disneyland provides good clean fun for good clean families. Trash, literally, and in terms of undesirable people, is excluded."[46]

Predictability and expectations

The design and organization of the parks have led to a kind of predictability that people have come to expect, based on the company's promotion, visitors' previous experiences, and the reputation that the parks have built over the years. Commentators have pointed to the safety and reliability of the Disney experience, which is designed to avoid the usual dangers and concerns of everyday life in the real world. As Hiassen observes:

> nobody provides a safer, more closely supervised brand of carefree than Team Rodent. Whether you're on a Disney ocean liner or a Disney log flume or the eighteenth fairway of a Disney golf course, you can be pretty sure nobody's going to sneak up and stick a real .45 in your back. That's not just a perception, it's a fact – and one reason that Disney's image as a benign enchanter-protector is now embedded in the collective parental psyche.[47]

But there are also expectations that involve the themes represented by the parks. Visitors come to *expect* that they will have a happy time in this magical place, that all of the "cast members" will be courteous and polite, that the streets will be clean and unlittered, that the themes and the fantasies will be complete and consistent.

There are numerous stories that illustrate these expectations. For instance, during a recent interview, a business reporter recalled a visit to Disneyland, where she observed one of the costumed characters being assaulted by unruly teenagers. The incident attracted the attention of the crowds, as well as park officials, as the character finally started slugging back. Later that day, while visiting the main desk at the park, the reporter witnessed a number of guests demanding their money back because the slugging episode had ruined their expectations of the park as "the happiest place on earth."

In a more publicized incident, a former Mouseketeer sued Disney in a 1995 incident which involved an armed robbery of her and her grand-children in the Disneyland parking lot. She was not as upset at the attackers as she was at the Disney employees after the incident, when "the children were rudely disillusioned" upon encountering a few of the disassembled characters backstage. The suit alleged that the company exposed the children to "the reality that Disney characters, were, in fact, make believe."[48]

Control, control, control

The predictability of a Disney park visit is possible because of the vigorous control exercised in managing the parks. In fact, nearly all of the park analysts identify control in one way or another as one of the fundamental themes of the Disney worlds.[49] Bryman identifies six levels of control at the parks, which helps to organize the numerous interpretations of this concept.[50]

1.   Control of the theme park experience   The parks' layouts, as well as most rides and exhibits, are designed to control the visitors' activities and experiences – an observation that is nearly unanimous among theme park analysts. It begins with the obligatory stroll down Main Street USA – the only entrance to the Magic Kingdom. Carefully landscaped paths lead visitors to specific destinations and Kodak Memories spots. Appropriate sound effects, music, and even aromas are carefully manipulated throughout the park.[51] The attractions and rides are usually "programmed shows," with visitors transported in either cars, boats, or trams through prearranged, unchangeable views, and carefully planned sounds and movements. As Bryman notes, "Each person will see the same as everyone else so that the experience of many theme park attractions is controlled and thereby standardized."[52]

2.   Control over the imagination   But it is not only visitors' movements and experiences that are controlled. An irony not often overlooked by theme park analysts is the passivity that is involved in most of the parks' activities, thus undermining the imagination motif that is prominently promoted in the company literature. Eco states it bluntly: "An allegory of the consumer society, a place of absolute iconism, Disneyland is also a place of total passivity. Its visitors must agree to behave like its robots."[53]

As Tom Carson, an *LA Weekly* journalist, writes:

> I love pop most for the democratic way it enlists its fans as collaborators. But Disneyland forbids this. Disneyland is unilateral, literally a control freak's paradise. It can't be experienced in any way, or yield any meanings, other

than those Walt meant it to. If Walt had really wanted our imaginations to soar, he would have given us wings, not mouse ears.[54]

Many critics have expanded on this theme, noting that activities and even thoughts are "channeled" and "controlled." As Hunt and Frankenberg explain:

> Disneyland operates through controlled imaging aimed at controlling controlled imaginations. . . . Ours is but to laugh at the jokes and to marvel at the genuine technical achievements of modellers and engineers. We too are reduced to the "ideal" child-like condition of being acted upon rather than acting. The excitements of reading (or being read to) have truly been doubly translated and betrayed.[55]

Meanwhile, Steve Nelson offers the following critique:

> In an age where the manufacture of concretized fantasy has reached new heights, Disney is certainly in the forefront. Films such as Roger Rabbit and Indiana Jones and parks like Disney–MGM Studios simulate the actuality of movie fantasies with great precision. But somehow they do it too well, leaving little room for the visitor's own imagination and personal sense of fantasy. Instead of having to wish upon a star, you may now see one from an orbiting spaceship. The technical prowess and complexity of Disney entertainment is in danger of overwhelming the humans they were designed to beguile.[56]

Furthermore, while the parks avoid any references to work or labor (to be discussed later), there are not any opportunities for real play either – no slides, swings, or other facilities that allow children (and others) to play independently or spontaneously. Hunt and Frankenberg conclude: "Here forms of play are, for both economic and ideological reasons, inseparably combined, served up prepackaged, timed, priced, and valued."[57]

3. Control as a motif Many of the park's attractions emphasize the theme of control, as well, and there is often little subtlety in the presentations. One of the attractions frequently cited to exemplify this point is Living with the Land, sponsored by Nestlé (previously, Listen to the Land, sponsored by Kraft Foods). Visitors are treated to a boat ride through displays that demonstrate how difficult nature can be unless tamed by technology and science. In discussing the attraction, Fjellman observes,

"The land is to be manipulated, tricked and beaten into submission, told what to be, and certainly not listened to."[58]

The control motif can be seen plainly at other sites around the parks, including the taming of the American West in Frontierland and the subjugation of the rest of the world in Adventureland. Bryman concludes his discussion of control as a motif by noting how it connects quite well with other park themes, such as corporatism and technological progress.[59]

4.   Control over the behavior of employees   Disney's control of employees was discussed in chapter 4. However, it is worth recalling the company's near obsession with theme park employees' appearance through the company's "Aryan-android dress code" (as Hiassen calls it), as well as the carefully monitored and structured behavior and the focus on "emotional labor," discussed previously. Obviously, this influences the park experience and its meaning, as the Disney Look and Disney Behavior contribute to the predictability that visitors expect, as well as reinforcing the all-American theme of the parks.[60]

The company is so concerned about the image of the park that employees are instructed to handle emergencies in precise ways, as discussed previously. For instance, the company goes to extreme lengths to avoid reporting any deaths in the park. One employee claimed that the medical staff is instructed to wait until they are off of the company's property to pronounce a person dead. Thus the official policy is that no one has ever died in the park.[61]

5.   Control over the immediate environment   As Kuenz observes, the company policy is to "let nothing enter or exit the property unregulated or uncontrolled."[62] But the parks and resorts themselves represent the company's ability to control the land, by "creating fantasy worlds out of orange groves or swamp lands."[63] Details about the construction of the parks and their attractions have been presented by many writers, as well as by the company itself. In particular, the construction of impossible or unnatural landscapes is a distinct feature of the parks and part of their appeal to visitors. A recent example is the new Animal Kingdom, where *unnatural* environments for *nonnative* animals have been constructed and then promoted as *natural*, as in the following promotional piece: "Celebrating man's enduring fascination with animals of all kinds, the new park provides natural habitats for more than 1,000 animals. . . . Rare and wonderful creatures, native to far-off lands . . . roaming freely. Natural barriers for safety are nearly invisible."[64]

Plate 5   Meet Mickey. One of the attractions of the Disney theme parks for both children and adults is meeting "live" Classic Disney characters. Here, Mickey Mouse greets a group of "guests" at Disneyland.
Photo by Jeremy Alden.

Even those features that are indigenous receive special treatment, so that the appropriate image is maintained. For instance, Hiassen explains how Disney World's Bay Lake was an inappropriate tea-color because of the bark from surrounding cypress trees. The company removed the trees, replaced the muck with imported sand, and refilled the lake with the bluish water that tourists expect.[65] More widely reported was the black buzzard incident in 1988, when the company was accused of killing the federally protected birds because their (natural) behavior was inappropriate for the desired Disney ambience. The company handled the resulting public relations fiasco by donating funds to Florida's game commission.[66]

Part of the allure of the Disney worlds is the carefully controlled environments that separate visitors from the "real world." But the company's control also extends far beyond the park gates, especially at Walt Disney World. The limitations of the original size of Disneyland alerted the company to the need to control much more than just the land for the

Florida park, so the company managed to purchase 24,000 acres for the Disney World complex, which now includes a wide range of hotels and other resort attractions. The connection between the hotels and the parks is fundamentally financial, but also (as Bryman points out) contributes to the control of the basic appearance of the entire area, as well as controlling Disney's competition.

6.   Control over its destiny   The Disney company has been successful generally at getting what it wants from governments, whether local, state, or national. As discussed in chapter 4, deliberate efforts are made to influence political decisions to favor the company's businesses, whether it be over copyright protection, import quotas, or tax exemptions. As noted previously, Disney has also been able to convince governments to contribute to the construction of its parks. In Florida, government-funded road improvements were made, while the French government contributed improved transportation links to Disneyland Paris.

However, the Reedy Creek Improvement District is the most appropriate symbol of the company's ability to control its own affairs. In 1967, the Florida legislature gave the Disney company "special treatment" through the creation of Reedy Creek, which meant that the company no longer needed to obtain building permits or pay certain government fees, but could maintain its own utilities, create its own building codes, and even levy taxes. In essence, Reedy Creek represents the company's ability to set up a private government. The company owns its own water supply, telecommunications facilities, fire department, and could even operate its own nuclear energy facility, if desired. Overt control over the facilities is provided by a security force of 800 uniformed "hosts" and "hostesses," otherwise known as security guards.[67]

While theme park analysts – especially Bryman – are quite perceptive in their discussions of various ways in which control is exemplified at the parks, they still underplay the point that control is a recurring theme *throughout* the Disney empire. Though Wilson makes this connection, he is still referring mostly to the parks: "The organizing principle of the Disney Universe is control. . . . This sort of thematic and directed space is a common one in our society [shopping malls, supermarkets], though seldom is it so systematically applied."[68]

It needs to be stressed more emphatically that the control visible at the parks is also characteristic of other aspects of the company's activities, as well as being represented in Classic Disney texts.

Classic Disney and beyond

Many commentators have observed that the parks are organized around narratives with distinct cinematic characteristics.[69] Thus, it is not surprising that the parks recycle the stories and characters in Classic Disney entertainment products, especially the animated films, contributing in important ways to the synergy mentioned previously and outlined in chapter 4. Stories and characters, especially from animated features, are recreated at the parks in new formats, such as rides, costumed characters, and parades, adding even further dimensions to Classic Disney themes and values. As Fjellman notes (referring specifically to Walt Disney World): "The ideological messages at WDW are wide-ranging and intricately woven and cross-referenced."[70]

A park visit itself is yet another representation of Classic Disney themes, as the following description of Disney World from the company's website stresses:

> Welcome to the most magical place on earth! Here in this incredible fantasy world, imagination takes flight and spirits soar as your favorite characters and lands of make-believe come alive just for you. Wondrous attractions thrust you into enchanting adventures. Lavish parades and shows leave you laughing along with characters from your favorite Disney classics. It's a kingdom where once upon a time is now, and a place to create cherished memories that last forever.

Many of the Classic Disney themes are celebrated here – fantasy, magic, escape, happiness, fun. The happiness theme is reiterated and expanded and, as noted above, becomes part of the parks' predictability. As Hunt and Frankenberg observe:

> You have seen the films, are familiar with the cartoon characters, and know that their trials and tribulations are humorous, and will eventually resolve into happy endings. You expect (and know that an omnipresent but unobtrusive management intends) a similar ending from the thrills and spills of your own visit.[71]

Still other themes are incorporated in attractions throughout the parks. For instance, many observers have noted that the parks celebrate the notion of individualism – overtly in the American Journeys and American Adventure attractions, but also by implication in the spirit of Frontierland and Tomorrowland. Adams has noted that everything is designed to promote a

sense of optimism, "a belief in progressive improvement toward perfection."[72] (Recall the previous discussion of the Carousel of Progress.)

The theme of escape, already discussed in Classic Disney films, is
strongly accentuated at the parks, where one is encouraged to forget
everyday cares and worries. As Lawrence Taylor, a former defensive
linebacker for the New York Giants, once commented, in explaining his
well-known problems with drugs, etc.: "We'd all like to go through life
without any trials or tribulations, but we don't live in Disneyland."[73] This
kind of thing is often said in everyday conversations, as Disneyland has
come to represent something that is unreal, escapist, or overly romantic.

Above all, the messages incorporated in the parks are clear and straight-
forward, as in Classic Disney films. "Its images, however complex the
network of representation and illusion involved, are clear and self explana-
tory living up to Disney's own continuing advice: 'Make it read!' meaning,
making the action distinct and recognizable. No contradictions, no ambi-
guities."[74] The meaning of the Disney worlds seems to be generally
understood by all and is tied rather neatly to Classic Disney themes. For
Hunt and Frankenberg, this means that:

> A good time can be had because all the visitors, courting couples, parents
> and their children are out of time: out of the routine, demands and conflicts
> of the daily timetable. What goes on here is not really serious; it does not
> count in the workaday world. At the same time, like other leisure activities,
> it carries a more or less concealed philosophical socialization for the family
> and for the ethnocentric white Anglo-Saxon tradition which masquerades as
> American values.[75]

While Classic Disney themes are evident, certain Disney ideals and
values have been accentuated and expanded at the parks, especially those
that pertain to the representation of the past and the future. As noted
previously, Disneyland provided Walt Disney even further opportunities to
depict his own version of America's past, as well as his vision of the future.
The next sections will expand upon these themes.

The past: Walt Disney's America

The original, overarching theme of Disneyland – as expressed in the
dedication plaque quoted in the first epigraph to this chapter – is the
celebration of the past and the promise of the future. The past is strongly
emphasized in many attractions in the Magic Kingdom, including Main

Street USA, Liberty Square, Frontierland, and Adventureland. Meanwhile, EPCOT's Future World and American Adventure feature explicit views of the past, even though they are often included in exhibits that are meant to be about the future.

The nostalgic appeal of the parks is highlighted by most writers, who often point out that Disney's version of the past never really existed. And, indeed, park designers agree. As one Imagineer explained, "What we create is a 'Disney Realism,' sort of utopian in nature, where we carefully program out all the negative, unwanted elements and program in the positive elements."[76] So, the Disney past is clean, happy, and, above all, organized. This is especially emphasized in discussions of Main Street USA, which is said to represent Walt Disney's turn-of-the-century hometown of Marceline, Missouri. Despite the irony that Walt's boyhood was apparently not so happy, Main Street USA represents the essence of small town USA that grounded his overall philosophy.

Some writers connect the presentation of the past directly with another major theme at the parks: namely, consumption. As Bryman explains: "The past is subject to heavy doses of nostalgia which not only results in a skewed account of the past, but also serves to link the warm feelings inspired by nostalgia to consumption." As Eco observes: "The Main Street façades are presented to us as toy houses and invite us to enter them, but their interior is always a disguised supermarket, where you buy obsessively, believing that you are still playing."[77]

Other commentators note that the parks' presentation of the past is typically portrayed in a comical, lighthearted, and, above all, entertaining manner, a style that Disney used in representations of the past in films and television programs.

In other ways, the historical detail in Disney's presentation is meticulous, as the company goes to extreme lengths to "get it right." For instance, for American Adventure, historians were consulted on how historical figures actually spoke; costumes for the robot impersonators were made in the exact manner as the originals, and the exact size of the cannon balls was calculated. The Imagineers' remarkable technology is employed to bring history to life.

However, the most common critique of the Disney version of history – which Wallace and Fjellman call "Distory" – pertains to what is *not* presented, especially in those attractions that feature sketches of American history. Bryman categorizes these omissions as those that deal with (1) problems created by industry and corporations; (2) issues pertaining to class, race, and gender; and (3) situations involving conflict.

Wallace points out how Disney's "selective reconstruction of the past" is reminiscent of other forms of historical representation found in nine-teenth-century wax museums and industrial expositions, where science and industry were hailed as the keys to progress in the future.[78] Furthermore, the various Disney exhibits have been influenced by specific historical contexts. The attractions created in the 1950s and 1960s (specifically, the Carousel of Progress and the Hall of the Presidents) represent a kind of corporate boosterism and patriotic fervor that was less acceptable in the 1970s, when EPCOT was built. The latter's attractions (especially Future World) actually acknowledge a few problems in the past (mostly relating to the environment), but find that the answers have been – and will continue to be – provided by corporations and technology. Thus, Disney embraces modernization to assure its middle-class visitors that all is well.

Wallace argues that by the 1980s, changes in public opinion influenced the presentation of EPCOT's American Adventure, where Frederick Douglas, Chief Joseph, and Susan Anthony are represented among the 35 Audio-Animatronic robots. The 29-minute presentation is explained in Birnhaum's guidebook:

> The idea is to recall episodes in history, both negative and positive, which most contributed to the growth of the spirit of America, either by engender-ing "a new burst of creativity" (in the designers' words) "or a better understanding of ourselves as partners in the American experience." The presentation is hardly comprehensive; instead, it's "a hundred-yard dash capturing the spirit of the country at specific moments in time."[79]

Nevertheless, as Wallace explains, it is still Disney history, which reinforces some of the Classic Disney values. It is upbeat, positive, optimis-tic, and relies on individualist explanations. Martin Luther King, for instance, is acknowledged "as an icon, not spokesman for a movement."[80] And the omissions are still glaring, including those social movements that are difficult to depict without attention to collective efforts (the labor movement) and those wars that cannot be portrayed optimistically (Viet-nam). As Michael Smith notes, it is "decontextualized history" which reduces reality to nostalgia and magic.[81]

For some critics, it is not that education (specifically, history) cannot and should not be conducted in more interesting and entertaining ways, as Wallace observes; but it becomes especially problematic when the past is presented selectively and unrealistically for the sake of entertainment. Perhaps it is more understandable now why many intellectuals and others were skeptical of Disney's proposals to create a park specifically designed to represent American history, as discussed in chapter 3.

Back to the future?

In addition to the nostalgic past, the Disney worlds claim to offer "the challenge and promise of the future." Tomorrowland includes fantasy adventures, such as Space Mountain, as well attractions, such as the Carousel of Progress, The Timekeeper, and Dreamflight. At EPCOT's Future World, Disney and its corporate partners present visions of the future in pavilions focusing on agriculture, communications, the ocean, energy, health, and the imagination.

Many Disney analysts have pointed out that attempts to envision the future are reminiscent of the world fairs, with unimaginative presentations that rarely compare to the fantasies and visions that science fiction writers regularly capture in their written work. The difficulty in presenting the future at a relatively permanent site is the obvious one of needing to constantly keep ahead of the present.

For the most part, Disney's efforts have not been all that successful. One of the main problems has been the overt connection with the corporations that sponsor the exhibits. While the Imagineers are responsible for the design of the exhibits, analysts have observed that the visions of the future are firmly tied to the sponsor's current products. The exhibits suggest that citizens of tomorrow can count on the technological solutions that corporate America will provide. As Jane Kuenz observes, "the future is simply presented; the social mechanisms producing it and the social consequences thereof are not."[82]

Most of the theme park analysts suggest that the future seems mainly to reflect the past, or Disney's version of the past, and thus celebrates a reification of existing social relations and the status quo, or, in other words, the present. Indeed, a conservative message seems clear and unmistakable. Although visitors do not actually confront the present at the parks, the representation of the past and the future serves as confirmation – more specifically, a class confirmation – of the ways things are. As Bryman concludes: "the suppression of the present has the effect of making visitors feel better about the world that they currently live in. By presenting rosy pictures of the past and the future, the problems of the present can be played down."[83] Again, it is an entertaining escape to an optimistic, comfortable future, a future that reaffirms the status quo.

Mobility/transportation   One of the less obvious themes of the Disney parks revolves around movement and transportation. As Sorkin notes, "movement is ubiquitous and central" at Disneyland and Disney World, which are called travel "destinations," but also feature a wide range of thematic transport systems (trains, monorails, gondolas, etc.).[84] "The visitor travels in order to travel," as most of the attractions move visitors through them as rides, rather than walk-through or staged events. Marling argues that Disneyland actually represents a critique of the auto-driven metropolis:

> In a society in which the ticket to adulthood was the driver's license, the Disneyland transportation system permitted regression to childhood through the simple expedient of inviting grown-ups to become passengers. And the destinations were no longer the office, the shopping center, or some sleazy, little amusement park. Disney's boats and trains went instead to the places of the heart, to a happy past, to memories or dreams of a perfect childhood.[85]

Postmodern analysis and synthetic experiences

A number of writers have discussed the Disney worlds as sites of post-modernism. In fact, Fjellman concludes his extensive study with ten basic theses, one of which states without any qualification that Walt Disney World is postmodern: "It is a seemingly endless mélange of discreet, bounded informational packets plopped down next to each other willy-nilly – Liberty next to Fantasy, Japan next to Morocco. It is so rife with differences and strange borders that the very concept of difference is obliterated."[86]

Although there is great variation and even confusion over the concept, Bryman, in a very un-postmodern style, identifies a few postmodern themes that are relevant to the Disney worlds, including an emphasis on pastiche and image, the dedifferentiation trend, and the notion of hyperreality.[87]

The Disney worlds are one of the most common references for the postmodern notion of pastiche. For example, in one of the more sensible discussions of postmodernism, Harvey discusses the timespace compression evident at the Disney parks.[88] It is easy to think of examples from the Disney worlds, where one can shift within minutes from a visit to the American Wild West to an adventure in space or back to Europe during the Middle Ages. Bryman observes, however, that this may not necessarily represent a peculiarly postmodern phenomenon, as late nineteenth-century exhibits and parks displayed similar tendencies. Nevertheless, it is worth noting the Disney parks' perfection of pastiche and that they are among the most common contemporary references to the concept.

The tendency of boundaries between institutional settings to collapse is called "dedifferentiation" by postmodernists and is represented in several ways by the Disney parks. The merging of theme park with shopping has already been mentioned, but it is also evident in the other direction, with the increased theming of shopping malls. Other examples are the distinct themes that characterize the Disney hotels, especially at Walt Disney World. Analysts have noted that recent developments in Las Vegas represents a similar dedifferentiation between hotels, casinos, and theme parks.

Further instances of dedifferentiation are the merging of work/play, actor/audience, entertainment/education. Perhaps the most fitting example is the dedifferentiation of reality and unreality, or representation, which has attracted a good deal of attention from Disney analysts. Harvey cites the Disney worlds as instances of experiencing the world as a simulacrum, while Baudrillard describes Disneyland as "a perfect model of all the entangled orders of simulation."[89] In this sense, Disney worlds aptly exemplify Jameson's characterization of postmodern culture as a breaking down of the signifying chain, or the relation between the signifier and the signified.[90] As Bryman observes: "There are real trees and flowers. There are real entertainers. But in the main, it is the unreal, the fabricated, that tends to be the most memorable."[91] The title of Fjellman's study – *Vinyl Leaves* – refers to the fabricated tree that (before 1999) held the Swiss Family Island Treehouse and is covered with 800,000 vinyl leaves. For Fjellman, then, reality/non-reality is a key theme of the Disney worlds.

Other analysts have pointed to the Disney parks as synthetic experiences, representing what Eco and others have called "hyperreality." Baudrillard writes that "Disneyland is presented as imaginary in order to make us believe that the rest is real, when in fact all of Los Angeles and the America surrounding it are no longer real, but of the order of the hyperreal and of simulation."[92] Bryman argues that this has been postmodernism's greatest contribution to understanding the parks, contributing "a sense of models as standing for themselves rather than for a reality that prompted them into being."[93]

Disneyfication/Disneyization   Postmodern discussions of the theme parks also refer to "Disneyfication," a term which has been applied both to literary works subjected to the Disney treatment (as discussed in chapter 5) and to an approach to urban planning.[94] While Isozaki notes that theme parks provide some of the only possibilities left for community planning,[95] there are others who claim that Disney represents "the person who has most influenced America's urban landscape. Disney and Disney-inspired design have moved out of the bounds of the theme park and planned community to take on the real city."[96]

Accordingly, Bryman and others have offered a more expansive frame of reference called "Disneyization": "the process by which the principles of the Disney theme parks are coming to dominate more and more sectors of American society as well as the rest of the world."[97] Bryman identifies four dimensions of Disneyization – theming, dedifferentiation of consumption, merchandising, and emotional labor – all themes that have been discussed in either this or previous chapters. He explores numerous examples of the applicability and prevalence of these themes, noting that the Disneyization trend is growing and may become even more significant in the future.

Celebration: Living in a Disney world

Walt's dream

The ultimate Disney park might be one in which people would actually live, rather than merely visit. Although not a theme park, the community of Celebration may be the closest thing to a live-in Disney world and could well serve as the quintessential example of Disneyization.

The original idea for EPCOT was Walt's dream of the perfect community: "EPCOT will be an experimental prototype community of tomorrow that will take its cue from the new ideas and new technologies that are now emerging from the creative centers of American industry." The futuristic community would be home to 20,000 residents, and include high-speed trains and even a massive umbrella that would protect residents from rain. However, plans for the project were dropped after Walt's death, and, as we have seen, another version of EPCOT became part of Walt Disney World.

But the idea of a perfect community reemerged at Disney in the early 1990s, and Celebration opened on 4 July 1996. The town is located on 4,900 acres, five miles from Walt Disney World. By the end of 1997, 1,500 people were living in the community, with plans to grow to a population of 20,000, as Walt originally envisioned.

Celebration is an example of New Urbanism, a planning movement which has attempted to rediscover the "lessons of Main Street" as solutions to the problems of the suburbs. The company insists that Celebration is "not just a housing development, but a community." Indeed, some commentators have noted that it is actually Disney's answer to the perceived lack of community in America.

Celebration includes a state-of-the-art school, pedestrian-friendly streets, attractive public spaces, a convenient downtown, etc. The choices of living accommodations include six types of home, with prices ranging from $200,000 to $1 million, as well as town house apartments renting for $600 per month and up. Home prices are reported to be 25–40 percent above comparable real estate in the area.[98] It is clear that Celebration does not include poor Americans, and obviously there are no homeless citizens. The town has also been described as "extremely white."

Disney's publicized goal was to create a community, but another goal has to be selling real estate. Claims have been made that the larger corporate strategy was a $2.5 billion real estate deal, or a "creative way of packaging and selling Florida swampland." Apparently, the company paid about $200 per acre in the 1960s for land that was sold for Celebration in quarter-acre lots at $80,000 each.

Celebration can also be viewed as a clever political move that may help Disney's government relations in Florida. It seems that the state-chartered, virtually sovereign municipality, the Reedy Creek Improvement District (discussed previously), contributes relatively little in the way of taxes to Osceola County, where Disney World is located. The addition of Celebration provides ready-made taxpayers, which may actually endear Disney to the state government.

Controlling Celebration

The power structure in the town of Celebration will probably not come as a surprise to those familiar with the Disney ethos. Michael Pollan, a *New York Times* journalist, wrote after his first visit to Celebration:

> From my research I knew that every last visual detail my eyes had taken in during my two-hour walk, from the precise ratio of lawn to perennials in the front yards to the scrollwork on the Victorian porches to the exact relationship of column, capital and entablature on the façades of every Colonial Revival, had been stipulated – had in fact been spelled out in the gorgeous and obsessively detailed "Pattern Book" that governs every facet of architectural and even horticultural life at Celebration. I knew all that, yet

now I felt it, too, and how it felt was packaged, less than real, somewhat more like a theme park than a town.[99]

The rules are spelled out in a document called "Covenants, Codes and Restrictions," the quasi-constitution that all home buyers are required to sign. Some examples:

- All visible window coverings must be either white or off-white (colored or patterned curtains look "icky", says a community newsletter).
- The proportion of perennials to grass is prescribed.
- Residents may hold only one garage sale in any 12-month period.
- A single political sign (measuring 18 by 24 inches) may be posted for 45 days prior to an election.
- Any activity that "detracts from the overall appearance of the properties" is prohibited – including the parking of residents' pickup trucks on the street.[100]

Political control of Celebration is firmly entrenched in the hands of the Disney company. As with other master-planned communities in the USA, the responsibility for the community is technically in the hands of a home-owners' association, whose board is elected by the residents. As Pollan observes, home-owners' associations represent "the fastest-growing form of political organization in the country, forming a kind of alternative political universe in which one of every eight Americans now resides."[101] However, even though Celebration residents elect the directors of the home-owners' association, the covenants dictate that the association cannot change any rule or restriction in Celebration "without prior notice to and the written approval of the Celebration Company." In addition, Disney maintains the right to control every aspect of the physical character of the community. As a lawyer and home-owners' association expert says: "It is absolute top-down control. The homeowners are powerless against the association and the association is powerless against Disney. I can't imagine anything more undemocratic."[102]

In addition, the community is organized around privatized municipal services, including garbage pickup, recreational facilities, public safety, and lighting. Celebration's town hall is privately owned by Disney. In other words, rather than being citizens of Celebration, residents are more like Celebration consumers. As Pollan concludes:

It may be Disney's boldest innovation at Celebration to have established a rather novel form of democracy, one that is based on consumerist, rather than republican, principles. For many of the people I met at Celebration, the measure of democracy is not self-rule but responsiveness – they're prepared to surrender power over their lives to a corporation as long as that corporation remains sensitive to their needs. This is the streamlined, focus-grouped responsiveness of the marketplace, rather than the much rougher responsiveness of elected government – which for many Americans was discredited a long time ago.[103]

Celebration defectors

Many residents have only positive things to say about living in Celebration, and the development has been one of the fastest-selling in its price range in the area. For instance, residents Douglas Frantz and Catherine Collins write about their experiences in *Celebration, U.S.A.*, concluding that the town is an exciting place to live, although "We would insist on more racial and economic diversity, not because it's morally right or politically correct, but because for us it makes life better, more interesting."[104]

Still other inhabitants have become disillusioned and have moved out, complaining about building problems, and the lack of suitable shops and amenities. For some residents, the utopian vision of a perfect community has definitely faded: "Celebration has indeed become a community: a messy, ever-changing and inevitably political town where some residents complain that the Disney company has failed to keep its promises and runs its settlement like a benign dictatorship."[105]

The community's school been especially problematic for some residents. The facility is described in promotional material as "a school of tomorrow" and "a model for education into the next century." Since Florida schools are notoriously impoverished, the promise of a "state-of-the-art school" in central Florida has been one of the town's strongest selling points. The Celebration school abounds with the latest information technologies and has been claimed as "the most wired campus on the planet."[106] However, some parents have had strong reactions to the progressive curriculum, multi-age classrooms, narrative assessments rather than grades, and few exams.

When a group of Celebration parents began organizing for school reform, they found little interest from Disney representatives, who (residents claimed) were not interested in the school, but only in selling real estate. Focus groups were held, rather than public meetings, and many residents began to defect. In 1997, it was reported that 16 percent of the children in the school withdrew, many enrolling in private schools in Orlando.

Leaving Celebration also became an eye-opener for disenchanted residents. According to the buyers' contract, a home owner is not allowed to make a profit if he or she has not lived in the house for more than a year, unless hardship is proved. At one point, the company offered to disregard the provision if departing home owners would not reveal why they were leaving the community. The defections and dissension may have accentuated the difference between consumers and citizens, as well as Disney's ability to manage reality. In other words, Disney may be able to create fantasy, but it is far more complex to create community. It is not clear whether the company has understood any of these problems, as the community continues with the same rules and regulations.

The future?

Disney executives say they have abandoned plans to adopt the Celebration model elsewhere in the USA. But even though there may be no future Celebrations, there will be more Disney-themed environments. Disney has made a major impact in Manhattan, with the transformation of a two-block area of Times Square into a Disney-themed location. Furthermore, DisneyQuests and ESPNZones are popping up around the country, joining the trend towards more and more location-based entertainment.[107]

In the next chapter, we move from Disney worlds to the people who make the Disney phenomenon possible – the fans, consumers, and audiences who inhabit the Disney universe.

Disney and the World

An adult cannot become a child again, or he becomes childish. But does the naiveté of the child not give him pleasure, and does he himself not endeavor to reproduce the child's veracity on a higher level?

Karl Marx[1]

Truly all ages – from children to the elderly, all nationalities, all races and all types of social systems are intoxicated by him with the same delight, surrender with the same fervor to his charm, with the same ecstasy allow themselves to be carried away by Disney's living drawings.

Sergei Eisenstein[2]

It has been claimed that "Disney is a primary force in the expression and formation of American mass consciousness" and that Disney characters "have a universal appeal."[3] While these and other assumptions may be broadly accepted, it is certain that there are far more complex responses to Disney's products and messages. A closer look raises some tough questions: What is the audience for Disney products? What do people actually think about the Disney universe? What do these products mean to consumers? And why are Disney products and characters still popular after all these years?

This chapter will consider some of these questions, first, by attempting to define the Disney audience and then by discussing the ways in which Disney audiences have been studied. The final section will present a range of Disney audience archetypes, as well as discussing various types of resistance to the Disney universe.

Defining Disney audiences

Just as it is difficult to generalize about the reach of the Disney empire, so it is difficult to assess the "audiences" for, and thus the "effects" of, Disney messages/products. In considering the notion of a "Disney audience," we must ask what we mean by "Disney," as well as what we mean by "audiences."

The Disney brand   As noted in the first few chapters, the Disney universe covers an extremely wide range of media/entertainment activities, from traditional television and film viewing, to theme park visits and sports event attendance. While audience reactions to specific examples of Disney products (especially Classic Disney films and theme parks) have been studied, it is also necessary to look at *Disney as a brand* and what meanings people associate with it.

Indeed, "Disney" represents an example of the kinds of brands that are being formed around media and entertainment products – that is, multi-dimensional products that cut across media and other forms of entertainment. Recall the quote from *The Economist*, cited in chapter 4? "The brand is a lump of content . . . which can be exploited through film, broadcast and cable television publishing, theme parks, music, the Internet and merchandising."[4] Kodak, Nike, and Coca-Cola may have explicit (or even covert) meanings attached to their products and/or their brand which are promoted through their advertising and public relations efforts. However, it might be argued that brands based on media products, such as Disney, present far more overt and often more complex values and forms of signification than these non-media-related brands.

It is also generally agreed that Disney is the most immediately recognized of any of the media brands. So, while audience reactions to specific Disney products or characters are certainly worth examining, it is also important to understand what audiences think about Disney, the brand.

Audiences or consumers?   The concept of "audience" has been chal-lenged recently by Vincent Mosco and Lewis Kaye, who point out that the notion is directly related to marketing research and should be used more carefully by critical researchers.[5] The relevance of their argument notwithstanding, how do we go about defining the people who experience and consume Disney products and services? While the term "audience" will be used in this discussion, it is probably more appropriate to refer to "consumers." It is almost always the case that individuals experience Disney via the consumption process, whether they are being bought and sold as audiences for advertising, or purchasing Disney products/services.

"Children of all ages."   So who is included in the "Disney audience"? While exposure to Disney products is typically strong during childhood, some of the same products are still enjoyed by adults, while other products are specifically designed for adults. Despite the oft-cited emphasis on children, Disney's products cut across age groups in assorted ways and thus may have multiple meanings. It is generally recognized that the theme parks, in particular, were designed not only for children but, to a great extent, for adults, as discussed in chapter 6. In fact, the ratio of adults to children who visit the parks is estimated at 4:1.[6]

As discussed in chapter 5, when we refer to "Disney," the association is ordinarily with those clearly labeled Disney products aimed at the "family" market and, more specifically, those products representing Classic Disney. Nevertheless, the point is that targeting families means attempting to appeal to *different* age groups, not just children. In addition, we need to remember that the company's diversified products reach, and thus potentially influence, a much wider audience or number of consumers than the "family" audience.

In other words, Disney's diversified activities are aimed at a variety of consumers, not just parents and children. This is especially the case for the theme parks and resorts, where a range of attractions are featured. For instance, the company has been especially active in hosting sporting events, such as marathons, auto races, and an assortment of sports tournaments (golf, football, volleyball, as well as in-line skating and skate-boarding). The industry publication, *Brandweek*, explains: "Disney has started hosting events to try to appeal to everyone from empty nesters and senior citizens to honeymooners and post-college singles."[7]

Another example is Disney's Winnie the Pooh franchise, which the company acquired in the 1960s.[8] Disney's products featuring Winnie the Pooh characters are pitched to a wide range of consumers. A Disney spokesman explains:

Disney now has three distinct Pooh lines, each targeted at a different market. Each line is aimed at a distinct demographic and market, but even within a product line there's segmentation. Individuals and even groups tend to make a connection to particular characters. Eeyore, for example, is most popular with teens, possibly because he is a little different from the others. But teens seem to be attracted to characters that are a little different.

With over 100 companies producing Pooh products, plus the promotion of Pooh across the company's other business sectors, the Pooh characters have recently started to outsell even Mickey, Minnie, and friends. As an industry trade journal reported: "Disney has done a magnificent job overall with Pooh, licensing and marketing products that appeal to a lot of different audiences and demographics."[9]

In summary, then, to understand "Disney audiences," it is necessary to consider the highly promoted image of Disney as a brand, the widespread availability and unique exposure to Disney products at different periods of peoples' lives, especially, but not only, during childhood, as well as other audience differences, including class, gender, race, and nationality. In light of these considerations, it may not be surprising that there is not much in the way of audience research that analyzes the Disney phenomenon in its entirety. The next sections will discuss examples of the different approaches taken to studying audiences in general, and the few attempts that have been made to study Disney audiences in particular.

Studying Disney audiences

Disney's market research

The Disney company itself has been very interested in the consumers of its products and has employed various ways to study them over the years. Several observers have noted that Walt Disney was sensitive to the reactions of audiences and was "willing to change a film based on audience response," whereas other studios were less willing to make such changes.[10] Ohmer has documented the history of Disney's audience research, from the informal studio previews in the 1930s, through the use of George Gallup's Audience Research Institute (ARI) beginning in the early 1940s.[11] In reviewing the ARI files at the Disney studio archives, Ohmer found that ARI research was used in every studio project from 1946 to 1957. The purpose of the research (as stated in the company's annual reports) was to hold down production costs, to allocate resources efficiently, and to maximize income. The research included studio screenings and questionnaires given to the company's own employees, who were thought to mirror the average American film viewer. The questionnaires led to the development of an "enjoyment rating" that was used in various ways during the production process. Ohmer concludes that the efforts by Disney and ARI "not only expose the work behind his seemingly 'instinctive' understanding of audiences, but can also make us more conscious of current efforts to manage viewer response."[12]

To be sure, the current Disney company now uses far more sophisticated marketing techniques, similar to other film and media companies.[13] Like other media companies, Disney decision-makers rely on data from their own research, in addition to commercial measurement companies, which provide broadcasting and cable ratings, purchasing surveys, etc.[14] Before the company releases a product, introduces new media or entertainment outlets, or adds to its existing businesses, marketing research attempts to predict consumer responses.

While Disney representatives have been notoriously tight-lipped about such marketing research, a few clues can sometimes be gleaned from press coverage of the company's business strategies. For instance, Disney hired Statistical Research, Inc. to conduct audience research in test markets and found that 60 percent of children between ages five and nine have radios in their rooms and often decide which station the radio in the family car is tuned to. In focus groups, children reported that they wanted "a station that was totally their own." Enter Radio Disney in October 1997. Because other ratings services do not measure children's radio programming, Statistical Research, Inc. now gathers radio audience shares for Disney's 36 radio stations, which reach an average of 1 million kids each week.[15]

Disney's Imagineering group is also especially active in research and development of new projects across the company's businesses, but especially at the theme parks and resorts. Their activities have been chronicled in numerous ways, by the Disney company itself as well as by Disney admirers.[16]

Besides continuous efforts to predict market behavior, Disney also participates in other kinds of audience research. For instance, the company commissioned a study released in 1998 claiming that the use of VCRs actually made children more, rather than less, sociable. Based on a poll of 300 parents in Britain, an Oxford clinical psychologist reported that children played games and drew pictures of scenes and characters after watching a film.[17] Of course, the findings were widely publicized in the press to assure parents that media consumption is safe for their children.

It is no mystery as to why the Disney company studies audiences in these ways. But what about other kinds of audience research? The next section considers the study of audiences outside of media corporations, especially in academic research.

Academic audience research

The study of media audiences has been the focus of an enormous amount of academic research over the years. In a recent collection dedicated to exemplifying audience research approaches, Dickinson and colleagues argue that

> All research which takes media processes as central to its analysis stems from an interest or concern with the consequences of the media for society, communities, publics, readers, listeners, viewers, consumers – audiences. The difference between approaches is, essentially, to do with the scale of analysis or the length of focus – micro or macro – chosen by the researchers in question.[18]

From early efforts to study the direct effects of propaganda to more recent attempts to identify the uses and gratifications that media serve for individual audience members, the study of audiences has been a major stronghold of mainstream communications research, especially in the USA, but also in other countries.[19] The dominant paradigm has shifted from assuming direct effects of media messages on individual audience members to more limited effects with intervening variables influencing audience responses. Such research has typically employed quantitative methods, such as surveys, questionnaires, experiments, and closed interviews.

More recently, the analysis of audiences has become the major focus of reception analysis, as well as a central theme in cultural studies, with more qualitative research methods employed (participant observation, ethnography, etc.). Such analysis has been influenced especially by Stuart Hall's encoding/decoding model, which argues that there are preferred textual messages encoded by producers, but that resistant and even emancipatory readings can be decoded by audiences.[20] These notions are pushed even further in John Fiske's discussion of active audiences constructing their own liberating meanings from polysemic, open texts.[21]

While Fiske's extreme active audience model has been challenged by critical researchers, as well as recanted to some degree by Fiske himself, there are still variations on the active audience in the audience research literature. In late 1998, Barker and Brooks identified the following four trends in the current state of audience research, which are useful in considering the research that has been done on Disney audiences:

- residual but not strong textual determinism, particularly from those still adhering to strong psychoanalytic approaches;
- an effortless freeing of audiences into multiple "readings" [*à la* Fiske];
- compromise: stress on dominance of contextual factors over "reading" processes, but range of responses is limited and still a "preferred reading";
- compromise: use of the concept of "interpretive communities" as a way of preserving a role for the text while preserving the social nature of responses.[22]

Versions of the first two approaches have been used in research on Disney focusing primarily on texts. For instance, some of the examples of textual analysis presented in chapters 5 and 6 assume specific "readings" of Disney texts by audiences. However, most often these studies do not include research to find out what audiences actually think about these texts. In a review of recent Disney studies which include these textual interpretations, Buckingham notes: "The underlying question here, of course, is the extent to which any of the covert ideological messages allegedly revealed by this kind of analysis – be they 'positive' or 'negative' – actually connect with what might be going on for the children who represent their primary audience."[23]

Actually, there is no dearth of research on children and media, which has been a major area of audience research over the years. In particular, there is a considerable body of research that has been directed at children and television, even though some of that work may be flawed in various ways.[24] But, despite the numerous studies of children and media, there has been little attention to Disney as a major and ongoing force in children's media.

While Buckingham bemoans the lack of attention to Disney's "primary audience," it might also be argued that the *entire* Disney audience has been neglected. There have been relatively few attempts to study the broad range of responses to the Disney universe by children and adults, connecting the texts presented by Disney to the audiences who experience them. The next sections will summarize some of the research that has been done.

Previous research on Disney audiences

Most of the past academic audience research that has been done on Disney has focused on distinct groups or specific media products/texts. The next section will present brief summaries of these studies, together with examples of recent research.

One of the best-known studies of Disney audiences was included in Michael Real's *Mass-Mediated Culture* in 1973.[25] Real administered questionnaires to 200 individuals (primarily students) from southern California who generally had high exposure to Disneyland, as well as a wide range of other Disney products. In addition to their exposure, respondents were asked about the values represented by Disney ("vices and virtues"), as well as its perceived influence. While there was some ambivalence in assessing influence, the identification of values represented by Disney was clear and unequivocal. Respondents mentioned many of the values previously discussed as part of the Classic Disney model, such as happiness, friendliness, honesty, innocence, industriousness, cleanliness, etc. On the other hand, most respondents agreed that Disney did not approve of sex, violence, greed, laziness, un-American activities, or leftist politics.

The Disney universe was considered by Real as an example of mass-mediated culture, in which meaning is structured as a semiological system, "fixing reality both by receiving and transmitting dominant patterns of perception, structures of feeling, cognitive maps and cultural norms." His study confirmed two major hypotheses: "that Disney attracts participants into mass-mediated utopian typifications and that Disney instructs through morality plays that structure personal values and ideology."[26] Above all, Real's research confirmed that the Disney universe is not value-free, as well as contributing to the argument that entertainment media, such as Disney, have definite effects on individuals and the social system.

Meanwhile, in her study of heroines in 1975, Kay Stone interviewed 40 women of different ages in three cities.[27] She found that many of the women admitted that they were influenced by fairy tales, but mostly through the Grimms' translations and Disney films. However, at least some of the women were not very impressed with the passive heroines of Disney and the Grimms and would have appreciated more active heroines, or at least more diversity, in these stories.

In another study, Jill May asked students at Purdue University about their favorite "family" film experience and found that students preferred Disney films four to one, and animated films three to one.[28] May also reported that Disney was favored by both young men and young women, who admitted that they wanted to expose their children to Disney's versions of classic stories and mostly enjoyed watching a Disney film more than reading the story in book form.

Replicating Real   More recently, there have been further attempts to look more closely at Disney audiences by focusing on young adults. In one effort at the University of Oregon, a questionnaire was given to students enrolled in a Journalism and Communication course in 1994.[29] More than 82 percent of the 45 respondents were white, 25 female and 20 male, and the median age was 21. Many of the questions were based on Real's survey, including those pertaining to respondents' past and future experiences with Disney products and their impressions of Disney's influence. A mixture of prompted and unprompted questions was used.

Participants were asked to identify their exposure to Disney products and then, later in the survey, asked whether they had been exposed to specific products. Comparing these prompted and unprompted answers revealed that the respondents seriously underestimated their exposure to the Disney universe – even the theme parks, which one would expect to be particularly memorable. Many were reluctant to admit that Disney currently had any effect on them.

The findings were most likely related to the specific audience surveyed – university students, with a median age of 21. Within this age range, Disney is often assumed to be childish, as indicated by one respondent: "I've grown up and Disney is no longer appropriate." Although these young adults generally disavowed any influence that Disney may have had on them, they were unanimous in their assessment that any influence was positive. Similarly contradictory attitudes were revealed in many respondents' interpretations of the general effects of Disney. Indeed, both positive and negative interpretations could be found even in the responses of the same person.

Overall, the strongest results related to exposure to Disney products. While respondents claimed that current interactions were low, their responses indicated both that they still had significant exposure and planned on continuing exposure, both for themselves and for future generations (their own children, nieces, nephews, etc.).

Global Disney/international audiences   Meanwhile, the Global Disney Audiences Project used a similar questionnaire, in part to analyze the reception of Disney products internationally.[30] The project involved researchers in 18 countries participating in a three-pronged research design:

(1) subject questionnaires and interviews; (2) individual country market analysis; (3) cross-cultural analysis.

The audience research portion of this study utilized two main research instruments: standardized questionnaires and in-depth interviews. The questionnaires were designed to ascertain respondents' level of contact with Disney and attitudes toward Disney at various age levels (pre-teen, teen, and adult), the types and number of Disney products with which each respondent had come into contact, the values that respondents attached to Disney, and the perspective from which Disney makes its offerings (American? Western? Global?). Volunteers from among those responding to the questionnaires were recruited to participate in in-depth interviews that explored the topics touched upon in the questionnaire.

The research was designed to examine the proliferation of Disney globally and to identify patterns of expansion. While the study did not claim statistical representativeness, it was still possible to glean interesting insights across cultures as the same sample frame was used in each country. The study hypothesized that while Disney may individualize certain product offerings to specific countries, the values represented by the company would be remarkably consistent across cultures, and that consumers would view Disney as essentially benign, but would tend to underestimate their own level of exposure to Disney. Thus, parents tend to view Disney as appropriate for their children without fully realizing the effects the company may have had on their own development. Interestingly, the results of the study tended to affirm these hypotheses.

The widespread exposure to Disney products was evident in the survey and interviews. The average respondent reported first being exposed to Disney when under five years of age. Less than 1 percent of respondents reported having no contact with Disney. Conversely, over 99 percent of respondents had seen a Disney film.

Furthermore, certain core values represented by Disney have been consistently received and understood across cultures. For example, when asked if Disney promotes or discourages such values or themes as family, imagination, good over evil, happiness, magic, and fun, more than 85 percent of respondents agreed that Disney promotes each of these values. Thus, despite cultural and language differences and certain individualized product offerings, Disney has been amazingly successful in consistently communicating specific values.

In-depth interviews indicated a growing awareness of Disney as a corporate entity. That is, respondents recognized that Disney is a business, and that, as a business, its first priority is to earn profits. While expressing some distaste for Disney the corporation – such terms as greed, cultural imperialism, manipulation, monopoly, etc. were often used – respondents seem to be able to compartmentalize their approach to Disney as business versus Disney as entertainment. While certain aspects of Disney as business were reported to be objectionable, Disney as entertainment was still considered to be wholesome, safe, and, most of all, fun.

Other contradictory or conflicting attitudes about Disney emerged in the research, especially during the interviews. Disney was often viewed as typically American, which carried both positive and negative connotations. On the other hand, some interviewees interpreted Disney messages or characters as representing their own culture. For instance, one of the Danish participants suggested that "Donald is so Danish." Others echoed the view that Disney is universal. The following Greek respondent unquestionably confirmed this belief: "Disney is universal. It belongs to (and promotes) the little souls of the children of the world. It cannot be put in borders. . . . It promotes the imagination and the sensitivity of children and all the people who stay children until they are 100 years old."

The results of the Global Disney Audience Project need to be qualified as a preliminary look at the international reception of Disney products, but the findings suggest the pervasiveness of the Disney brand, as well as the variations and complexity involved in interpreting its meaning for different audience members.

Disney confessions   Another study involved an assignment given to students at the beginning of a course on Disney at the University of Oregon in Eugene, Oregon. Before reading any of the course material or listening to any lectures, students were asked to write brief personal histories about their interest, experiences, and/or impressions of Disney and/or Disney products.

Again, these students represent a specific type of Disney audience. Many were avid Disney fans; all of them had at least passing interest in Disney, as the course was not required. But the comments provide insights into the reception of Disney products, many of the accounts echoing and further elaborating some of the themes discussed in previous chapters.[31]

Most identify strong memories of Disney as children, recalling their first encounters with Disney products, their favorite characters, and their first trip to one of the theme parks. Other common themes included praise for "the genius" behind it all, Walt Disney, as well as awe for the company's success (although a good number of students also called attention to the recent expansion by the Disney company and its negative corporate reputation). Many of the students also made clear that though they may not be into Disney at the moment, they look forward to introducing their future families to Disney experiences.

The students often recalled Disney memories and experiences very closely connected with their families.

> My exposure to "Disney" began when I was a small child. Disney has always been a source of entertainment and fun to both myself and my family. I see Disney as a world of fantasy that both children and adults can enjoy. The adventure and excitement of Disney movies allows the viewer to escape into a world of imagination and fulfillment.

> My sister and I loved Disney. We even named the family station wagon Chitty Chitty Bang Bang. When Chitty Chitty Bang Bang was the movie of the week, my sister and I made my dad set up a TV in the garage so the car could watch the movie.

Disney's universal appeal was echoed in other accounts which emphasized that Disney products and parks are cherished by literally everyone.

> Disney. When I hear this word I think of fun. I think of everything that Disney is a part of, and to me that means something that makes people happy. I don't think I have ever heard anyone say they hate Disneyland. How could you? It is a fun and happy place which generates a good feeling inside of a person. This feeling is what everything Disney is involved with is supposed to and does generate.

Very often, respondents' memories of Disney experiences as children were quite vivid and strong. The following accounts represent recollections from childhood, as well as echoing some Classic Disney themes.

> As a shy, only child growing up in a big city, watching Disney films gave me the power and imagination to believe. By watching Disney's animated feature-length movies, Disney instilled in me a belief that I could do anything I wanted. I never thought of Disney as anything more than that "magic" that happened when I watched a movie. I didn't think about the products, or have very much desire to go to the theme parks, because what I wanted were the fantasies. And I believed with all my heart that I could have them. The bright lively characters on the screen told me that I could be as happy as them if I could only dream as they do. And through catchy sing-along songs, the characters made sure I knew to believe in myself in order to make my dreams come true. Therefore, believing in myself, I wished on a star

every night, knowing that if I wished hard enough my wishes would someday come true. Undoubtedly, Disney had cast its spell on me.

A dream is a wish your heart makes is a phrase that will forever remain in my heart. As a young child and into adulthood, the imagination that Disney has encouraged me (and others) to obtain is enlightening. Disney is the very essence of imagination and dreams. Though it may not be reality, it is an escape into fairytale and illusion that one can engage in without the ridicule of others for being childlike. Disney represents the "family." It has created a place for families to spend time with each other, and share laughter. Adults and children combined can feel comfortable in Disney's world. There are not races, or classes within the Disney kingdom. Everyone can feel the comfort of a dream!

Again, while these memories are from a specific age group, it is still possible to glean insights into the appeal of Disney for many consumers. The association with childhood and family, as well as the attraction of escaping to fun-filled, fantasy worlds, are compelling themes that still appeal to these young adults and are not simply promotional slogans asserted by the Disney company. However, we need to look more carefully at a wider range of reactions to the Disney universe. The next section will discuss different audience types and propose a scheme to categorize Disney audiences.

Disney audience archetypes

Based on these previous studies, as well as on unsystematic research for several years, it is possible to categorize most people's positions vis-à-vis the Disney universe and suggest a range of audience archetypes. Marketing researchers have developed consumer categories; however, they are generally not all that helpful in understanding the entire Disney audience.[32]

The following archetypes/categories apply mostly to Americans, although there may be similarities in other countries. Because virtually every American has experienced or heard of Disney in some way, at some time, an attempt has been made to categorize or represent the entire population, not just those who represent consumers or fans. (In this sense, the notion of "Disney audience" is deceptive here, as some of these categories are *not* part of the Disney audience.) Also, the designations may not apply as neatly with children, as most seem to be highly enthusiastic about Disney. As indicated from the research discussed previously, it seems

Box 7.1 Disney Audience Archetypes

fanatic fan Consumer cynic uninterested resister antagonist
  • enthusiastic
  • admiring
  • reluctant

that people's relationship with Disney typically changes during their life-time. For instance, as we have seen, many children are extremely positive about Disney, but sometimes lose interest as they mature. It might be noted that there are often crossovers or merging of types, as well as variations in intensity within categories. And without more extensive research, it is difficult, if not impossible, to estimate the number or type of people in each category.[33] However, it is still important to at least describe these various categories, if only to establish a system of differentiation of responses to Disney. (See box 7.1.)

Disney fanatics

First, we can identify fanatical and zealous Disney fans, who strongly, sometimes obsessively, adore anything Disney and arrange their lives accordingly. They have been profoundly affected by the Disney universe and proclaim their allegiance to The Mouse in numerous ways, from body adornments and life-style choices to club membership and on-line activities.

The illustrated fan   One of the most extreme Disney fanatics is 44-year-old postal worker, George Reiger, who had more than 1,000 tattoos of Disney characters on his body in August 2000. He claims that he is the no. 1 Disney fan, and it is possible that many would agree with his claim. In addition to his tattooed torso, Reiger's self-proclaimed credentials are included in a biography that he has distributed to the media:

• He has made 284 visits to the Disney theme parks.
• He claims to be the only person known to have kissed the ground of each Disney property.
• His will states that his ashes are to be spread in the Seven Seas Lagoon and the Pirates of the Caribbean ride at Disney World.
• His home is a "Disney shrine" with over 13,000 (another account claims 15,000) Disney collectible items displayed.

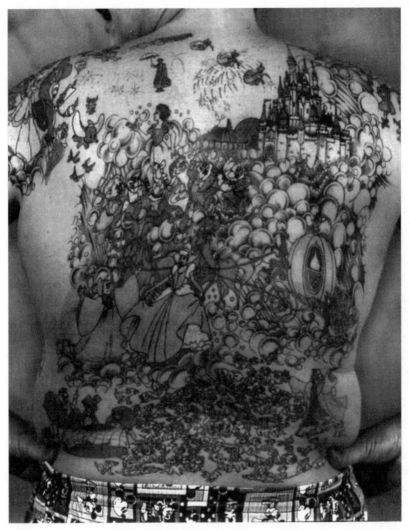

Plate 6 Disney's Number 1 Fan. George C. Reiger sports more than 1,000 Disney tattoos and spends most of his expendable income on theme park visits and Disney memorabilia.
Photo courtesy of George C. Reiger.

- After basic living expenses, every cent he earns is spent on Disney, which, by 1993, totalled over $500,000.[34]

Reiger explains: "This is my religion. This is my life. . . . Every cent I have goes to Disney." His tattoos include all 101 Dalmatians (in fact, 103), as well as 10 tattoos that he doesn't show anyone (although one might assume that his former five wives and his current sixth wife may be familiar with the hidden images).

Another fanatic, tattoo artist, Jim Jones, barely competes with Reiger, with a mere 57 Disney images adorning his body. Jones declares: "I'm a Disney freak. This is my personal tribute to Walt. This is my way of being a fan. I want to take this to the grave."[35]

While one might think that the Disney company would appreciate such zealous fans, neither Reiger nor Jones has impressed the company, which attempted to enforce its copyright and prevent Jones from adding additional images to his body. The company is careful not to comment on Reiger, but apparently security guards regularly follow him during his frequent visits to the parks.

Disney as life-style   While other Disney fanatics are typically unwilling to make of their own bodies Disney shrines, Reiger's other activities are characteristic of Disneyphiles or self-proclaimed "Disney freaks," who visit the parks often, own huge collections of Disney memorabilia, and decorate their homes in Disney themes. For instance, Todd Parker of Tustin, California, has visited Disneyland over 1,000 times and owns more than 1,000 Fantasia items; meanwhile, in Paris, Didier Ghez owns more than 3,000 Disney comics and books.

The Disney company has its own designation for Disney fanatics and features an "Ultimate Disney Fan" on its website each month. For instance, the Ultimate Disney Fan for July 1999 was Carol Thompson, who lives in her "Disneyfied home" in Tumwater, Washington, with two dogs that are often dressed in Mickey ears and Mickey T-shirts with their names on them.[36]

Disney fanatics are big consumers of Disney products and services and organize their important life events, such as birthdays and weddings, around Disney. These extreme fans have been known to design their weddings around Disney themes, including music and wedding vows based on Disney films. With the Classic Disney emphasis on romance, it is not surprising that devotees (as well as less intense fans) often arrange honeymoons at one of the Disney theme parks. Disney World is said to be the number one honeymoon destination in the USA.

However, since 1991 it has been possible to actually arrange wedding ceremonies at Disney World. Every year about 2,300 couples pay to have their marriage vows conferred in "Disney's Wedding Pavilion, surrounded by sparkling water and an unforgettable view of Cinderella Castle." While every couple planning a wedding at Disney World may not be considered Disney fanatics, those who are would certainly make every attempt to tie the knot in the Magic Kingdom. As of 1998, 10,000 weddings had been "hosted" at Walt Disney World.[37]

There are a range of options and settings for the blessed events from an "intimate wedding" (starting at $2,500) to a customized affair (beginning at $12,500) complete with Cinderella's horse-drawn carriage, trumpeters, and hundreds of guests.[38] The average expenditure is $19,000; however, the cost can be as high as $250,000. It is also possible to arrange weddings at the Disney–MGM Studios or at EPCOT. And, of course, there are special honeymoon packages available, featuring "the enchantment of the Walt Disney World Resort with the romance of a sea voyage" on the Disney Cruise Line.

Disneyana   The buying and selling of Disney merchandise has developed as a major activity of many collectors around the world and is a typical preoccupation of Disney fanatics. In a volume published by Disney's Hyperion Press, the author explains, "The use of the term *Disneyana*, a play on *Americana*, as a catch-word has come to be equated with the zealous collecting of the wide variety of Walt Disney character merchandise manufactured from the 1930s right up to the present era of new 'instant' Disney collectibles."[39] Some have traced the "Mickey fashion trend" to the 1960s and the "youth revolution," when Mickey watches accounted for over $7 million in sales in 1970 alone. In 1975, Disneyana became a "standout antiques investment," exemplified by the sale of a German Mickey Mouse windup for $3,105, a record price for a Mickey toy at that time. The same toy sold for $18,700 in 1993.[40]

Several thousand collectors gather yearly at the Offical Disneyana Convention, which features seminars, speeches, and auctions. Very often, the convention is held at one of the theme parks, which enables "ConventionEars" to buy more merchandise during visits to the parks.

Collectors may not necessarily be avid Disney fanatics, but may become involved in Disneyana for investment purposes. However, most collectors are at least Disney fans, and many qualify as true fanatics.

Fan clubs   There are numerous examples of Disney fan clubs, both those organized by the company and those set up by fans themselves. The Disney Company organized Mickey Mouse Clubs as early as 1930, with club meetings arranged around Saturday matinees at local movie theaters. As deCordova reports, the growth of the clubs was substantial, with estimates of over one million members by 1932.[41] Currently, the company organizes Mickey Mouse Clubs in many countries.

But there are also clubs organized by Disney fans themselves, most often including people who classify themselves not merely as fans, but as Disney "freaks" or "addicts." One example is The National Fantasy Fan Club (NFFC): The Club for Disneyana Enthusiasts, organized in 1984 "by a small group of Disneyana enthusiasts who wanted to share their love of Disney with others." By mid-1999, the organization had expanded into an international organization with over 7,500 members, with its main goal "to help spread the magic of Disney." The club features local chapters, as well as a website which publishes a monthly newsletter, called the FantasyLine Express. Many of the largest NFFC chapters are close to the Disney theme parks; however, groups in other parts of the world are active, as well. For instance, the Castle Keepers Chapter includes members primarily around Philadelphia, who are "fascinated by anything and everything that is Disney: theme parks, live and animated films, television productions, collectibles and much more." The club meets regularly to share stories and display Disneyana items.

There also are several associations, mostly outside the USA, where the Duck comics are immensely popular, organized around the Disney Ducks or Carl Barks, with members calling themselves "Donaldists."[42] For instance, in Germany, there is the Deutsche Organisation Nicht-kommerzieller Anhänger des Lauteren Donaldismus (D.O.N.A.L.D.), and in Sweden, the National Donaldist Society of Sweden (also called "quack").

Fan magazines   Similar to popular media programs such as *Star Trek*, there are Disney fan magazines produced by committed Disney fanatics. In the USA, fan magazines include *The Duckburg Times*, *The "E" Ticket*, *The Duck Hunter*, and *The Barks Collector*. However, many others are published outside the USA by some of the "Donaldists": *Carl Barks & Co.* (in Denmark); *NAFS(K)uriren* (in Sweden); *Donaldisten*, *Duckmite*, and *Carl Barks and the Old Master's Secret* (in Norway); and *Der Donaldist* (in Germany).

On-line activities   There is an abundance of activity relating to Disney that takes place on-line that is not produced by the Disney company, but provides fascinating insights into Disney fanaticism. A variety of chat sites or newsgroups offer fans and fanatics the chance to share information about Disney history, theme parks, and merchandise. Indeed, many of the on-line sites feature a profusion of messages about Disney items for sale. (See box 7.2.)

One chat group in particular clearly illustrates the Disney fanatic. The newsgroup alt.disney.disneyland was created in 1995 and discusses only Disneyland – "from the paint in ToonTown and Hidden Mickeys, to the current park management and Disneyland's role in American society." The group attracted such adamant Disneyland fans that a website and other activities were added. As the site explains,

> ADD'er is the general term given to anyone who frequents alt.disney.disneyland. Because A.D.D. is such a friendly and sometimes very interesting newsgroup, many people have been ADDicted for some time now. Some ADD'ers have become so dedicated that they meet at Disneyland every week. Being an ADD'er can be seen as an affliction that is only cured with death . . . and sometimes not even then.

Many ADDicts are local to Disneyland and meet every Sunday afternoon at the park (wearing special buttons to recognize each other); however, regional groups also have been formed. A particularly interesting feature is the newsgroup's ongoing "message thread" called "You know you are ADDicted when . . ." There are literally hundreds of responses that have been offered by ADDicts; only a few will be given here, to provide even further insights into Disney fanatics:

You know you are ADDicted when . . .

you wear at least 5 lbs of Disneyland pins, buttons, and badges at any given time.

you spend your entire 6½ hour drive to Disneyland listening solely to Disney music.

your significant other makes you choose between having a relationship with them or going to Disneyland; your status changes to 'single'.

you see life as the time you spend between DL [Disneyland] trips.

you have more Disney Park Annual Passes than pictures of your family in your wallet.

Box 7.2   Disney Fans On-Line

Disney fan sites

- "Forgotten Disney: The Lost Legacy" – a website devoted to now-defunct Disney rides and shows
- Arielholics Anonymous – a site for "people who are obsessed with Ariel"
- Yesterland – former attractions, shops, and restaurants at Disneyland
- "Trash Cans of Disney" – an exhaustive inventory of facts about waste disposal and trash can architecture on Disney sites
- Hidden Mickeys of Disney
- FANtasEARS Disney Fan Club
- Disney on Display – a collection of free backgrounds and graphics for personal Disney web pages
- John's Twilight Zone Tower of Terror Site – "everything you ever wanted to know about the old Tower of Terror"
- Our Disney Holiday Photos
- Badger's Disney Countdown – "enter the date of your trip to Walt Disney World and watch it count down the days remaining until you arrive"
- FCDMuck – "online virtual community where Disney fans can play the roles of their favorite Disney characters and chat with other fans"
- I'm Mad about the Mouse

and Andy's, Crystal's, Doug & Lisa's, Frank's, Holly's, Kathy's, Kevin's, Laura's, Michelle's, Myra's, Palmer's, Phil & Patti's, Sue's . . . Disney Pages.

Disney link sites

- A World of Disney Web Ring
- The Best of the Best Disney Web Sites
- Net Disney – "Home of the Greatest Disney Website Election and the Disney Webmaster Alliance"
- The Ultimate Disney Link Page
- Christine's Disney Links

Box 7.3 Disney Newsgroups

alt.disney.disneyland	rec.arts.disney.misc	alt.disney.beauty+beast
rec.arts.disney.parks	alt.disney	alt.disney.tech
rec.arts.disney.parks	alt.disney.beanies	alt.disney.the-evil-empire
rec.arts.disney.announce	alt.disney.secrets	alt.fan.disney
rec.arts.disney.animation	alt.disney.vacation-club	alt.music.disney
rec.arts.disney.merchandise	alt.fan.disney.afternoon	alt.binaries.multimedia.disney
alt.disney.disneyworld	alt.disney.criticism	fj.rec.disney
alt.disney.collecting	alt.fan.disney.gargoyle	japan.disney

you're so used to touching trees and things at DL to see if they're real that you start doing it where ever else you go, too.

your youngest daughter hums "It's a Small World" while she nurses.

you scotch tape large black ears to your gerbil.

Walt Disney's opening day speech comes on when you turn on your computer.

when you decorate your Kitchen in Gourmet Mickey, dining room in Lion King/Disneyland, living room in all Disney Characters and movies, guest room in 101 Dalmatians, bathroom in Classic Mickey, and Master bedroom in Disneyland, WDW. (Yes, this is just how my house is decorated.)

Through hundreds of other home pages and websites, enthusiasts declare their Disney allegiance in various ways.[43] Many of the websites focus on the theme parks, with descriptions and photos from recent visits or information and trivia about the parks. Some of the most amusing examples include Hidden Mickeys, Trashcans of DisneyWorld, and The Happiest Poddies on Earth. (See box 7.3 for other examples.)

It might be assumed that most of the people who create Disney websites are quintessential cases of Disney fanatics (although there may be a disproportionately large number of young males, who tend to dominate Internet activity generally). Many sites include personal information, providing a glimpse into the lives of some Disney fanatics. Some examples:

The webmaster of Net Disney:

My name is Steve Marshall. I am 18 years old, and a junior in High School. Yeah, I know, you wouldn't imagine an 18-year-old running a Disney website, but what can I say? I love it. Other than maintaining this web site,

I am on my High School's track & field team (I run the short sprint races). I also enjoy playing the guitar (I am not good at it though), listening to Hard/Classic Rock (my favorite band is Led Zeppelin). After High School I would like to continue on with Web site design. . . . In January of 1999, I quit my job to devote my time to my Disney website.

Scott M. Leonard, creator of "The Disney Phenomenon" website:

My life is pretty much divided between my work, classes, Disneyland, and my girlfriend. (Any guess which one takes priority?) . . . When I'm not at class, or working, I'm probably at Disneyland. I've been a Deluxe Annual Passholder for several years now, so you've probably seen me around the Park and never known it. . . . I'm one of the guys with the digital camera taking photos of Tomorrowland's construction. I even have a small site (The WWW Disney Phenomenon) dedicated to the Happiest Place on Earth. . . . And then there's Julie, my girlfriend. . . . We met at Disneyland, and grew to love each other over several special dates . . . She's also very talented . . . a great writer. Some of her Hunchback of Notre Dame fanfictions can be found at her page, Opal's Tent.

And, finally, Kevin and Adrienne Krock, the ADDicts who created "The Happiest Poddies on Earth" website, which includes not only locations and details about all of the toilets at Disneyland, but ratings and trivia, as well:

Let's face it: when you visit Disneyland as often as we do, you start to notice these things. Thus the idea for the page was born. An opportunity to have fun with our Disney obsession as well as to contribute to the information available for other Disney enthusiasts . . .

From these various accounts, it seems clear that Disney fanatics exemplify Dallas Smythe's notion of audience labor – they are going far beyond the passive audience category and participate and even work at their media experiences.[44] It seems clear, as well, that these audiences have clearly accepted the intended or encoded messages in Disney's products.

Disney fans

Beyond the Disney fanatics or Disneyphiles, there are probably millions of unwavering Disney fans who wear T-shirts emblazoned with Disney characters, visit the parks often, and enthusiastically consume other Disney products.

From one respondent on a chat site called Yoo Hoo!:

Yoo Hoo! I love Walt Disney. I think it's the best company ever. I have been collecting Disney stuff for a while now. I love all Walt Disney movies. I get them as soon as they come out. My children and my husband, and I are big fans.

Another fan reports her involvement with Disney:

From the time I was born up until now, Disney has been a significant factor in my life. The first movie I ever saw in a theater was *Pinocchio*, and I have been hooked on Disney animation ever since. I have seen just about every Disney movie. No other set of characters has impressed me the way Disney's have. This runs in my family; my mother is a huge fan of Disneyland and has been there at least once a year since she was 16 years old. Subsequently, I have been there every year of my life. While I know Disney is far more than a park and magnificent animation, I still see it as magic. . . . I believe there is a Disney character to match almost every real person I have ever met. . . . I know in my family each member's favorite character reminds me of them. This may sound far fetched, but I really think of Disney as a metaphor for life.

Disney fans typically defend the Disney image as sacred and untouchable, expressing their love of specific characters and admiration of the Disney company's success. As one fan declares:

I am a bit of a Disney champion. Not everybody is, but I can respect that. I will almost always defend Disney. I refuse to wear incessantly skeptic blinders when examining corporations, be they entertainment conglomerates or clothing magnates. Disney is successful because they create solid family entertainment. And they do a damn fine job at it, thank you.

Disney consumers

There are many different types of consumers for Disney products, some more enthusiastic than others. Only three types will be identified here, although it is certain there are other kinds.

Enthusiastic consumers Literally millions of Americans accept Disney as a distinct and attractive brand, regularly attend films or buy Disney products, and have visited at least one of the theme parks, perhaps as a child. In fact, for many Americans, it is assumed that it is "normal" to grow up with Disney experiences, including at least a visit to one of the theme parks. If they haven't visited the parks, they add "tragically" or "unfortunately" to their explanations.

> I always felt like I was a deprived child because I have never been to Disneyland, Disney World or any other Disney magical dreamland. I still have visions of what it must be like. Today, it doesn't bother me – I'm almost proud of the fact. I guess just because it makes me a little unique.

Another consumer who has seen many of the films and visited two theme parks explains:

> While I know there are peers out there who are much greater fans of Disney than myself, there are those out there who care a whole lot less than myself. I think I would put myself right in the middle of the Disney influence scale, when it comes to your average kid growing up in the 70's and 80's America.

Disney consumers typically feel that Disney is a special brand and use descriptions that are frequently drawn directly from the company's own promotional rhetoric.

> I went to Disneyland for the first time when I was 17 years old with my family. I enjoyed my recent visit at the age of 23 much more than my first visit. I not only realized what Disney means to me, but I was amazed by the great appreciation and sense of awe I felt for Disney and the culture it embodies. Disney has become a symbol of wholesomeness, innocence, and fantasy that is virtually untainted by the trappings of the outside world. It seems to embody all that is good, after all, it is the happiest place on earth . . . the name Disney has become synonymous with the idea of family. Disney's products appeal to such a wide audience, and it is one of the few things left in our society that is suitable for the whole family to enjoy.

As noted in the above account, adults are often fond of Disney for nostalgic reasons, recalling memories from childhood, and especially family visits to the parks. It is also significant that Disney has deliberately incorporated these nostalgic elements into its products and their promotion, as mentioned in the discussion of the theme parks in chapter 6.

Among Disney patrons are parents who choose to expose their children to Disney products because they are perceived as "safer" and less problematic than other media fare. In other words, the Disney brand is predictable for parents.

> Taking the kids to WDW (and DL, for that matter) when they were little always seemed worth it for a couple of reasons. The main one was that you knew what you were going to get, and it was worth the money. I'd compare it to going to McDonald's – you know what to expect, and they deliver it. It's extremely unlikely that there are going to be any unpleasant surprises. It's going to be a safe place to take the kids. The other is that it meets the kids' expectations, given the amount of hype it gets from advertising, entertainment tie-ins, word of mouth, etc. Even when the kids were preschoolers, they knew "Disney." You get a sort of parental satisfaction that you're meeting the kids' expectations, even if you're hassling with crowds and lines and pressures to consume food and souvenirs.

Indeed, there is sometimes a certain pressure on parents to engage in Disney consumption, especially to arrange visits to the theme parks. As a more mature university student recalls:

> As a child, Disney was a word that represented excitement and ambiguity. Disney elicited two distinct perceptions in my mind growing up: the Disney that we could afford to experience and the Disney that we could not. . . . To visit Disneyland Park in Anaheim was always my wish when I blew out my birthday candles every year. . . . To this day my father still measures his worth as a decent parent by the fact that he could never afford to take his children to Disneyland. The cost of going to the movie theater increased the gap between our family and the Disney experience.

Admiring consumers   There are also those who become consumers because of their admiration of Disney products for aesthetic or creative reasons. For instance, many people are in awe of, or even express reverence for, the quality of Disney's animation, or the creativity and organization of the theme parks, and thus become consumers to admire these qualities. They may be less enthusiastic about the sentiments or values expressed in these Disney products, as the following account reveals:

> I've never cared much for Disney plots (well, maybe Pinocchio) – but I love the animation. I'm a fan of illustration and animation is a form of moving illustration. For me, Disney's animation has an amazing quality. It makes things look real without them looking real. It's professional because it replicates life without duplicating it. But I really don't care about the plots or messages.

Reluctant consumers   The prevalence and popularity of Disney products sometimes means that people who may not necessarily be interested in
consuming Disney products find themselves compelled to do so. This is
especially the case with parents, who may find that their only choices are
Disney products for their children. As one "reluctant parent" reports:

> The books, clothes, movies, videos, that surround us are largely Disneyfied.
> For example, the hand-me-down clothes we received from my sister for our
> two-year-old son have Disney monograms with Mickey Mouse as the most
> prominent. When people greet him on the days he is wearing the shorts
> with the Mickey Mouse monogram, they say "Oh, you are wearing Mickey
> Mouse." Our five-year-old son hears about the newest Disney movie at
> preschool and asks if I will take him. Our public library carries all the
> Disneyfied classics, which have become occasional visitors to our house.
> Although surrounded, we do offer our boys a "critical stance" as we invite
> them as they enter the age of reason to vibrate the Disney image against
> values of inclusion, compassion, and empathy.

Disney cynics

During the last decade, there has been a definite backlash to Disney's
intense expansion, as some consumers have come to view the Disney
Company as behaving in an overtly greedy and overly materialistic manner.
The Disney cynics are typically still involved as consumers of Disney
products, but are critical of the increases in theme park prices and the
intense marketing and merchandising efforts. While they still enjoy Disney
and its products, they describe Disney as having gone past the point of
good corporate behavior. As one of the Oregon students writes:

> Our frequent trips south to see my grandparents and other family members
> (in California) resulted in mandatory trips to Disneyland. I believe that if
> you did not go Mickey Mouse and Scrooge McDuck would meet you at
> the airport and beat you with Pluto's leash. As one can see, I do have much
> cynicism directed towards the Disney corporation. I find it amusing that the
> name Disney is associated with wholesomeness and true American values
> when the company employs sweatshop workers to make their products. . . .
> While what I call the business aspect of Disney makes me somehow leery of
> the company, I must admit that I am enchanted with Disney movies and
> products.

Many say that they didn't notice such intense commercial practices
when they were children or that the Disney company has become much

more commercialized since Team Disney took over. While many identify Michael Eisner as the culprit, most still remain in awe of Walt Disney and the Classic Disney era. As a few cynics explain:

> Walt Disney has always intrigued me. . . . I love that he was not a greedy man and the whole reason he created The Magical [sic] Kingdom was because he was a loving father who wanted to create the ultimate family oriented theme park for his kids. . . . One only has to look at the Disney enterprise now, which I feel is run by many money hungry people who are not just out for the families of the world, a lot of them are just out for themselves. Walt Disney had never run his company in this manner and I think he would turn over in his grave if he saw some of the decisions made these days.

> I have grown up and have become a fairly cynical person and this might be the reason behind my questioning of Disney's motives. I have always wanted to believe in Disney but they keep coming up with unusual movie choices, like *Pocahontas* and *The Lion King*. The unrealistic drawings and story line of *Pocahontas* does not socially enrich children but instead creates untrue stereotypes of the past. How can Disney be so nonchalant about a historical event as to manipulate it to their own desires? Why didn't they just come up with an original story instead of distorting a true one? They must realize the power they have over children. Why aren't they more careful with it? Disney was a place of magic, and for most 3- to 14-year-olds, it still is, but for me it has become just another huge conglomerate to be scared of and closely watched.

Uninterested

Is it possible that there are Americans who have been unaffected or untouched by Disney's empire? Indeed, there *are* those who are detached, disengaged, or dispassionate about the Disney phenomenon. They are often uninterested in or unable to distinguish products or characters as "Disney" and probably have never been to any of the theme parks.

It is far more difficult to find information about Disney nonpartisans than about Disney fanatics, who are most often quite public about their "addiction." Rather, the Disney uninterested would rather *not* talk about Disney and have very little to say when they do.[45] For instance, the following respondent was much more interested in talking about the non-Disney experiences in his life:

I am one of those rare citizens who lived 18 years in Southern California and never went to Disneyland. And I also must admit that I have never much of an inkling to go to the Magic Kingdom. I have done some considerable world traveling. I have seen the Eiffel Tower, the Houses of Parliament in London, I have walked the Stroget in Copenhagen and I have sailed under the Golden Gate Bridge. But I have never been to the Mouse House.

Not once did I go to Disneyland for a simple reason. I never had the inclination. Disneyland and its attendant movies and products have never appealed much to me because growing up in a sports family, other activities and values were much more compelling. Mickey Mantle and the New York Yankees was much more appealing than Mickey Mouse and the Disney characters, as were Darrell Royal and the Texas Longhorns and Roger Staubach and the Dallas Cowboys.

Some of the negative responses to Disney have strong ties to elitist cultural attitudes, as Disney is associated with popular and mass culture. This attitude is represented in a comment contrasting Mexican and American culture by a Mexican-American woman who has been a teacher in South Texas for over 20 years: "Mexican culture has a rich, historical legacy in the Aztec, Mayan and Toltec civilizations. What I'm saying is that Mexico has ancient pyramids – what does the US have? Disneyland."

It may also be important to distinguish between those who are aware and uninterested and those who are unaware that they are being exposed to Disney products. "I own a few shares in the Disney company, so I'm interested in the company doing well. But I'm really not very interested in any of the Disney products – although I didn't realize until recently that Disney owned ESPN or ABC, and I watch a lot of sports on television."

Disney resisters

This group includes those who prefer other products or brands, or have grown out of Disney and its "magic spell" and now basically reject Disney and its products. The sentiments expressed are fed by a strong degree of cynicism towards the Disney company, as well. Again, it is difficult to estimate the numbers here, as Disney rejecters are far less visible and vocal than Disney fanatics and fans.

Examples of those who simply prefer other brands:

In my mind, Bugs Bunny would win over Mickey Mouse any day. Disney cartoons lack several characteristics I admired in cartoons. For example, I found the shenanigans of Bugs Bunny and Elmer Fudd to be entertaining because of the violence. In Disney films, everything is fantasy. There is never the combination of violence and comedy as there are in Warner Bros. cartoons. Instead, the jokes and gags are "clean." Secondly, I never found Warner Bros. cartoons attempting to impose any kind of values or morals. Every Disney film and many of the cartoons end with some kind of lesson. Of course, this was Walt Disney's idea.

I have to confess that I'm a diehard Bugs Bunny fan. I much prefer the mischief, sarcasm and slapstick of the Warner Bros. characters over the sweetness and innocence of Disney's.

Then there are the former fans who have been recently disillusioned by the company's greed, such as this newlywed, who spent her honeymoon at Disneyland:

I can't say that I didn't have a good time there. . . . But I don't know that I can say I felt I was in "The Happiest Place on Earth." I'm sure my credit card company will be happy with the money I spent there, but I'm a bit disillusioned personally. . . . I am discontented mostly because of the fact that our tickets lied to us. On the tickets it says "Where everyone can be a kid again." Disneyland is not a place for children. It's a place for their parents to feed into the great big Disney profit machine.

Others may have experienced Disney during their childhood, but now reject most everything it stands for:

I think I am too jaded to be fully touched by the Disney phenomenon. I've gone to sleep too many times without being awakened and changed by a kiss, I've wished on too many stars without my dreams coming true. Next to the biting satire of *The Simpsons*, Disney cartoons seem like they are trying to pull a fast one on me and make me believe in something that doesn't exist. Not to say that I don't believe in magic. I do very much. I just doubt that magic can be created and sustained by a corporate entity that insists on depicting life in terms of cuteness and perfection.

In terms of what the word "Disney" now invokes, I tend to think of forced wholesomeness and sanitized imagination. In the world of Disney (and Disneyland), everything is clean, litter-free, and clearly marked. Good is represented by youth, purity, beauty, determination, seriousness, and conformity. Even *Beauty and the Beast*, which gives lip service to nonconformity by having Belle fall in love with the ugly but noble Beast, reinforces these values as the Beast reverts to a young, handsome prince at the end of the movie. And Disney protagonists are never funny – it is the foolish minor characters who provide the humor. For me, the childhood cloud of idealism that surrounded Disney is quite gone and I do not miss it.

Disney antagonists

The final category of audience reaction is one of antagonism and, interestingly, includes those at the extremes of the political spectrum. These are not the folks who simply dismiss, ignore, or reject Disney, but in some way actually work against the company and its products.

Dissin' Diz on the Left   The disenchantment with Disney from the left can be seen as part of a more general critique of media corporations and their promotion of consumerism. A recent example was the December 1998 issue of the *New Internationalist*, which focused on Disney and the spread of global culture.[46] While the editor confesses to be a "former Disney addict" in the issue's preface, the collection of articles proceed to tear the company and its products limb from limb, critiquing everything from Disney's animated heroines to the Disneyfication of urban environments and the corruption of global culture.

Disney antagonists also include groups that sometimes organize opposition to the Disney company, including those who actually work (or have worked) for the company (for example, NABET/CWA workers who worked without a contract with the ABC television network for many months). Their campaigns include distributing material that emphasizes some of the same issues as the leftist critics mentioned above. Likewise, there a number of exposés written by people who have worked at the theme parks, revealing elements of the parks' management that are not all that innocent.

Among Disney antagonists might also be included those groups that work to protect consumers' interests. Public interest groups, such as the Center for Media Education, Action for Children's Television, and the Media Education Foundation, are active in critiquing the corporate domination of children's media through lobbying, press releases, educational videos, and research reports. While Disney has not necessarily been a major focus of these groups, the company is sometimes included as one of their corporate targets.

Goodbye New York, Hello Goofy

Plate 7 Disney Go Home. James Victore created posters that were hung around Times Square in 1998 to protest the Walt Disney Company's invasion of Times Square and "the destruction of anything original and unique to New York, for a cheap, plastic knock off of 'Malltown USA'". Courtesy of James Victore.

Another interesting example is the short video produced by Australian John Safran at Disneyland, calling attention to specific negative elements that are avoided at the park, as well as asking some tough questions during face-to-face encounters with Disney workers.[47]

The Mouse that Whored   At the other end of the political spectrum is the religious right in the USA and the moral outrage that has fueled an organized boycott of the Disney company. In August 1996, the Assemblies of God began urging their 2.5 million members to boycott the Disney products and theme parks for "abandoning the commitment to strong moral values." The nation's fifteenth largest denomination urged Disney "to return to the values that strengthen and build this nation, such as honesty, respect, integrity, decency and trust."

On 18 June 1997, the Southern Baptist Convention meeting in Dallas, Texas, called for a nationwide boycott of Disney and its subsidiaries. The Southern Baptists were joined by other groups in condemning Disney's policy of extending benefits to domestic partners of its gay and lesbian employees, allowing gays to visit and hold events at the theme parks, and featuring a gay character on its network television series, *Ellen*.[48] As more groups joined the boycott (including the American Family Association and the Catholic League), other issues were added beyond those focusing on gays and homosexuality.

The "Official Disney Boycott Site" includes information about "Disney's true agenda including Michael Eisner's war on the American family and religion," and describes Disney as anti-religion, anti-family, anti-union, violent, racist, pro-abortion, as well as promoting paganism, witchcraft, a homosexual agenda, corporate greed, sex in children's films, sweatshops, and media control.[49] Another site, the Disney Boycott Web-Ring, links sites that support the boycott in order to show that "a diverse number of individuals . . . have taken steps to protect their families from indoctrination through the Entertainment propaganda machine."

While the boycott initially gained a good deal of media publicity, with features on shows such as *60 Minutes*, there have been different claims about its effectiveness. The company explains that the boycott has had little effect, although Eisner has been called upon to comment in several instances. Among Southern Baptists, only 30 percent polled in March 1998 said they participated in the boycott. Still, as of mid-1999, boycotters stated that their efforts would continue, and that one of their aims was to draw attention to specific issues.

The Disney boycott represents a form of extreme right-wing backlash that actually has some similarities to extreme leftist critiques. Both criticize the company for being overly greedy (corporate greed), issues relating to labor (sweatshops, child labor, and union bashing[50]) and promoting problematic morals. Both criticize media control, albeit typically for different reasons. Also, both often assume that the messages or ideology represented by corporate mass culture directly influences audiences.

Appropriating and subverting The Mouse

The repetitive messages and themes in Disney products seem so blatant and obvious that it is difficult to imagine that they could be interpreted in any way other than as intended. However, there are important examples of people taking the Disney style, images, or meanings and reworking them in new ways. Not only have artists used Disney imagery in their work, but other kinds of appropriation can be found – despite the Disney company's penchant for strict copyright enforcement. At times, deliberate subversion has been involved, as when images have been taken over and given new meanings that are antithetical to the Disney ideology and style.

Reworking/appropriating The Mouse   A sizable number of artists, from Andy Warhol and Keith Haring to Charles Schulz and R. Crumb, have featured Disney characters – especially Mickey Mouse – in their work. Of course, it's not surprising in that The Mouse has become a popular American icon and "one of the most recognized faces in modern history."[51]

Other less famous artists who regularly incorporate these images into their work, or, actually, into their play, are the millions of children who use Disney characters in their own drawings, as discussed by Willis.[52] Along these lines, there are other examples of resistance to Disney's control of experiences and memories, especially by some visitors to the theme parks, as Klugman reminds us.[53]

Referencing and subverting The Mouse   With the proliferation of Disney products, along with the repetitive and easily recognizable elements of Classic Disney, there has been a plethora of intertextual references to Disney in other media products/texts. Historically, the Warner Brothers cartoons often included Disney references, but one now finds them throughout the media. For instance, a few examples from recent television programs include numerous examples from *The Simpsons* (Itchy & Scratchy Land, etc.), a vacation spot called the Disney Planet referred to in *Babylon 5*, and an episode of *Ally McBeal*, which blamed Disney for American women's belief that they must get married and be saved from life's rigors by a man.

Plate 8 Reclaiming Disney. Children's drawings, such as this one of the Lion King by Martina Russial, illustrate one way that audiences respond to Classic Disney.
Courtesy of Martina Russial.

Other examples represent overtly subversive parodies or satires of the Disney universe. A classic example of Disney subversion was the 1960s poster first published in the *Progressive* depicting Disney characters in very un-Disney-like situations (smoking dope, engaging in sex, etc.). Similarly, Swedish Charlie Christensen's Arne Anka (a takeoff on Donald Duck) smokes, drinks, and enjoys other less-than-wholesome activities.[54]

Other examples include Jamie Malanowski's "When Disney Ran America: A Speculative History of the Near Future," in *Spy* magazine ("A nation in crisis appealed to Disney chairman Michael Eisner to accept the presidency of the United States – and he agreed"); and Peter David's "Transcript of the Disney Heroine Round Table," held in King Stefan's Banquet Hall at Disney World, with Snow White moderating (Ariel: "It's exciting to meet you, Snow." Snow: "Thank you. Uhm, you're dripping on my clean floor.")[55]

Lately, there have been a variety of Internet sites that can definitely be labeled Disney subversion. One example is www.losdisneys.com, which includes a game that is set in 2010, when the USA has sold Florida to the Disney Company and the entire state has been transformed into a theme park (called Los Disneys). The site also includes a message board where visitors add "Disney Conspiracy Theories" – everything from the (Walt) Disney on Ice myth to stories about the deaths of theme park visitors. The site notes that such information was previously included in an underground publication, called *Disney World Babylon*, which included "true stories of the theme park that were too gruesome for Disney to allow the media to publicize."

While researchers have identified this phenomenon in relation to specific films or television series, such as *Star Wars* and *Star Trek*, as well as specific TV genres, such as soap operas, little work has been directed at those fans who reinterpret and/or subvert Disney products.[56]

Certainly, much more work is needed in analyzing Disney audiences, especially in identifying examples of reinterpretation, resistance, and subversion, which are often far more difficult to find than Disney fanatics and fans, who not only accept Disney messages as intended, but embrace them as a way of life.

This chapter has explored the concept of a Disney audience, and has presented a wide array of responses to the Disney phenomenon, ranging from the fascination of Disney fanatics to the repulsion of those who oppose Disney in various ways. From this discussion, plus the few studies that have been done, it may be possible to conclude that responses to

Disney are certainly not automatic and mechanical, or universal and ubiquitous, but complex, somewhat diverse, and often contradictory.

Yet, despite this variation, one of the most amazing aspects of the Disney phenomenon is the consistently uniform understandings of the essence of "Disney." There seems to be an almost universally accepted awareness of what "Disney" means, as well as a recognition of the basic characteristics of Classic Disney – even though people may differ as to whether or not they agree with or embrace these meanings or values, or to what extent they may engage in Disney experiences.

But this may not be too surprising, either, as these characteristics are those that the Disney company consistently and emphatically insists upon in its own self-definition and in its incessant promotion and marketing. The company repeats endlessly that it is about "family," "magic," "happiness," and "fun." And, over and over, people refer to Disney as "family," "magic," "happiness," and "fun." People's similar understandings of Disney suggest that there is relatively little room for active or alternative readings of texts, like Disney's, which are carefully coded and controlled, and not polysemic and open.[57]

The final chapter will summarize some of the major points that have been covered in the book and consider whether these discussions have moved us any further along in understanding Disney.

8 Living Happily Ever After?

The study of popular culture and the Disney universe can no longer be considered a Mickey Mouse enterprise, but an important component of our understanding of the world today. Despite what company officials and some audience members may say, Disney is not merely entertainment – the manufacture of fantasy by a company like the Disney corporation has implications for the reinforcement of societal norms and values. Trying to understand how this process works, however, can be a difficult and complex matter. In fact, in the process of examining the entire Disney phenomenon, more questions may have been raised than have actually been answered.

Understanding Disney in review

This book has attempted to cover different, yet overlapping approaches to understanding the Disney phenomenon. While it is difficult to present the depth that some scholars have provided in their studies, the aim has been to look at Disney in its totality, from production to consumption, as well as the historical and current status of the company.

Chapter 2 attempted to sort through the various historical presentations of Walt Disney and focus on the foundation and evolution of the Disney company. Although most of the histories of the Disney company focus on the genius of Walt Disney, it is important to go beyond the great man approach to understand the Disney phenomenon. Even though he contributed greatly to the success of the Disney enterprise, it is nevertheless important to distinguish the company's achievements from the legend that surrounds the individual, Walt Disney.

Certainly there is little disagreement on the immediate popularity of Disney's products with the introduction of Mickey Mouse cartoons in the early 1930s. The company was able to build and maintain its reputation for quality animation and cutting-edge techniques, including sound, color, and animated features. And though it didn't achieve major status until late in the century, looking more closely at the company's history helps to explain how the New Disney was able to build a globalized, diversified empire. In many ways, the groundwork was laid with the establishment and mainten-ance of the Disney brand over the years, as well as the company's diversification into merchandising, television, theme parks, and other film projects.

The current Disney empire was explored in chapters 3 and 4, providing a basis for understanding not only what businesses the New Disney controls, but how the company operates and who benefits from its activities. The current Disney company must be viewed in relation to the rest of the media and entertainment industry, which increasingly represents a concentrated, overlapping, profitable sphere. Disney has been able to build on its established, diversified activities, as noted above, and has joined other media conglomerates in exploiting new entertainment and com-munication technologies, both in the USA and in other countries. The Disney company, however, also represents one of the best examples of the synergy that is taking place through the cross-ownership of media and entertainment outlets, as well as the recycling of products across these businesses.

In addition, the company has worked to establish control over its empire in various ways, including strong copyright enforcement, enlisting state support for its businesses, strict employment policies, and creative promo-tional and marketing techniques in both domestic and foreign markets.

Chapter 5 and 6 explored various interpretations of Disney products, specifically some of the Classic Disney films and theme parks. The focus of most textual or content analysis has been on Classic Disney – a specific set of aesthetic, stylistic, and thematic characteristics that are generally recog-nized and identified with Disney. A wide array of Classic Disney themes have been discussed by critics, including individualism, the work ethic, goodness triumphing over evil, innocence, and ultimate optimism, plus a range of expectations and assumptions about the roles of women and men in society. The theme parks especially represent Disney's assumptions about the past, as well as exemplifying the theme of control in a number of different ways. While Disney content has been studied from various interpretive perspectives, most often analysts have found clear, conspicuous representations of these themes in Classic Disney products.

Finally, chapter 7 considered different types of audiences for Disney products. The little audience research that has been done indicates that there is general agreement on what Disney represents, not only in the USA but in other countries. In other words, the Classic Disney characteristics, or preferred meanings, are clearly communicated by the products. However, there are different types of responses to the Disney phenomenon. Those who have actually adopted Disney life-styles (or those who fully accept the preferred meanings) are contrasted with those who have resisted, rejected, or attempted to subvert Disney. Nevertheless, a huge number of Americans, at least, seem to accept Disney unquestioningly, accepting the preferred meanings and generally embracing the ideology promoted by Classic Disney products.

So, what have we learned about Disney?

Obviously, a wide range of issues and questions emerges from the study of the "the whole Disney," some of which have been highlighted in the previous chapters. A few other queries will be addressed to conclude this examination of the Disney universe.

The universal Disney

It is generally assumed that there is "universal" recognition of what "Disney" represents. There is an assumption – by the company and by those who support it – that Disney and Mickey Mouse are not only recognized, but loved around the world. In considering this issue, one might begin with a definition that was provided once by Walt Disney:

> Disney is a thing, an image in the public mind. Disney is something they think of as a kind of entertainment, a kind of family thing, and it's all wrapped up in the name Disney. If we start pulling that apart by calling it "A Bill Walsh Production for Walt Disney" or "A Jim Algar True-Life Adventure for Walt Disney," then the name Disney won't mean as much any more. We'd be cutting away at what we've built up in the public mind over the years. You see, I'm not Disney any more. I used to be Disney, but now Disney is something we've built up in the public mind over the years.

It stands for something, and you don't have to explain what it is to the public. They know what Disney is when they hear about our films or go to Disneyland. They know they're gonna get a certain quality, a certain kind of entertainment. And that's what Disney is.[1]

This explanation reveals one of the keys to Disney's presumed universality: "what we've built up in the public mind over the years." The Disney brand has been carefully nurtured and controlled, as well as marketed and promoted globally. Thus, if Mickey Mouse lives in the hearts and minds of people all over the world then it is because The Mouse and other Disney characters have been carefully manufactured and effectively distributed to reach the hearts and minds of people all over the world.

The Disney Company has grown and expanded by vigilantly controlling its products, characters, and images and developing its reputation as a company that produces positive, wholesome, family and children's entertainment. The Disney company takes advantage of its reputation by presenting the corporation as special and different. Its brand recognition has been built and zealously protected, allowing the company to expand into whatever new areas develop, drawing on its strong reputation. As Eisner boasts: "It doesn't matter whether it comes in by cable, telephone lines, computer, or satellite. Everyone's going to have to deal with Disney."[2]

The company has been built on a strong historical base, taking advantage of global trade opportunities that have expanded its empire far and wide, to the point where it is possible for company representatives and others to claim that Disney and Mickey Mouse are universal. But we also need to remember that this "universality" is neither automatic nor natural, but has been – and continues to be – deliberately manufactured and carefully controlled.

The sacred Disney

How has Disney developed and maintained such a sacred aura that many refuse to criticize? It has to have something to do with the link to childhood and innocence. Disney products typically become a part of every child's life, in one form or another (at least in the USA). Thus, they are intimately and strongly associated with childhood and retain a special place in people's memories of childhood. As Susan Davis has suggested:

> It is interesting how deeply one company and all its products have penetrated and defined the experience of childhood. There is almost universal agreement that this company's products mean wholesome, mentally healthy, happy childhood, America, conflict free, conflict resolution, closeness, togetherness, family bonds . . . on and on. What other company has ever accomplished this? The amazing thing is the thoroughness with which everyday life has been penetrated by these overlapping products.[3]

So, is this why adults also enjoy Disney products? Are the products popular with adults because of their associations with childhood memories, or because they have come to represent fun, happiness, and pleasure? Are Disney products deliberately aimed at "the child in everyone"? And, if we are experiencing "the disappearance of childhood" (along the lines that Neil Postman argues[4]), why is Disney still popular?

The meaning of Disney is most often tied directly to the notion of fantasy and imagination. Indeed, the role of pleasure is a natural and important element in human nature, as some media analysts have noted in recent work. We have a natural inclination to seek pleasure and escape, and to look for utopian experiences. The Disney brand of fantasy is a ready-made, highly promoted, and powerfully seductive option, often assumed to be one of the few "acceptable" options available.

However, the problem with Disney's version of fantasy, imagination, and pleasure is the direct connection with a specific set of values. In other words, the products are hardly "innocent" – whether one is considering the proliferation of Disney products in our consumer culture or the mainstream American values represented by those products.

Disney's fantasies are offered as commodities, produced and manufactured in accordance with specific commercial parameters. While this is never forgotten by those who control the Disney company, the consumers who experience the pleasure, fun, and magic often overlook these motivations. Increasingly, our lives revolve around the accumulation of an enormous array of commodities and engagement in commercial activities that come to signify basic human relations – hence the association of warm family memories with visits to Disneyland, and the fond recollections of Disney characters and products. Clearly, pleasures and memories have become associated with activities that have lost their connection to their original motivation or their inherent commercial nature.

Furthermore, definite and often unmistakable themes and values are represented in Classic Disney products. As noted in chapters 5 and 6, Classic Disney fantasies are anything but open-ended and imaginative;

rather, they are neatly tied into a conservative vision of the world and are linked directly with consumer culture. Indeed, the legacy of Walt Disney and the Disney company itself have been especially adept at representing what America represents: business, progress, individual initiative. Disney has incorporated the American personality, as fun-loving, innocent, optimistic, and with a sense of fair play and what is right. In addition, the success of the Disney company has come to represent American ingenuity and cleverness.

The problem is that these attributes also form the basis of many American values that have either been mythologized or are not necessarily embraced by everyone. Indeed, Disney values can also be associated with such all-American traits such as conservatism, homophobia, Manifest Destiny, ethnocentricity, cultural insensitivity, superficiality, lack of culture, etc. Disney did not create these traits, but it is possible to argue that the Disney empire helps to perpetuate them. Is it the only company that does so? Of course not. But it does it very well and (at least for many) in an appealing, seductive, and enjoyable way.

Many analysts have pointed out that the themes emphasized by Disney culture are reminiscent of a past America and may have less to do with the reality of America today. As we have seen, those able to take a trip to Disneyland or see a Disney film are able to escape from an everyday reality that is not always pleasurable or fun, and may well pose challenging dilemmas. In real life, not every story has a happy ending. In other words, Disneyland is not just further down the freeway from the inner-city reality of south central Los Angeles – it's a world away.

Disney divergence

When we look more closely at the company, its history, and its products, we see that Disney is ripe with tensions and contradictions. Disney is seen as a major component of children's culture, yet adults are important consumers of Disney products, as well. While some celebrate Disney's unique successes, others celebrate its failures.[5] As we learned in chapter 7, even though multitudes of consumers still idolize the Disney company and its products, many former Disney fans are disillusioned by the New Disney and the perceived over-commercialization promoted by the company. Furthermore, even though there is a good deal of acceptance of the Disney ideology, there is also ambiguity, contradiction, and sometimes outright rejection.

To some Disney defenders, it may seem that everywhere one turns these days, Disney is being dissected, deflowered, and deconstructed. In fact, the company's products are finally drawing the attention of academics, who have discovered that Classic Disney is an enduring and significant part of our media and cultural landscape. However, much of the analysis has focused on reading Disney texts, and more work is needed linking textual interpretations to corporate imperatives, as well as assessing how Classic Disney themes are received, accepted, and/or reworked by consumers or audiences.

The most stinging assaults on the Disney company (from both conservative and leftist critics) often advocate a knee-jerk rejection of the products and themes. Some analysts argue that the real challenge is to use Disney products as pedagogical tools to further understand the culture in which they are embedded. Critics, such as Henry Giroux and others, have argued persuasively along these lines, suggesting that, "Challenging the ideological underpinnings of Disney's construction of common sense is the first step in understanding the ways in which corporate culture has refashioned the relationship between education and entertainment, on the one hand, and institutional power and cultural politics, on the other."[6] In other words, a critical understanding of Disney must be seen as a part of a more general critique of corporate and consumer culture.

But the study of Disney also provides an opportunity to analyze an entire popular cultural phenomenon from various perspectives, and thus more fully understand and develop a range of cultural analytic tools. While this volume may not have fully developed all the possible approaches, or answered all the questions and addressed all the issues that emerge from this one cultural phenomenon, it may still provide a model to use in further examining the Disney universe, as well as other cultural products and their significance.

Notes

Chapter 1   Introducing the Disney Universe

1   *Register Guard*, 27 Nov. 1997, p. 1A.
2   *Register Guard*, 7 Jan. 1998, p. 1C. James Simpson isn't the only one to wish for a trip to Disneyland or Disney World as their final dream. An entire foundation is based on funding terminally ill children's trips to one of the Magic Kingdoms. The Make-A-Wish Foundation, which has 82 US chapters and 13 affiliates in other countries, was formed in 1980 and by 1996 had organized about 37,000 trips and other events for terminally ill children. The most popular wish is reported to be a visit to either Disney World or Disneyland, which are provided by the Disney corporation. Meanwhile, Stanley Wilkins's novel *Magic Kingdom* (New York: E. P. Dutton, 1985) is about seven terminally ill children visiting Disney World before they die.
3   Michael Real, *Mass-Mediated Culture* (Englewood Cliffs, N.J.: Prentice-Hall, 1973).
4   Kathy Merlock Jackson, *Walt Disney: A Bio-Bibliography* (Westport, Conn.: Greenwood Press, 1993); Lynn Gartley and Elizabeth Leebron, *Walt Disney: A Guide to References and Resources* (Boston: G. K. Hall, 1979).
5   Ariel Dorfman and Armand Mattelart, *How to Read Donald Duck* (New York: International General, 1975); Herbert I. Schiller, *The Mind Managers* (Boston: Beacon Press, 1973).
6   In "Dissin' Disney: Critical Perspectives on Children's Media Culture," *Media, Culture and Society*, 19, 2 (Apr. 1997), pp. 285–93, David Buckingham discusses several recent books on the Disney phenomenon, pointing out how the studies include economic, textual, and (sometimes) audience research, albeit rarely integrating these forms of analysis. He notes: "Of course, it would be asking too much to expect any single book to incorporate

all these dimensions." I take Buckingham's comment as one of my justifications for the length of time it has taken to produce this book.

Chapter 2   Disney History(ies)

1   "Walt Disney Issue," *Wisdom*, 32 (1959), p. 46; cited in Steven Watts, *The Magic Kingdom: Walt Disney and the American Way of Life* (New York: Houghton Mifflin, 1997), p. 58.

2   William Irvin McReynolds, "Walt Disney in the American Grain" (Ph.D. dissertation, University of Minnesota, 1971).

3   One of the most commonly cited sources in Disney biographies is Diane Daisy Miller, *The Story of Walt Disney* (New York: Dell, 1956), written by Disney's daughter. Watts, *Magic Kingdom*, reports that close acquaintances said that Disney was "preoccupied" by his own history, and that it is clear that "Disney mythologized his past and presented it to the public" (p. 7).

4   Richard Schickel, *The Disney Version: The Life, Times, Art and Commerce of Walt Disney* (New York: Simon & Schuster, 1968, (repr. 1985).

5   Joel Taxel, "A Literature Review of the Impact of Walt Disney Productions Inc. on American Popular Culture and Children's Literature," in University of Georgia, Department of Language Education, 1982 (ERIC Document Reproduction Service no. ED 213648).

6   The most frequently cited biographies are probably Schickel, *Disney Version*, and Bob Thomas, *Walt Disney: An American Original* (New York: Simon & Schuster, 1976). See also Leonard Mosley, *Disney's World* (Briarcliff, N.Y.: Stein and Day, 1985), Katherine Greene and Richard Greene, *The Man behind the Magic: The Story of Walt Disney* (New York: Viking, 1991), and Marc Eliot, *Walt Disney, Hollywood's Dark Prince* (New York: Birch Lane Press, 1993). More recently, Watts, *Magic Kingdom*, has presented a relatively thorough discussion of Disney, relying on primary sources from the Disney Archives. Kathy Merlock Jackson, *Walt Disney: A Bio-Bibliography* (Westport, Conn.: Greenwood Press, 1993), includes a biography, a biographical essay, and "Key Disney Sources." She notes that "an exhaustive treatment of Disney resources is not possible nor even desirable by virtue of the fact that much of it is inaccurate." Jackson lists the most important biographical articles, including a sample list of 12 cover stories on Disney.

7   The most glowing accounts have received the Disney company's "seal of approval" and have benefited from the cooperation of the company and access to the Walt Disney Archives, an extensive library of historical materials housed at corporate headquarters in Burbank. By contrast, authors of many of the more critical biographies have been denied such resources, and their works have sometimes been greeted by vehement denials and protests from the Disney company and family: e.g. Eliot, *Walt Disney, Hollywood's Dark Prince*, and Schickel, *Disney Version*. For background on the archives by their chief archivist, see David R. Smith, "The Walt Disney Archives: It All

Started with a Mouse," *Historical Journal of Film, Radio and Television*, 16, 1 (1996), pp. 13–18.

8   Leonard Maltin, *The Disney Films* (New York: Crown, 1973), p. 11.

9   Graham Murdock, "Large Corporations and the Control of the Communications Industries," in *Culture, Society and the Media*, ed. Michael Gurevitch, Tony Bennett, James Curran, and Janet Woollacott, (London: Methuen, 1982), pp. 118–50, at p. 125. See also Eileen Meehan, "Critical Theorizing on Broadcast History," *Journal of Broadcasting and Electronic Media*, 30, 4 (Fall 1986), pp. 109–13.

10   Even the events of Disney's birth have been disputed, Eliot's controversial biography asserting that Walt may actually have been adopted from a Spanish immigrant. The evidence is shady and inconclusive, but Eliot argues that the possibility of such an adoption haunted Disney for much of his life.

11   Watts, *Magic Kingdom*, pp. 11–14.

12   One of the few books focusing primarily on Roy is Bob Thomas, *Building a Company: Roy O. Disney and the Creation of an Entertainment Empire* (New York: Hyperion, 1998).

13   "History of the Walt Disney Company," mimeo distributed by Walt Disney Company, p. 2.

14   Ibid.

15   Eliot, *Walt Disney, Hollywood's Dark Prince*, p. 49.

16   Schickel, *Disney Version*, p. 139.

17   Robert Heide and John Gilman, *Disneyana: Classic Collectibles 1928–1958* (New York: Hyperion, 1995), p. 37.

18   Ibid., pp. 37–9.

19   For more on the Mickey Mouse Clubs, see Richard deCordova, "The Mickey in Macy's Window: Childhood, Consumerism, and Disney Animation," in *Disney Discourse: Producing the Magic Kingdom*, ed. Eric Smoodin (New York: Routledge, 1994), pp. 203–13.

20   For more details about Disney and Technicolor, see Richard Neupert, "Painting a Plausible World: Disney's Color Prototypes," in *Disney Discourse*, ed. Smoodin, pp. 106–17.

21   Alan Bryman, *Disney and his Worlds* (London: Routledge, 1995), pp. 26–32, identifies lack of recognition of pre-Disney animation as one of the many omissions and equivocations in biographical accounts. Others include the neglect of Roy Disney's contribution to the company, the 1941 strike, and Walt's business acumen. Walt's involvement with the Hollywood blacklist, HUAC, and the FBI might be added to Bryman's list.

22   Watts, *Magic Kingdom*, p. 32.

23   For more background on the film industry during this period, see Tino Balio, *The American Film Industry* (Madison, Wis.: University of Wisconsin Press, 1985).

24   Douglas Gomery, "Disney's Business History: A Reinterpretation," in *Disney Discourse*, ed. Smoodin, pp. 72–3.

25 Bryman, *Disney and his Worlds*, p. 14.

26 Personal attributes discussed by Eliot, including impotence, alcoholism, nervous ticks, and compulsive cleanliness, make it easy to understand why the Disney family publicly decried the release of Eliot's book.

27 Watts, *Magic Kingdom*, p. 46.

28 "The Big Bad Wolf," *Fortune*, Nov. 1934, p. 146; cited in Watts, *Magic Kingdom*, p. 47.

29 There are numerous sources for this point, including Schickel, *Disney Version*, pp. 33–4; Watts, *Magic Kingdom*, p. 50.

30 Watts, *Magic Kingdom*, pp. 32–3.

31 Ibid., p. 59.

32 "History of the Walt Disney Company," p. 3.

33 A number of the specific products are discussed in Heide and Gilman, *Disneyana*, pp. 145–55, including doll sets, marionettes, music boxes, toy pianos, lamps, children's furniture, sleds, Halloween masks, tea sets, beach toys, lunch boxes, glasses, purses, watches, jewelry, fabrics, tablecloths, napkins, towels, baby pants, rattles, notepads, stationery, soaps, socks, hankies, rubber boots, canvas sneakers, pajamas, snowsuits, Valentine cards, Bagatelle and pinball games, card games, and jigsaw puzzles.

34 Cited in Watts, *Magic Kingdom*, p. 162.

35 McReynolds, "Walt Disney in the American Grain," p. 42.

36 Schickel, *Disney Version*, p. 23.

37 Thomas, *Walt Disney: An American Original*, pp. 165–6.

38 Watts, *Magic Kingdom*, p. 167.

39 See Janet Wasko, "Challenges to Hollywood's Labor Force in the 1990s," in *Global Productions: Labor in the Making of the "Information Society"*, ed. Gerald Sussman and John A. Lent (Cresskill, N.J.: Hampton Press, 1998), pp. 173–89.

40 Watts, *Magic Kingdom*, pp. 204–9; Holly Allen and Michael Denning, "The Cartoonists' Front," *Southern Atlantic Quarterly*, 92, 1 (1993), pp. 89–119, at p. 95.

41 See Julianne Burton-Carvajal, " 'Surprise Package': Looking Southward with Disney," in *Disney Discourse*, ed. Smoodin, pp. 131–47; Lisa Cartwright and Brian Goldfarb, "Cultural Contagion: On Disney's Health Education Films for Latin America," in *Disney Discourse*, ed. Smoodin, pp. 148–80.

42 Watts, *Magic Kingdom*, pp. 226–7.

43 Ibid., p. 441.

44 Ibid., pp. 240–1. See also "The Testimony of Walter E. Disney before the House Committee on UnAmerican Activities," in Danny Peary and Gerald Peary, *The American Animated Cartoon: A Critical Anthology* (New York: E. P. Dutton, 1980), pp. 92–7.

45 Watts, *Magic Kingdom*, p. 349, claims it was the 1950s; Eliot, *Walt Disney, Hollywood's Dark Prince*, p. 165, says that it was the early 1940s.

46 Watts, *Magic Kingdom*, p. 349.

47   Allen and Denning, "Cartoonists' Front," p. 89.

48   Watts, *Magic Kingdom*, p. 228.

49   See Cartwright and Goldfarb, "Cultural Contagion," for more discussion of the educational films on health and sanitation produced at the Disney studios by the government for export to Latin America.

50   For more on Disney's wartime films, see Richard Allen Shale, "Donald Duck Joins Up: The Walt Disney Studio during World War II" (Ph.D. dissertation, University of Michigan, 1976), and Eric Smoodin, *Animating Culture: Hollywood Cartoons from the Sound Era* (New Brunswick, N.J.: Rutgers University Press, 1993).

51   Jackson, *Walt Disney: A Bio-Bibliography*, p. 42; Thomas, *Walt Disney: An American Original*, p. 193. For more on Disney's relationship with the Bank of America, see Janet Wasko, *Movies and Money: Financing the American Film Industry* (Norwood, N.J.: Ablex, 1982), pp. 172–5.

52   See Michelle Hilmes, *Hollywood and Broadcasting: From Radio to Cable* (Urbana, Ill.: University of Illinois Press, 1990); and Janet Wasko, *Hollywood in the Information Age: Beyond the Silver Screen* (Cambridge: Polity Press, 1994), pp. 11–13.

53   Quoted in Jackson, *Walt Disney: A Bio-Bibliography*, pp. 49–50.

54   The company obviously underestimated the success of the series, as Disney explained: "We had no idea what was going to happen to 'Crockett.' Why, by the time the first show finally got on the air, we were already shooting the third one and calmly killing Davy off at the Alamo. It became one of the biggest overnight hits in TV history, and there we were with just three films and a dead hero" (Maltin, *Disney Films*, p. 122).

55   Schickel, *Disney Version*, p. 28. The Paramount decrees refer to the antitrust suit against the five fully integrated Hollywood majors and three other distributors in the 1940s, which was settled through a series of consent decrees beginning in 1948. The majors were required to divorce their production and distribution activities from exhibition, to refrain from price setting and other anti-competitive agreements, and to distribute their films "theater by theater, picture by picture." For more details, see Michael Conant, *Antitrust in the Motion Picture Industry* (Berkeley, Calif.: University of California Press, 1960).

56   Jackson, *Walt Disney: A Bio-Bibliography*, p. 66. In addition to the hundreds of articles that chronicled Disney during his life, there were further discussions of his life and his effect on American culture after his death, many of which have already been referred to in this chapter. See also John Gardner, "Saint Walt: The Greatest Artist the World Has Ever Known, Except for, Possibly, Apollonius of Rhodes," *New York*, 12 Nov. 1973, pp. 64–6; and James Morrow, "In Defense of Disney," *Media and Methods*, Apr. 1978, pp. 31–2.

57   http://disney.go.com/disneyatoz/read/walt/index.html.

58   Bryman, *Disney and his Worlds*, pp. 32–3.

59 Miriam Stillwell, "The Story behind Snow White's $10,000,000 Surprise Party," *Liberty*, 9 Apr. 1938, p. 8; quoted in Jackson, *Walt Disney: A Bio-Bibliography*, p. 28.

60 Ronald Grover, *The Disney Touch* (Homewood, Ill.: Business One Irwin, 1991), p. 10.

61 Bryman, *Disney and his Worlds*, p. 33.

62 http://disney.go.com/disneyatoz/waltdisney/home.html.

63 This is one of the most common myths (or urban legends) about Disney, even internationally. Many authors discuss Disney's interest in cryogenics before his death, including Bryman, *Disney and his Worlds*; Thomas, *Walt Disney: An American Original*; and Steven Fjellman, *Vinyl Leaves: Walt Disney World and America* (Boulder, Colo.: Westview Press, 1992).

64 Gomery, "Disney's Business History," p. 86.

Chapter 3   The Disney Empire

1 Dallas Smythe, "The Political Economy of Communication," *Journalism Quarterly* 37 (1960), pp. 563–72.

2 Graham Murdock and Peter Golding, "For a Political Economy of Mass Communications," in *The Socialist Register*, ed. Ralph Miliband and John Saville (London: Merlin Press, 1974), pp. 105–234.

3 Vincent Mosco, *The Political Economy of Communication: Rethinking and Renewal* (London: Sage, 1996), p. 25.

4 Cited in Kim Masters, *The Keys to the Kingdom: How Michael Eisner Lost his Grip* (New York: William Morrow & Co., 2000), p. 42.

5 Walt Disney World College Program, Finance & Marketing, p. 1.

6 Ronald Grover, *The Disney Touch* (Homewood, Ill.: Business One Irwin, 1991); John Taylor, *Storming the Magic Kingdom* (New York: Knopf, 1987); Douglas Gomery, "Disney's Business History: A Reinterpretation," in *Disney Discourse: Producing the Magic Kingdom*, ed. Eric Smoodin (New York: Routledge, 1994), pp. 71–86; Jon Lewis, "Disney after Disney: Family Business and the Business of Family," in *Disney Discourse*, ed. Smoodin, pp. 87–105; and Richard Schickel, *The Disney Version: The Life, Times, Art and Commerce of Walter Disney* (New York: Simon & Schuster, 1968, repr. 1985).

7 Steven Fjellman, *Vinyl Leaves: Walt Disney World and America* (Boulder, Colo.: Westview Press, 1992); Alan Bryman, *Disney and his Worlds* (London: Routledge, 1995).

8 See Janet Wasko, *Hollywood in the Information Age: Beyond the Silver Screen* (Cambridge: Polity Press, 1994).

9 It is interesting to note the disparate reports about how Eisner became CEO at Disney and who was mostly responsible for selecting him.

10 Bryman, *Disney and his Worlds*, ch. 3.

11 Michael Eisner, *Work in Progress* (New York: Random House, 1998).

12 In considering the company's impressive financial success, it should be noted that Disney is known for using accounting policies that show the best possible earnings record, or what some have called "Mickey Mouse accounting." It includes the use of *pro forma* earnings, or adding earnings from merged companies before the acquisitions have actually taken place, as Disney did with their 1995–6 statements. Another tactic is called "purchase price accounting," which allows the company to write down program costs before release and thus show a larger profit if the program is successful. (See Lisa Gubernick, "Mickey Mouse, CPA," *Forbes*, 10 Mar. 1997, p. 42.)

13 See Wasko, *Hollywood in the Information Age*, for changes in Hollywood in the 1980s and 1990s.

14 Christopher Knowlton, "How Disney Keeps the Magic Going," *Fortune*, Dec. 1989, p. 128.

15 Gomery, "Disney's Business History," pp. 81–2.

16 See Janet Wasko, *Movies and Money: Financing the American Film Industry* (Norwood, N.J.: Ablex, 1982), esp. ch. 5.

17 Interestingly, Eisner's list did not include the Celebration project, which opened in July 1996. More on this development later in this chapter and in chapter 6.

18 J. Max Robins and Martin Peers, "Goliaths Reel at Disney Deal," *Variety*, 21 Aug. 1995, p. 1.

19 The Walt Disney Company, *1998 Annual Report*, p. 9.

20 Eisner's 1998 letter to shareholders reiterates the point: "Disney's overall corporate mission – to offer quality entertainment that people will seek out." He then explains how such investments will "create significant growth," and will "enrich our company."

21 The company's *1999 Annual Report* provides the following overview of the company's goals: "to maximize earnings and cash flow from existing businesses and to allocate capital profitably toward growth initiatives that will drive long-term shareholder value" (p. 10).

22 For a good overview of these issues, see Maurice Zeitlin, "Corporate Ownership and Control: The Large Corporation and the Capitalist Class," *American Journal of Sociology*, 79 (Mar. 1974), pp. 1073–1119.

23 As of 28 Dec. 1998, there were 2,048,862,650 shares of common stock outstanding for the Walt Disney Company (Proxy, filed 4 Jan. 1999).

24 Taylor, *Storming*, p. 249.

25 John A. Byrne and Ronald Grover, "The Best and Worst Boards," *Business Week*, 8 Dec. 1997, p. 90.

26 "Four Studies Analyze Executive Pay Raises," *Report on Salary Surveys*, June 2000, p. 3.

27 Since the company continuously adds (and sometimes, eliminates) new lines of business, the organization of its operating segments changes periodically. For instance, with the addition of ABC, a new Broadcasting Division was

formed, and Consumer Products was folded into Creative Content, thus creating three divisions: Creative Content, Theme Parks and Resorts, and Broadcasting. However, in 1999, the broadcasting segment was renamed Media Networks (and further broken down into cable and broadcasting businesses), and Creative Content was split into three different segments: Studio Entertainment, Consumer Products, and Internet and Direct Marketing.

28 Touchstone Pictures was formed in 1984, before the management/ownership shuffle, and its first release was *Splash*.

29 Gomery, "Disney's Business History," p. 81.

30 In the Form 10-K for 1990 (p. 2), the company reported that its film library included 194 full-length live-action features, 29 full-length animated colour features, and 529 cartoon shorts. In 1997, the totals were 480 full-length live-action features, 35 full-length animated color features, and approximately 476 cartoon shorts.

31 *Variety*, 11 Jan. 1999, p. 20.

32 Quoted in "Are You All Ears?", *DVD Newswire*, 12 Nov. 1999.

33 According to Disney's 1997 Form 10-K (p. 2), "approximately 1,100 produced and acquired titles, including 531 feature films and 408 cartoon shorts and animated features, were available to the domestic marketplace."

34 Carl Hiassen, *Team Rodent: How Disney Devours the World* (New York: Ballantine, 1998), speculates that the whole affair may have been staged deliberately to further perpetuate the Disney image.

35 http://www.disney.com/DisneyCareers/WhoWeAre/DisneyConsumrProducts.html. 14 Oct. 1998.

36 Charles Solomon, *Enchanted Drawings* (New York: Alfred A. Knopf, 1989), p. 92.

37 Ibid., p. 96.

38 See Norma Odom Pecora, *The Business of Children's Entertainment* (New York: Guilford Press, 1998); Janet Wasko, Mark Phillips, and Christopher Purdie, "Hollywood Meets Madison Ave.: The Commercialization of US Films," *Media, Culture and Society* 15, 2 (1993), pp. 271–93. Mark Yates, "Toying with Movies: Motion Picture Based Merchandising and the Commodification of Cinematic Images" (M.A. thesis, University of Oregon, 1999).

39 Stephen Koepp, "Do You Believe in Magic?," *Time*, 25 Apr. 1988. Disney's merchandising activities are regularly discussed in the trade publication *The Licensing Letter*.

40 B. Hulin-Salkin, "Movie Tie-ins," *Incentive*, June 1989.

41 For more, see Elizabeth Bell, Lynda Haas, and Laura Salls, (eds), *From Mouse to Mermaid: The Politics of Film, Gender, and Culture* (Bloomington, Ind.: Indiana University Press, 1995), p. 6.

42 Marc Grasner, "Mouse Clicks on Toysmart.com Site," *Variety*, 26 Aug. 1999, p. 3.

43 Robert Heide and John Gilman, *Disneyana: Classic Collectibles 1928–1958* (New York: Hyperion, 1995), p. 7.

44 The Walt Disney Company, *1993 Annual Report*, p. 4.

45 The Walt Disney Company, 1998 Form 10-K , p. 4.

46 The deal is meticulously explained in a 484-page proxy statement/prospectus issued by the company 30 Sept. 1999 to Disney and Infoseek stockholders.

47 F. Rose, "Mickey Online," *Fortune*, 28 Sept. 1998, pp. 273–6. "Unique visitors" represent an estimate of the number of people who visit a site, not how many times they visit.

48 Ron Grover, "The Wonderful World of Disney.Com," *Business Week*, 2 Mar. 1998, p. 78.

49 Rose, "Mickey Online"; Grover, "Wonderful World."

50 See Sumana Kasturi, "Constructing Childhood in a Corporate World: A Cultural Pedagogy Analysis of the Disney Web Site," paper presented at the Association for Education in Journalism and Mass Communications, New Orleans, 6 Aug, 1999; Randy Nichols, "Ideology and Manufactured Environments: An Analysis of the Disney Home Page," paper presented at the Association for Education in Journalism and Mass Communciation Conference, Phoenix, Ariz., Aug. 2000.

51 Penny Gill, "The Disney Stores Blend Retailing and Entertainment," *Stores*, June 1991, 20–4.

52 http://www.disney.com/DisneyCruise/DisneyCruise_F/Home_F/index.html; 28 Aug. 1998.

53 The Walt Disney Company's 1997 Form 10-K, p. 11. For more on the Imagineers, see The Imagineers and C. E. Jones, *Walt Disney Imagineering: A Behind the Dreams Look at Making the Magic Real* (New York: Hyperion, 1998), and Karal Ann Marling (ed.), *Designing Disney's Theme Parks: The Architecture of Reassurance* (Montreal: Canadian Center for Architecture, 1997).

54 An interesting wrinkle at the time for the Disney company, which mostly had stayed out of the arena of news and information production, was an innovative three-hour prime-time news format on KCAL.

55 The Walt Disney Company, *1998 Annual Report*, p. 44.

56 The Walt Disney Company, *1999 Annual Report*, pp. 12–13.

57 Christopher Knowlton, "How Disney Keeps the Magic Going," *Fortune*, Dec. 1989, p. 130.

58 The Walt Disney Company, *1998 Annual Report*, p. 11.

59 The Walt Disney Company, *1999 Annual Report*, p. 41.

60 Dana Flavelle, "Mounties Disney-fied Official RCMP Merchandise Beginning to Hit Store Shelves," *Toronto Star*, 29 June 1996, p. A2. See also "RCMP–Disney Deal Anything but Goofy," *Toronto Star*, 28 June 1998, p. A11.

61 Colin Nickerson, "Mounties Find Mickey Always Gets his Man," *Boston Globe*, 23 July 1996, p. A1.

62 *Business Week*, 5 Mar. 1990, p. 32.

63 The Walt Disney Company, *1999 Annual Report*, p. 23.

64 By mid-1999, there were Disney Channels in Taiwan, the UK, Australia, Malaysia, France, the Middle East, Spain, Italy, Germany, and Brazil. The channel in the Middle East features Disney programming 7 days a week, 24 hours a day, to 23 countries throughout the Middle East and North Africa.

65 William Kunz, "A Political Economic Analysis of Ownership and Regulation in the Television and Motion Picture Industries" (Ph.D. dissertation, University of Oregon, 1998).

66 "The National Entertainment State," *The Nation*, 3 June 1996; "The Crushing Power of Big Publishing: The National Entertainment State II," *The Nation*, 17 Mar. 1997; "Who Controls the Music? The National Entertainment State III," *The Nation*, 25 Aug.–1 Sept. 1997; "Who Controls TV?: The National Entertainment State IV," *The Nation*, 8 June 1998. For further discussion of media concentration, see Edward S. Herman and Robert W. McChesney, *The Global Media: The New Missionaries of Corporate Capitalism* (London: Cassell, 1997); Ben H. Bagdikian, *The Media Monopoly*, 5th edn (Boston: Beacon Press, 1997); Leo Bogart, *Commercial Culture: The Media System and the Public Interest* (New York: Oxford University Press, 1995).

Chapter 4 Corporate Disney in Action

1 "Size Does Matter," *Economist*, 23 May 1998, p. 57.

2 James Zoltak, "Aggressive Marketing, Disney Synergy Keys to Disneyland's Banner '95 Season," *Amusement Business*, 8 Jan. 1996, p. 5.

3 The discussion of the promotion of *Hercules* is drawn from coverage in a wide array of newspapers and trade magazines, especially *Variety*, *The Hollywood Reporter*, *Business Wire*, *PR Newswire*, *Amusement Business*, and the *Los Angeles Times*. Specific citations will be made for direct quotes and exclusive sources.

4 Danny Biederman, "Disney's 'Hercules' Promises Big Summer Muscle," *Children's Business*, Feb. 1997, p. 24.

5 "Disney on Ice" is produced by Feld Entertainment, a Virginia company that produces other live entertainment events, including the Las Vegas illusion shows by Siegfried & Roy and the Ringling Bros and Barnum & Bailey Circus. The company had 11 productions touring the world in the 1999–2000 season. "Private Companies," *Washington Post*, 24 Apr. 2000, p. F57.

6 *Hercules* is not the first film to feature its own merchandise; similar scenes spoofing movie merchandise were included in *Space Balls*, *Wayne's World*, and *Jurassic Park*.

7 Cited in Biederman, "Disney's 'Hercules'," p. 24.

8 Ibid.

9   Cited in Mark Yates, "Toying with Movies: Motion Picture Based Merchandising and the Commodification of Cinematic Images" (M.A. thesis, University of Oregon, 1999), p. 89.

10   Cited in Biederman, "Disney's 'Hercules'," p. 24.

11   Gannett News Service, 7 July 1997.

12   James Peltz and Michael Hiltzik, "Of Mouse and Yen: Disney's Still a 'Do' . . .," *Los Angeles Times*, 21 July 1998, p. D7.

13   Elaine Dutka, "No Herculean Gross; Why?," *Los Angeles Times*, 19 July 1997, p. F1.

14   John Horn, "Can Anyone Dethrone Disney?," *Los Angeles Times*, 1 June 1997.

15   For example, see Ben J. Bagdikian, *The Media Monopoly*, 5th edn (Boston: Beacon Press, 1997); Edward S. Herman and Noam Chomsky, *Manufacturing Consent: The Political Economy of the Mass Media* (New York: Pantheon Books, 1988).

16   Leo Bogart, "What Does it All Mean?," in *Media Mergers*, ed. Nancy J. Woodhull and Robert W. Snyder, (New Brunswick, N.J.: Transaction Publishers, 1998), pp. 17–28.

17   See Ronald V. Bettig, *Copyrighting Culture: The Political Economy of Intellectual Property* (Boulder, Colo.: Westview Press, 1996), for a thorough analysis of these issues.

18   Cited in "Disney Sues 200 People for Copyright Infringement," UPI Regional News release, 6 Oct. 1988.

19   "Disney Files Suit against 123 California Cos., 99 Oregon Cos.," *The Entertainment Litigation Reporter*, 22 July 1991.

20   Tom Baldwin, "Mandelson Mustn't Take Mickey," *Sunday Telegraph*, 18 Jan. 1998.

21   "Cartoon Character Controversy," *Asbury Park Press* (Neptune, N.J.), 21 Dec. 1997.

22   Jonathan D. Salant, "Copyright Extended for Mickey Mouse," AP story, 16 Oct. 1998.

23   Ibid.

24   Sabra Chartrand, "Congress Has Extended its Protection for Goofy, Gershwin and Some Moguls of the Internet," *New York Times*, 19 Oct. 1998.

25   http://www.disney.com/Legal/conditions_of_use.html.

26   Interview with Matt Dyste, Director of Merchandise Marketing and Licensing, University of Oregon, Eugene, Oregon, July 1998.

27   "Disney Employees Report on Work Culture at VaultReports.com," *Business Wire*, 25 Aug. 1999.

28   John Lent, "The Animation Industry and its Offshore Factories," in *Global Productions: Labor in the Making of the "Information Society*," ed. Gerald Sussman and John Lent (Cresskill, N.J.: Hampton Press, 1998), pp. 239–54, at p. 241. See also N. M. Klein, *7 Minutes: The Life and Death of the American Animated Cartoon* (London: Verso, 1993).

29 Lent, "Animation Industry," p. 245.

30 Cited, ibid.

31 Ibid., p. 252.

32 The discussion in this section is drawn from material distributed during the summer internship program at Walt Disney World, plus Jane Kuenz, "Working at the Rat," in *Inside the Mouse: Work and Play at Disney World*, ed. Project on Disney (Durham, N.C.: Duke University Press, 1995), pp. 110–62. Other sources on working at the parks include David Koenig and Art Linkletter, *Mouse Tales: A Behind-the-Ears Look at Disneyland* (Irvine Calif.: Bonaventure Press, 1995); David Koenig and Van Arsdale France, *More Mouse Tales: A Closer Peek Backstage at Disneyland* (Irvine, Calif.: Bonaventure Press, 1999); and Thomas Connelan, *Inside the Magic Kingdom: Seven Keys to Disney's Success* (Austin, Tx.: Bard Press, 1997).

33 The company has developed seminars and courses based on the Traditions model for managers and educators. More discussion of these courses is included in chapter 6.

34 Eve Zibart, *The Unofficial® Disney Companion* (New York: Macmillan, 1997), p. 177.

35 Cited and discussed in Alan Bryman, "The Disneyization of Society," *Sociological Review*, 47, 1 (1999), p. 28.

36 Apparently, there are numerous stories of accidents and other incidents, whether true or not, that "cast members" are forbidden to discuss, on pain of being "fired on the spot." Kuenz (pp. 115–16) discusses some examples; others are included on the Los Disneys website (www.losdisneys.com) discussed further in chapter 7.

37 *Cast Member's Handbook*, Walt Disney Company publication.

38 Kuenz talked to one worker who spends much of his time during the summer driving around the park, picking up passed-out characters. See Kuenz, "Working at the Rat," pp. 134–7; Zibart, *Unofficial® Disney Companion*, p. 182.

39 Wayne Ellwood, "Service with a Smile," *New Internationalist*, Dec. 1998, p. 17.

40 Kuenz, "Working at the Rat," p. 117.

41 http://www.VaultReports.com/links/Disney.

42 Ellwood, "Service with a Smile," p. 18, claims that two-thirds of the workers at the park make $6.57 an hour or less.

43 "Top Dogs Should Toss their Workers a Bone," *Los Angeles Times*, 10 Mar. 1996, p. D–2.

44 Kuenz, "Working at the Rat," p. 122.

45 Ibid., pp. 119–20.

46 Ibid., p. 117.

47 Jon Lewis, "Disney after Disney: Family Business and the Business of Family," in *Disney Discourse: Producing the Magic Kingdom*, ed. Eric Smoodin (New York: Routledge, 1994), p. 94, reports that turnover at the lower

management level is encouraged, to bring in fresh and enthusiastic new employees.

48 Zibart, *Unofficial® Disney Companion*, p. 177.

49 In addition, Hollywood film companies such as Disney have taken advantage of non-union production, although there are differing reports as to its prevalence. According to IATSE reports, 65 percent of films produced in Southern California in 1989 were made with non-union crews. More recently, IATSE claimed that only 31 percent (121 out of 400) of the pictures released in the USA in 1993 were made with union labor; in 1992, 109 out of 390 flms (27.9 percent) released were produced by union workers. See Janet Wasko, "Challenges to Hollywood's Labor Force in the 1990s," in *Global Productions*, ed. Sussman and Lent, p. 178–9.

50 See "Actors' Equity Concludes Initial Accord Covering Performers at Walt Disney World," *Daily Labor Report*, no. 166 (1990), p. A-7.

51 Walt Disney World College Program material, "Human Resources," p. 5.

52 Harry Bernstein, "Hollywood May Take the Drama Out of Settling Disputes," *Los Angeles Times*, 11 Apr. 1989, p. 1.

53 http://www.VaultReports.com/links/Disney.

54 Lewis, "Disney after Disney," p. 94.

55 More examples are discussed by Lewis, "Disney after Disney," pp. 87–94, and Ronald Grover, *The Disney Touch* (Homewood, Ill.: Business One Irwin, 1991), pp. 237–54.

56 Quote from "Suing Disney is Like Suing God in the Vatican," *San Diego Union Tribune*, 5 Mar. 1985, p. D–1.

57 Lewis, "Disney after Disney," pp. 89–90.

58 Paul Richter, "Disney's Tough Tactics," *Los Angeles Times*, 8 July 1990, p. D–1.

59 Christopher Knowlton, "How Disney Keeps the Magic Going," *Fortune*, Dec. 1989, p. 128.

60 For discussions of the historical background of the relationship between Hollywood and the US government, see the various studies by Thomas H. Guback, including *The International Film Industry: Western Europe and America since 1945* (Bloomington, Ind.: Indiana University Press, 1969); "Non-Market Factors in the International Distribution of American Films," in *Current Research in Film*, vol. 1, ed. Bruce A. Austin (Norwood, N.J.: Ablex, 1985), pp. 111–26.

61 See Janet Wasko, *Hollywood in the Information Age*, pp. 229–33.

62 See Janet Wasko, "Jurassic Park and the GATT: Hollywood and Europe— An Update," in *Democracy and Communication in the New Europe: Change and Continuity in East and West*, ed. Farrel Corcoran and Paschal Preston (Cresskill, N.J.: Hampton Press, 1995), pp. 157–74.

63 See Shawn Tully, "The Real Estate Coup at Euro Disneyland," *Fortune*, 28 Apr. 1986; Barry James, "Not without Qualms, France Cedes Space to Disney's World," *International Herald Tribune*, 9 Apr. 1992.

64 "Business Browser," *Arizona Republic*, 14 Sept. 1999, p. E2.
65 See Sussman and Lent (eds), *Global Productions*, for more discussion of trends in globalization of labor in communication and media industries.
66 James F. Tracy, "Whistle While You Work: The Disney Company and the Global Division of Labor," *Journal of Communication Inquiry*, 23, 4 (1999), pp. 374–90.
67 Murray MacAdam, "Working for the Rat," *New Internationalist*, Dec. 1998, pp. 15–17.
68 Tracy, "Whistle While You Work," p. 380.
69 Ibid., p. 386.
70 "100 Leading National Advertisers," *Advertising Age*, 28 Sept. 1998, pp. s3–s50.
71 "Top Global Marketers," *Advertising Age*, 9 Nov. 1998, pp. 15–20.
72 The Walt Disney Company, *1997 Annual Report*, p. 45.
73 Carl Hiassen, *Team Rodent: How Disney Devours the World* (New York: Ballantine, 1998), p. 60.
74 Don Groves, "Disney Goes Ape on Tarzan Dubs," *Daily Variety*, 14 June 1999, p. 12.
75 Personal correspondence, Oct. 1994.

Chapter 5 Analyzing the World According to Disney

1 See Kathy Merlock Jackson, *Walt Disney: A Bio-Bibliography* (Westport, Conn.: Greenwood Press, 1993), pp. 173–4, for references to early critical pieces on Disney animation.
2 See, e.g. Karl Erik Rosengren (ed.), *Advances in Content Analysis* (Beverly Hills, Calif.: Sage Publications, 1981); Klaus Krippendorf, *Content Analysis: An Introduction to its Methodology* (Beverly Hills, Calif.: Sage Publications, 1980).
3 For a review of different approaches to qualitative research in general, and textual analysis specifically, see Norman K. Denzin and Yvonna S. Lincoln (eds), *Handbook of Qualitative Research* (London: Sage Publications, 1994).
4 Leo Braudy and Marshall Cohen, *Film Theory and Criticism: Introductory Readings* (New York: Oxford University Press, 1999), pp. xv–xviii.
5 See Kathy Merlock Jackson, "Walt Disney: Its Persuasive Products and Cultural Contexts," *Journal of Popular Film and Television*, 24, 2 (1996), p. 50.
6 Robert Sklar, "The Making of Cultural Myths – Walt Disney," in *The American Animated Cartoon: A Critical Anthology*, ed. Danny Peary and Gerald Peary (New York: E. P. Dutton, 1980), pp. 58–65.
7 Richard Schickel, *The Disney Version: The Life, Times, Art and Commerce of Walt Disney* (New York: Simon & Schuster, 1968, repr. 1985), p. 154.
8 Ibid., pp. 153–5.

9   Robert Heide and John Gilman, *Disneyana: Classic Collectibles 1928–1958* (New York: Hyperion, 1995).

10 See Frank Thomas and Ollie Johnston, *Disney Animation: The Illusion of Life* (New York: Abbeville Press, 1984), and Christopher Finch, *The Art of Walt Disney: From Mickey Mouse to Magic Kingdoms* (New York: Harry N. Abrams, Inc., 1975).

11 Michael Real, *Mass-Mediated Culture* (Englewood Cliffs, N.J.: Prentice-Hall, 1973).

12 Jackson, *Walt Disney: A Bio-Bibliography*, p. 10.

13 For instance, see Chris Rojek, "Disney Culture," *Leisure Studies: The Journal of the Leisure Studies Association*, 12, 2 (Apr. 1993), pp. 121–9.

14 Timothy R. White, "From Disney to Warner Bros.: The Critical Shift," *Film Criticism*, 16, 3 (Spring 1992), pp. 3–16; Kevin Sandler, *Reading the Rabbit: Explorations in Warner Bros. Animation* (New Brunswick, N.J.: Rutgers University Press, 1998).

15 Steven Watts, *The Magic Kingdom: Walt Disney and the American Way of Life* (New York: Houghton Mifflin, 1997), pp. 104–5.

16 David Bordwell, Janet Staiger, and Kristin Thompson, *The Classical Hollywood Cinema: Film Style and Mode of Production to 1960* (New York: Columbia University Press, 1985), p. 35.

17 See Sandler, *Reading the Rabbit*, for a comparison of Warner Bros and Disney animation traditions.

18 Don Hahn, *Animation Magic: A Behind-the-Scenes Look at How an Animated Film is Made* (New York: Disney Press, 1996), p. 13.

19 Jason Cochran, "Sum of their Parts?," *Entertainment Weekly*, 6 Feb. 1998, pp. 64–5.

20 Some feminists agree with this reading, e.g., see Pamela Colby O'Brien, "The Happiest Films on Earth: A Textual and Contextual Analysis of Walt Disney's 'Cinderella' and 'The Little Mermaid'," *Women's Studies in Communication*, 19, 2 (1996), pp. 155–84; Marina Warner, "Beauty and the Beasts," *Sight and Sound*, 2, 6 (1992), pp. 6–12. However, other writers have argued that the more recent Disney heroines are more independent and thus more empowered than in the past. See Keisha L. Hoerrner, "Gender Roles in Disney Films: Analyzing Behaviors from Snow White to Simba," *Women's Studies in Communication*, 19, 2 (1996), pp. 213–29; Sharon D. Downey, "Feminine Empowerment in Disney's 'Beauty and the Beast'," *Women's Studies in Communication*, 19, 2 (1996), pp. 185–213.

21 Schickel, *Disney Version*, p. 156.

22 Joel Taxel, "A Literature Review of the Impact of Walt Disney Productions Inc. on American Popular Culture and Children's Literature," University of Georgia, Department of Language Education, 1982 (ERIC Document Reproduction Service, no. ED 213648, p. 14.

23 Marc Eliot, *Walt Disney, Hollywood's Dark Prince* (New York: Birch Lane Press, 1993) p. 72.

24 Frances Clarke Sayers and Charles M. Weisenberg, "Walt Disney Accused," *Horn Book Magazine*, Nov./Dec. 1965, pp. 602–11 at p. 610.

25 Henry A. Giroux, "Are Disney Movies Good for Your Kids?," in *Kinderculture: The Corporate Construction of Childhood*, ed. Shirley R. Steinberg, and Joe L. Kincheloe (Boulder, Colo.: Westview Press, 1997), pp. 119–31.

26 Hahn, *Animation Magic*, p. 20.

27 For example, see Tim O'Sullivan, John Hartley, Danny Saunders, Martin Montgomery, and John Fiske, *Key Concepts in Communication and Cultural Studies*, 2nd edn (London: Routledge, 1994).

28 See David Low, "Leonardo da Disney," *New Republic*, 5 Jan. 1942, pp. 16–18. Dorothy Grafly, "America's Youngest Art," *American Magazine of Art*, July 1933, p. 337.

29 Mark Langer, "Animatophilia, Cultural Production and Corporate Interests," in *A Reader in Animation Studies*, ed. Jayne Pilling (London: John Libbey, 1997), pp. 143–62.

30 Christopher Finch, *The Art of Walt Disney: From Mickey Mouse to Magic Kingdoms* (New York: Harry N. Abrams, Inc., 1975), p. 13.

31 Hahn, *Animation Magic*, p. 12.

32 See Watts, *Magic Kingdom*, p. 105.

33 Thomas and Johnston's *Disney Animation* has been called "the definitive text on Disney animation." Carl Barks, the main force behind the Donald Duck comics, also received more attention in the 1970s and 1980s, in such works as Michael Barrier, *Carl Barks and the Art of the Comic Book* (New York: M. Lilien, 1981). See Jackson, *Walt Disney: A Bio-Biography*, pp. 166–8, for sources on other Disney animators.

34 Cited in Watts, *Magic Kingdom*, p. 97.

35 Cited in Jackson, *Walt Disney: A Bio-Bibliography*, p. 109.

36 See Jay Leyda (ed.), *Eisenstein on Disney* (London: Methuen, 1988). Anne Nesbet, "Inanimations: 'Snow White' and 'Ivan the Terrible'," *Film Quarterly*, 50, 4 (1997), pp. 20–32, details how Eisenstein's *Ivan the Terrible*, in particular, was influenced by the music and techniques used in *Snow White*.

37 Watts, *Magic Kingdom*.

38 See Jackson, *Walt Disney: A Bio-Bibliography*, pp. 213–38.

39 Robert Feild, *The Art of Walt Disney* (New York: Macmillan, 1942). Watts, *Magic Kingdom*, pp. 101–2, describes how Feild was dismissed from the Art Department at Harvard University because of his attention to Disney's "art."

40 Alan Cholodenko (ed.) *The Illusion of Life: Essays on Animation* (Sydney: Power Publications, 1991); Langer, "Animatophilia."

41 Pilling, *Reader in Animation Studies*, p. xii.

42 Langer, "Animatophilia," p. 146. Langer cites examples of books that focus on the art of Walt Disney.

43 Langer's discussion of *Ren & Stimpy* indicates that the creators of the series and Nickelodeon had different ideas for the animated series. "Nickelodeon

looked towards Disney and Warner Bros. as models. Kricfalusi and his staff leaned towards the early Mad approach to culture" (ibid., p. 157).

44 Philip Kelly Denslow, "What is Animation and Who Needs to Know?," in ed. Pilling, *Reader in Animation Studies*, pp. 2–3.

45 Langer, "Animatophilia," p. 149.

46 Arata Isozaki, "Theme Park," *Southern Atlantic Quarterly*, 92, 1 (1993), pp. 175–82.

47 Jackson, *Walt Disney: A Bio-Bibliography*, pp. 181–3, lists some of the most important articles written about The Mouse since his appearance in the late 1920s.

48 For a useful summary of Benjamin's references to Disney, see Miriam Hansen, "Of Mice and Ducks: Benjamin and Adorno on Disney," *Southern Atlantic Quarterly*, 92, 1 (Winter 1993), pp. 27–61. Erich Fromm, *Escape from Freedom* (New York: Farrar and Rinehart, 1941). See also Mary Bancroft, "Of Mouse and Man," *Psychological Perspectives*, Fall 1978, pp. 115–24; and John Murray, "Mickey Mouse: A Brief Psychohistory," *Television and Children*, Summer 1983, pp. 28–35.

49 See Bob Thomas, *Disney's Art of Animation: From Mickey Mouse to Hercules* (New York: Hyperion, 1992, repr. 1997), p. 12.

50 Robert W. Brockway, "The Masks of Mickey Mouse: Symbol of a Generation," *Journal of Popular Culture*, 22 (Spring 1989), pp. 25–34. Neoteny is also discussed in Stephen Jay Gould, "Mickey Mouse Meets Konrad Lorenz," *Natural History*, May 1979, pp. 30–5.

51 Elizabeth A. Lawrence, "In the Mick of Time: Reflections on Disney's Ageless Mouse," *Journal of Popular Culture*, Fall 1986, pp. 65–72.

52 See Jill May, "Walt Disney's Interpretation of Children's Literature," *Language Arts*, 58, 4 (1981), pp. 463–72.

53 Sayers and Weisenberg, "Walt Disney Accused," p. 610. For an opposing view, see Robert T. Sidwell, "Naming Disney's Dwarfs," *Children's Literature in Education*, Summer 1980, pp. 69–75.

54 Sayers and Weisenberg, "Walt Disney Accused."

55 May, "Walt Disney's Interpretation," p. 465. See also Jill May, "Butchering Children's Literature," *Film Library Quarterly*, 11, 1 and 2 (1978), pp. 55–62; and Lucy Rollin, "Fear of Faerie: Disney and the Elitist Critics," *Children's Literature Association Quarterly*, 12 (1987), pp. 90–3.

56 Jack Zipes, "Breaking the Disney Spell," in *From Mouse to Mermaid: The Politics of Film, Gender, and Culture*, ed. Elizabeth Bell, Lynda Haas, and Laura Sells (Bloomington, Ind.: Indiana University Press, 1995), p. 40.

57 Colin Sparks, "From the Hundred Aker Wood to The Magic Kingdom," Professorial Lecture Series, University of Westminster, 14 Oct. 1998.

58 Ariel Dorfman and Armand Mattelart, *How to Read Donald Duck* (New York: International General, 1975), p. 35.

59 Zipes, "Breaking the Disney Spell," p. 39.

60 Zipes discusses the Disney version of *Puss in Boots* as an example; ibid., pp. 31–3.

61 List based on ibid., pp. 39–40.

62 Other writers have addressed the role that Disney products play in children's education; e.g., see Henry A. Giroux, *The Mouse that Roared: Disney and the End of Innocence* (Lanham, Md.: Rowman & Littlefield, 1999); A. R. Ward, "Lion King's Mythic Narrative: Disney as Moral Educator," *Journal of Popular Film and Television*, 23, 4 (1996), pp. 171–81; Joel Sisenwine, "Aladdin, The Lion King, and Jewish Values: What is Walt Disney Teaching our Children?," *Jewish Spectator*, 59, 3 (Winter 1995), pp. 9–12.

63 Zipes, "Breaking the Disney Spell," p. 34.

64 Kay Stone, "Three Transformations of Snow White," in *The Brothers Grimm and Folktale*, ed. James M. McGlathery (Champaign, Ill.: University of Illinois Press, 1988), pp. 52–65.

65 Ibid., p. 60.

66 Zipes, "Breaking the Disney Spell," p. 39.

68 Terri Martin Wright, "Romancing the Tale: Walt Disney's Adaptation of the Grimm's 'Snow White'," *Journal of Popular Film and Video*, 25, 3 (1997), pp. 98–109.

68 See Sara Halprin, "Beauty as White as Snow," in *"Look at My Ugly Face!" Myths and Musings on Beauty and Other Perilous Obsessions with Women's Appearance* (New York: Viking, 1995), ch. 2.

69 Gaye Tuchman, "The Symbolic Annihilation of Women by the Mass Media," in *The Manufacture of News*, ed. Jock Young and S. Cohen (London: Constable, 1981), pp. 134–49.

70 See H. Leslie Steeves, "Feminist Theories and Media Studies," *Critical Studies in Mass Communication*, 4, 2 (1987), pp. 95–135; L. Van Zoonen, "Feminist Perspectives on the Media," in *Mass Media and Society*, ed. James Curran and Michael Gurevitch (London: Edward Arnold, 1996), pp. 31–52.

71 See Dominic Strinati, *An Introduction to Theories of Popular Culture* (London: Routledge, 1995), ch. 5.

72 An entire issue of *Women's Studies in Communication* (Summer 1996) is devoted to feminist analysis of Disney products. A number of other works that address feminist issues but are not cited specifically in this discussion include Gayanne Ramsden, "Sleeping Beauty as a Case Study of the Demonic and the Carnivalesque Grotesque" (Ph.D. dissertation, Brigham Young University, 1992); P. Tabor Dyke, "Recurring Images from Past to Present: Feminist Consciousness and Disney's 'New' Heroine" (unpublished honors thesis, Arizona State University, 1990); C. A. Stanger, "*Winnie the Pooh* through a Feminist Lens," *Lion and the Unicorn*, 11, 2 (1987), pp. 34–50.

73 Kay Stone, "Things Walt Disney Never Told Us," *Journal of American Folklore*, 88 (1975), pp. 42–50 at pp. 44, 45.

74 Hoerrner, "Gender Roles in Disney Films."

75 Zipes, "Breaking the Disney Spell," p. 40.

76 Giroux, *The Mouse that Roared*, p. 99.

77 Roberta Trites, "Disney's Sub/Version of Anderson's *The Little Mermaid*," *Journal of Popular Film and Television* 18, 4 (Winter 1991), p. 150.

78 Ibid., p. 152.

79 Laura Sells, "Where do Mermaids Stand?," in *From Mouse to Mermaid*, ed. Bell, Haas, and Sells, pp. 176–7.

80 Ibid., p. 181. For other readings of *The Little Mermaid*, see James Livingston, "What does a Mermaid Want?," *Cineaste*, 18, 1 (1990), pp. 17–20; Susan White, "Split Skins: Female Agency and Bodily Mutilation in *The Little Mermaid*," in *Film Theory Goes to the Movies*, ed. Jim Collins, Hilary Radner, and Ava Preacher Collins (New York: Routledge, 1993), pp. 182–95; E. Tseelon, "*The Little Mermaid*: An Icon of Woman's Condition in Patriarchy and the Human Condition of Castration," *International Journal of Psychoanalysis*, 76 (1995), pp. 1017–30.

81 Trites, "Disney's Sub/Version," p. 150.

82 Niels and Faith Ingwersen, "Splash!: Six Views of 'The Little Mermaid': A Folktale/Disney Approach," *Scandinavian Studies*, 62 (1990), pp. 403–29.

83 See Tim O'Sullivan et al., *Key Concepts in Communication*, for more detailed discussion of these approaches.

84 Michael Brody, "The Wonderful World of Disney—Its Psychological Appeal," *American Imago* 33 (1976), pp. 350–60; Schickel, *Disney Version*; Bruce MacCurdy, "The Child Hero in Walt Disney's *Snow White*, *Pinocchio*, and the 'Sorcerer's Apprentice' Sequence of *Fantasia*," (Ph.D. dissertation, Syracuse University, 1983). See also Richard Schickel, "The Films: No Longer for the Jung at Heart," *Time*, 30 July 1973.

85 Other interpretations of Pinocchio include Jack Zipes, "Towards a Theory of the Fairy-Tale Film and Carlo Collodi and Walt Disney: The Case of Pinocchio," *Lion and the Unicorn*, 20, 1 (1996), pp. 1–24; J. Stone, "Pinocchio and Pinocchiology," *American Imago*, 51, 3 (1994), pp. 329–42; J. M. Brandon, "Pinocchio's Progeny: Puppets, Marionettes, Automatons, and Robots in Modernist and Avant-Garde Drama," *Theatre Studies*, 42 (1997), pp. 99–100.

86 Brody, "Wonderful World of Disney," p. 354.

87 David Berland, "Disney and Freud: Walt Meets the Id," *Journal of Popular Culture*, no. 22 (Spring 1982), pp. 93–104.

88 For overviews of issues relating to race and the media, see Clint C. Wilson II and Félix Gutierrez, *Race, Multiculturalism, and the Media* (Thousand Oaks, Calif.: Sage Publications, 1995); Gail Dines and Jean M. Humez (eds), *Gender, Race and Class in Media* (Thousand Oaks, Calif.: Sage Publications, 1995).

89 Betsy Sharkey, "Beyond Teepees and Totem Poles," *New York Times*, 11 June 1995, sec. 2, p. 2.

90 Russell Means, quoted ibid.

91 Schickel, *Disney Version*, p. 95.

92 Thomas St John, "Walter Elias Disney: The Cartoon as Race Fantasy," *Ball State University Forum*, June 1981, p. 64.

93 Schickel, *Disney Version*, p. 176.

94 See Peggy A. Russo, "Uncle Walt's Uncle Remus: Disney's Distortion of Harris's Hero," *Southern Literary Journal*, 25, 1 (1992), pp. 19–33; James Snead, "Trimming Uncle Remus's Tales: Narrative Revisions in Walt Disney's *Song of the South*," in *White Screens/Black Images: Hollywood from the Dark Side*, ed. Colin MacCabe and Cornel West (New York: Routledge, 1994); and *idem*, "Everything is Not Satisfactual," in *Ceramic Uncles and Celluloid Mammies: Black Images and Their Influence on Culture*, ed. Patricia A. Turner (New York: Anchor, 1994), pp. 5–19.

95 Quoted in Sharkey, "Beyond Teepees." One exception is Margaret J. King's article, "The Recycled Hero: Walt Disney's Davy Crockett," in *Davy Crockett: The Man, the Legend, the Legacy 1786–1986*, ed. Michael Lofaro (Knoxville, Tenn.: University of Tennessee Press, 1985), pp. 137–57.

96 The offending lyrics were in the opening song, "Arabian Nights": "I come from a land / From a faraway place / Where the caravan camels roam. / Where they cut off your ears / If they don't like your face. / It may be barbaric, but hey, it's home."

97 Erin Addison, "Saving Other Women from Other Men: Disney's *Aladdin*," *Camera Obscura*, no. 31 (1993), pp. 4–25.

98 Ibid., p. 19.

99 Leslie Felperin Sharman, "New Aladdins for Old," *Sight and Sound*, 3, 11 (1993), pp. 12–15.

100 Gary Edgerton and Kathy Merlock Jackson, "Redesigning Pocahontas: Disney, the 'White Man's Indian,' and the Marketing of Dreams," *Journal of Popular Film and Television*, 24, 2 (1996), pp. 90–9.

101 See Kellee Weinhold, "A Cultural Analysis of *The Lion King*" (unpublished paper, University of Oregon, 1997).

102 Sharkey, "Beyond Teepees."

103 Edgerton and Jackson, "Redesigning Pocahontas," p. 90.

104 This remark was actually used by the company to promote the film in some markets. See Jacquelyn Kilpatrick, "Disney's 'Politically Correct' Pocahontas," *Cineaste*, 21, 4 (1995), pp. 36–8.

105 Edgerton and Jackson, "Redesigning Pocahontas," p. 92.

106 Derek T. Buescher, "Civilized Colonialism: 'Pocahontas' as Neocolonial Rhetoric," *Women's Studies in Communication*, 19, 2 (1996), pp. 127–54.

107 Kilpatrick, "Disney's 'Politically Correct' Pocahontas," p. 37.

108 With the emphasis on Pocahontas as the main character and the preponderance of love songs, some young boys reportedly had a hard time staying awake.

109 Edgerton and Jackson, "Redesigning Pocahontas," p. 99. See also Kathleen Merlock Jackson, "Walt Disney: Its Persuasive Products and Cultural Con-

texts," *Journal of Popular Film and Television*, 24, 2 (1996), pp. 50–3, and Kathi Maio, "*Pocahontas*: Disney Does It (to Us) Again," *Sojourner*, 20, 12 (Winter 1995), pp. 27–34.

110   Don Lazere, "Mass Culture, Political Consciousness and English Studies," *College English*, 38 (April 1977), p. 755.

111   David Kunzle, introduction to Dorfman and Mattelart, *How to Read Donald Duck*, p. 12.

112   The English version of the book cites the Center for Constitutional Rights' lawyers who defended the publisher: "the seizure of the books is a classic case of abuse of the laws to suppress political dissent and unpopular opinions." Ibid., p. 1.

113   Kunzle, introduction to Dorfman and Mattelart, *How to Read Donald Duck*, p. 14.

114   See Julianne Burton-Carvajal, " 'Surprise Package': Looking Southward with Disney," in *Disney Discourse: Producing the Magic Kingdom*, ed. Eric Smoodin (New York: Routledge, 1994), 131–47; José Piedra, "Pato Donald's Gender Ducking," in *Disney Discourse*, ed. Eric Smoodin, pp. 148–68; Mitsuhiro Yoshimoto, "Images of Empire: Tokyo Disneyland and Japanese Cultural Imperialism," in *Disney Discourse*, ed. Smoodin, pp. 181–202.

115   Dorfman and Mattelart, *How to Read Donald Duck*, p. 48.

116   Ibid., pp. 61–4.

117   Ibid., p. 66.

118   Kunzle, introduction to ibid., p. 11.

119   The Ducks have also been featured in the syndicated television cartoon series, *Duck Tales*, which appeared in 1987. For some of the background on the series, see the special *Duck Tales* issue of *Duckburg Times*, nos 24/25 (1 Aug. 1992).

120   Among the works on Disney comics are Frank Reilly, "The Walt Disney Comic Strips," *Cartoon Profiles*, Winter 1969, pp. 14–18; Stan Molson, "Disney Comics in the Seventies," *Comic Art News and Reviews*, 1974, pp. 4–7; David Kunzle, "Dispossessed by Ducks: The Imperialist Treasure Hunt in Southeast Asia," *Art Journal*, 49 (Summer 1990), pp. 159–66; Dave Wagner, "Donald Duck: An Interview," *Radical America*, 7, 1 (1973), pp. 1–19; Mike Barrier, "The Duck Man," in *The Comic-Book Book*, ed, Don Thompson and Dick Lupoff, (New York: Arlington, 1973), pp. 302–21; Martin Barker, *Comics: Ideology, Power and the Critics* (Manchester: Manchester University Press, 1989); and Reinhold Reitberger and Wolfgang Fuchs, *Comics: The Anatomy of a Mass Medium* (Boston: Little, Brown, 1972).

121   See, e.g., William Paul, "Art, Music and Nature," *Movie*, 24 (Spring 1977), pp. 44–52. *Bambi* is considered in A. Waller Hastings, "Bambi and the Hunting Ethos," *Journal of Popular Film and Television*, 24, 2 (1996), pp. 53–60; Ralph H. Lutts, "The Trouble with *Bambi*: Walt Disney's *Bambi* and the American Vision of Nature," *Forest and Conservation History*, 36 (Oct. 1992), pp. 160–71; and Ollie Johnson and Frank Thomas, *Walt Disney's*

Bambi: The Story and the Film (New York: Stewart, Tobori, and Chang, 1990). Other interesting analyses of Disney's representation of nature in animated work include Peter Vujakovic, "The Nature of Fantasy," *Geographical Magazine*, 68, 3 (1996), pp. 18–21, which examines why viewers have strong emotional reactions to Disney's landscapes.

122 Schickel, *Disney Version*, pp. 12–13. The Disney company's educational products have expanded greatly, as has the company's interaction with educational institutions. Disney's website pitches a wide range of educational products and services for teachers and parents.

123 Leonard Maltin, *The Disney Films* (New York: Crown, 1973), p. 276; Bob Thomas, *Walt Disney: An American Original* (New York: Simon & Schuster, 1976), p. 249.

124 Cited in Jackson, *Walt Disney: A Bio-Bibliography*, p. 81. For another positive assessment of the educational potential of the *True-Life Adventures*, see Robert De Roos, "The Magic Worlds of Walt Disney," *National Geographic*, Aug. 1963, pp. 159–207.

125 Jack Alexander, "The Amazing Story of Walt Disney, Part II," *Saturday Evening Post*, 7 Nov. 1953, p. 26.

126 Margaret J. King, "The Audience in the Wilderness: The Disney Nature Films," *Journal of Popular Film and Television*, 24, 2 (1996), pp. 60–9.

127 Maltin, *Disney Films*, p. 19.

128 Cited in Jackson, *Walt Disney: A Bio-Bibliography*, p. 186. For more on Disney's own views on these films, see his essays, "Why I Like Making Nature Films," *Woman's Home Companion*, May 1954, pp. 38–9; and "What I've Learned from the Animals," *American Magazine*, Feb. 1953, pp. 22–3.

129 Jackson, *Walt Disney: A Bio-Bibliography*, p. 87.

130 Rick Barry, "Lemmings Myth Debunked—The True Story Behind Disney's Not-So True-Life Adventure," *Tampa Times*, 29 Jan. 1978, pp. 13–14.

131 Kenneth Brower, "Photography in the Age of Falsification," *Atlantic Monthly*, May 1998, p. 108. For more on photofakery, see Tom Wheeler, *Phototruth or Photofiction? Ethics and Media Imagery in the Digital Age* (New York: NTC/ Contemporary, 2001).

132 Schickel, *Disney Version*, pp. 290–1.

133 Cited, ibid., p. 245.

134 King, "Audience in the Wilderness," p. 64.

135 Ibid., p. 60.

136 Ibid., p. 63.

137 Thanks to Susan Davis for sharing this insight.

138 Herbert I. Schiller, *The Mind Managers* (Boston: Beacon Press, 1973), p. 99.

Chapter 6   Dissecting Disney's Worlds

1 An exclamation sometimes made by athletes and teams during interviews after winning championship games or tournaments. Arrangements for pay-

ment (as high as $60,000) are made with the athletes by the Disney company *before* the game is played.

2 Richard Schickel, *The Disney Version: The Life, Times, Art and Commerce of Walt Disney* (New York: Simon & Schuster, 1968, repr. 1985), p. 13.

3 Alexander Wilson, "The Betrayal of the Future: Walt Disney's EPCOT Center," in *Disney Discourse: Producing the Magic Kingdom*, ed. Eric Smoodin (New York: Routledge, 1994), pp. 118–30.

4 Judith A. Adams, *The American Amusement Park Industry: A History of Technology and Thrills* (Boston: Twayne Publishers, 1991), pp. 57–67; also Susan G. Davis, *Spectacular Nature: Corporate Culture and the Sea World Experience* (Berkeley: University of California Press, 1997), pp. 20–1.

5 Alan Bryman, "The Disneyization of Society," *Sociological Review*, 47, 1 (1999), pp. 25–35, at p. 30.

6 Davis, *Spectacular Nature*, p. 25.

7 Schickel, *Disney Version*, p. 236. Karal Ann Marling, "Disneyland, 1955," *American Art*, 5 (Winter/Spring 1991), pp. 188–92, includes a studio sketch for a "magical little park," as well as a photo from the Disneylandia project.

8 See Richard J. Barnet and John Cavanaugh, *Global Dreams: Imperial Corporations and the New World Order* (New York: Simon & Schuster, 1994), ch. 1; Davis, *Spectacular Nature*; Adams, *American Amusement Park Industry*.

9 Marling, "Disneyland, 1955," pp. 180–5. Also see Davis, *Spectacular Nature*, pp. 20–1.

10 Stephen F. Mills, "Disney and the Promotion of Synthetic Worlds," *American Studies International*, 28, 2 (1990), pp. 66–78.

11 There are numerous tourist guides to the Disney worlds, such as Stephen Birnbaum (ed.), *Birnbaum's Walt Disney World* (New York: Hyperion and Hearst Business Publishing, 1995). Steven Fjellman, *Vinyl Leaves: Walt Disney World and America* (Boulder, Colo.: Westview Press, 1992), provides a detailed description of Disney World, as well as an analysis of its significance; while Alan Bryman in *Disney and his Worlds* (London: Routledge, 1995) includes a chapter that briefly describes the basic features of the Disney parks.

12 Shelton Waldrep, "Monuments to Walt," in *Inside the Mouse: Work and Play at Disney World*, ed. Project on Disney (Durham, N.C.: Duke University Press, 1995), p. 203, notes that analysis of Disney's rapidly expanding resort facilities outside the theme parks is lacking, although his article is a good beginning for such research.

13 Greil Marcus, in "Forty Years of Overstatement: Criticism and the Disney Theme Parks," in *Designing Disney's Theme Parks*, ed. Karal Ann Marling, pp. 201–7, chastises theme park critics for producing "treatises" that are "polemical, ideological, or merely self-congratulatory, smug . . ."

14 Julian Halévy, "Disneyland and Las Vegas," *The Nation*, 7 June 1958. Schickel calls the article "an annoyingly attitudinizing piece" in his annotated bibliography (*Disney Version*, p. 370).

15 Schickel, *Disney Version*, pp. 295–337.

16 Herbert I. Schiller, *The Mind Managers* (Boston: Beacon Press, 1973); Michael Real, *Mass-Mediated Culture* (Englewood Cliffs, N.J.: Prentice-Hall, 1973).

17 *Journal of Popular Culture*, Summer 1981; also Umberto Eco, *Travels in Hyperreality* (New York: Harvest/HBJ, 1983); Jean Baudrillard, *Simulations* (Brooklyn, NY: Autonomedia, 1997).

18 Some examples include *Inside the Mouse*, ed. Projection Disney; Mills, "Disney and the Promotion"; Fjellman, *Vinyl Leaves*; Alexander Moore, "Walt Disney World: Bounded Ritual Space and the Playful Pilgrimage," *Anthropological Quarterly* 53 (1980), pp. 207–18; Mike Wallace, *Mickey Mouse History and Other Essays on American Memory* (Philadelphia: Temple University Press, 1996); Alexander Wilson, *The Culture of Nature: North American Landscape from Disney to the Exxon Valdez* (Toronto: Behind the Lines, 1991); Sonja and Ann Gill Foss, "Michel Foucault's Theory of Rhetoric as Epistemic," *Western Journal of Speech Communicaton*, 51 (Fall 1987), pp. 384–401; Arata Isozaki, "Theme Park," *South Atlantic Quarterly* 92, 1 (1993), pp. 175–82; Michael Sorkin, "See You in Disneyland," in *Variations on a Theme Park: The New American City and the End of Public Space*, ed. Michael Sorkin (New York: Hill and Wang, 1992).

19 Bryman, *Disney and his Worlds*, p. 82, also notes that the parks may differ in some ways, as well as change over time, but one can still identify ongoing themes that apply to all of them.

20 For a discussion of Disneyland and television, see Marling, "Disneyland, 1955," pp. 204–5.

21 Susan G. Davis, "Theme Park: Global Industry and Cultural Form," *Media, Culture & Society*, 18, 3 (1996), pp. 399–422.

22 Fjellman, *Vinyl Leaves*, p. 11.

23 Davis, *Spectacular Nature*, p. 24.

24 Schickel, *Disney Version*, p. 320.

25 Susan Willis, "Disney World: Public Use/Private State," *Southern Atlantic Quarterly*, 92, 1 (1993), p. 191.

26 Fjellman, *Vinyl Leaves*, pp. 178–83.

27 Alan Bryman, "The Disneyization of Society," *Sociological Review*, 47, 1 (1999), p. 156.

28 Ibid., pp. 165–9.

29 Alexander Wilson, "Technological Utopias," *Southern Atlantic Quarterly*, 92, 1 (1993), pp. 157–73.

30 Fjellmann, *Vinyl Leaves*, p. 181.

31 Wallace, *Mickey Mouse History*, p. 140. See also Fjellman, *Vinyl Leaves*, pp. 80–4.

32 Cited in Wallace, *Mickey Mouse History*, p. 144.

33 Fjellman, *Vinyl Leaves*, p. 9.

34 Ann Oldenburg, "Spending a Fortune for Fun: The Cost of Entertainment is Rising," *USA Today*, 2 Apr. 1999, p. 1E, cites a US Labor Department survey.

35 "Empire of the Sun," *US News & World Report*, 28 May 1990, p. 48.

36 Adams, *American Amusement Park Industry*, pp. 102–4.

37 Fjellman, *Vinyl Leaves*, p. 10.

38 Bryman, *Disney and his Worlds*, pp. 95–8, presents these two variations on the pilgrimage theme as discussed in M. J. King, "McDonald's and Disney," in *Ronald Revisited: The World of Ronald McDonald*, ed. M. Fishwick (Bowling Green, Oh.: Bowling Green University Press, 1983), pp. 106–19; Moore, "Walt Disney World," pp. 207–18; Fjellman, *Vinyl Leaves*; and Pauline Hunt and Ronald Frankenberg, "It's a Small World: Disneyland, the Family and Multiple Re-representations of American Childhood," in *Constructing and Reconstructing Childhood: Contemporary Issues in the Sociological Study of Childhood*, ed. Allison James and Alan Prout (London: Falmer Press, 1990), pp. 99–117.

39 Bryman, *Disney and his Worlds*, p. 98.

40 Adams, *American Amusement Park Industry*, p. 154.

41 The company now offers tours of these facilities, called "Keys to the Kingdom" or "Backstage Magic." See Eve Zibart, *The Unofficial® Disney Companion* (New York: Macmillan, 1997), pp. 80–3.

42 Ibid., pp. 82–3.

43 Birnbaum (ed.), *Birnbaum's Walt Disney World*, p. 94.

44 *1999 Open Enrollment Catalog, Business & Management Programs, Disney Institute*. See also Bill Copodagli and Lynn Jackson, *The Disney Way: Harnessing the Management Secrets of Disney in Your Company* (New York: McGraw-Hill, 1999).

45 "Disney Culture Covers the Globe," *Arizona Republic*, 23 Apr. 1994, p. A8.

46 Hunt and Frankenberg, "It's a Small World," p. 109.

47 Carl Hiassen, *Team Rodent: How Disney Devours the World* (New York: Ballantine, 1998), p. 49. Perhaps this is why there is alarm at reports of accidents at the parks; it also explains (in part) the company's attempts to cover them up, as Hiassen and other authors report.

48 Willis, "Disney World," pp. 195–6, relates another experience with a "disassembled character."

49 See Adams, *American Amusement Park Industry*, p. 97; Fjellman, *Vinyl Leaves*, pp. 12–13.

50 Bryman, *Disney and his Worlds*, pp. 99–117.

51 Zibart, *Unofficial® Disney Companions*, p. 84, describes a few of Disney's "smellitzers," including sulphur around the volcanoes at the Universe of Energy and chocolate chip cookies near the shop that sells them on Main Street.

52 Bryman, *Disney and his Worlds*, p. 100.

53 Eco, *Travels in Hyperreality*, p. 48.

54 Tom Carson, "To Disneyland," LA *Los Angeles Weekly*, 27 Mar.–2 Apr. 1992, pp. 17–26, at p. 17.

55 Hunt and Frankenberg, "It's a Small World," pp. 110–11.

56 Steve Nelson, "Reel Life Performance: The Disney–MGM Studios," *TDR: The Drama Review*, 34, 4 (1990), pp. 60–78, at p. 77.
57 Hunt and Frankenberg, "It's a Small World," p. 115.
58 Fjellman, *Vinyl Leaves*, p. 270.
59 Bryman, *Disney and his Worlds*, p. 107.
60 See Sorkin, "See You in Disneyland," p. 228.
61 Jane Kuenz, "Working at the Rat," in *Inside the Mouse*, ed. Project on Disney, p. 115. See also Zibart, *Unofficial® Disney Companion*, pp. 182–3.
62 Kuenz, "Working at the Rat," p. 115.
63 Bryman, *Disney and his Worlds*, p. 113. See also Adams, *American Amusement Park Industry*, pp. 87–104.
64 Quoted in Hiassen, *Team Rodent*, p. 69.
65 Ibid., p. 18.
66 Ibid., pp. 70–2; Zibart, *Unofficial® Disney Companion*, pp. 162–5.
67 Hiassen, *Team Rodent*, p. 18, provides examples some of the WDW security forces' capers.
68 Wilson, "Technological Utopias," p. 166.
69 See Christopher Finch, *The Art of Walt Disney: From Mickey Mouse to Magic Kingdoms* (New York: Harry N. Abrams, Inc., 1975); Hunt and Frankenberg, "It's a Small World," pp. 103–4.
70 Fjellman, *Vinyl Leaves*, p. 64.
71 Hunt and Frankenberg, "It's a Small World," p. 107.
72 Adams, *American Amusement Park Industry*, p. 97.
73 Interviewed on ABC's *Monday Night Football*, 9 Mar. 1999.
74 Hunt and Frankenberg, "It's a Small World," p. 111, citing Bob Thomas, *Walt Disney: An American Original* (New York: Simon & Schuster, 1976), p. xv.
75 Hunt and Frankenberg, "It's a Small World," p. 116.
76 Cited in Wallace, *Mickey Mouse History*, p. 137.
77 Eco, *Travels in Hyperreality*, p. 43.
78 Wallace, *Mickey Mouse History*, pp. 140–2.
79 Birnbaum, *Birnbaum's Walt Disney World*, p. 154.
80 Wallace, *Mickey Mouse History*, pp. 152–3.
81 Michael L. Smith, cited in Adams, *American Amusement Park Industry*, p. 150.
82 Kuenz, "Working at the Rat," p. 78.
83 Bryman, *Disney and his Worlds*, p. 127.
84 Sorkin, "See You in Disneyland," p. 215.
85 Marling, "Disneyland, 1955," p. 176.
86 Fjellman, *Vinyl Leaves*, pp. 400–1.
87 Bryman, *Disney and his Worlds*, ch. 5.
88 David Harvey, *The Condition of Postmodernity* (Oxford: Basil Blackwell, 1989), p. 300.
89 Ibid., Baudrillard, *Simulations*, p. 23.

90   See Fjellman, *Vinyl Leaves*, p. 401.

91   Bryman, *Disney and his Worlds*, p. 173.

92   Baudrillard, *Simulations*, p. 25.

93   Bryman, *Disney and his Worlds*, p. 174.

94   S. Warren, "Disneyfication of the Metropolis: Popular Resistance in Seattle," *Journal of Urban Affairs*, 16 (1994), pp. 89–107.

95   Isozaki, "Theme Park," p. 176.

96   Linda Mack, "Themes Like Old Times," *Star Tribune*, 11 Jan. 1998, p. 9F.

97   Bryman, "Disneyization," p. 25.

98   Hiassen, *Team Rodent*, p. 52.

99   Michael Pollan, "Town-Building is no Mickey Mouse Operation," *New York Times*, 14 Dec. 1997, p. 56. Another visitor to Celebration was Andrew Ross, who wrote about his year-long stay in the planned community in *The Celebration Chronicles: Life, Liberty, and the Pursuit of Property Values in Disney's Celebration* (New York: Ballantine Books, 1999).

100 Pollan, "Town-Building."

101 Ibid.

102 Ibid.

103 Ibid.,

104 Douglas Frantz and Catherine Collins, *Celebration, U.S.A.* (New York: Henry Holt & Co., 1999), p. 119.

105 Pollan, "Town-Building."

106 David Kushner, "The Dog Ate My Hard Drive," *Spin*, Dec. 1998, pp. 118–21.

107 Susan G. Davis, "R&D for Social Life: Entertainment–Retail and the City," paper presented at Society for Cinema Studies Conference, San Diego, 1998.

Chapter 7   Disney and the World

1   Karl Marx and Frederick Engels, *The German Ideology, Part One* (New York: International Publishers, 1972), pp. 150–1.

2   Sergei Eisenstein, *Eisenstein on Disney*, ed. Jay Leyda, trans. Alan Upchurch (London: Methuen, 1988).

3   Christopher Finch, *The Art of Walt Disney: From Mickey Mouse to Magic Kingdoms* (New York: Harry N. Abrams, Inc., 1975), inside book jacket notes.

4   "Size Does Matter," *The Economist*, 23 May 1998, p. 57.

5   Vincent Mosco and Lewis Kaye, "Questioning the Concept of the Audience," in *Consuming Audiences? Production and Reception in Media Research*, ed. Ingunn Hagen and Janet Wasko (Cresskill, N.J.: Hampton Press, 1999), pp. 31–46.

6   Alan Bryman, "The Disneyization of Society," *Sociological Review*, 47, 1 (1999), p. 25.

7   T. L. Stanley, "Disney Pitch: 'Not Just Mickey Mouse'," *Brandweek*, 13 Feb. 1995, p. 18.

8   For a discussion of the development of Disney's version of Winnie the Pooh, see Colin Sparks, "From the Hundred Aker Wood to The Magic Kingdom," Professorial Lecture Series, University of Westminster, 14 Oct. 1998; also, A. Thwaite, *The Brilliant Career of Winnie-the-Pooh* (London: Methuen, 1992).

9   Jerry Hirsch, "Winnie the Pooh Gains Momentum across Disney Product Lines," *Knight–Ridder/Tribune Business News*, 4 Jan. 1999.

10 For instance, Shamus Culhane, *Talking Animals and Other People* (New York: St Martin's Press, 1986), pp. 113–14, and Leonard Maltin, *Of Mice and Magic: A History of American Animated Cartoons* (New York: New American Library, 1980), pp. 34–5.

11 Susan Ohmer, "Measuring Desire: Walt Disney and Audience Research in Animation," paper presented at Society for Cinema Studies conference, Washington, D.C., 1990, and *idem*, "Measuring Desire: George Gallup and Audience Research in Hollywood," *Journal of Film and Video*, 43, 1–2 (1991).

12 Ohmer, "Measuring Desire," p. 9.

13 See Justin Wyatt, *High Concept: Movies and Marketing in Hollywod* (Austin, Tex.: University of Texas Press, 1994), for a discussion of marketing techniques used by Hollywood companies. Another interesting discussion of film marketing is included in Martine Danan, "Marketing the Hollywood Blockbuster in France," *Journal of Popular Film and Television*, 23, 3 (1995), p. 131, which points out that marketing techniques no longer focus simply on the particular movie, but on "the public's receptiveness to advertising themes, trailers, posters, and other promotional materials, and helps devise effective campaigns geared toward film's potential audiences." Danan also notes the lack of cooperation from Disney in her study, citing an executive who "declared that it was a company-wide policy never to discuss its marketing decisions."

14 An example of these efforts is a request from a researcher at Nickelodeon, who expressed interest in an academic paper on Disney audiences, explaining that he was "interested in learning more about the methodologies you used and findings in your study of the 'meaning' of the Disney brand and how audiences relate to it. . . . We're periodically involved in studies looking at what our brand means to parent and kid audiences and it's always great to get methodological ideas."

15 Marc Fisher, "Mouse Ears on the AM Radio Dial," *Washington Post*, 29 July 1997, p. E07; Rachel X. Weissman, "Mouse in the House," *American Demographics*, Feb. 1999, p. 7.

16 See The Imagineers and C. E. Jones, *Walt Disney Imagineering: A Behind the Dreams Look at Making the Magic Real* (New York: Hyperion, 1998).

17 Eileen Murphy, "Videos are Good for Children, says Disney," *Newcastle Chronicle & Journal*, 5 June 1998, p. 18.

18 Roger Dickinson, Ramaswami Harindranath, and Olga Linné (eds), *Approaches to Audiences: A Reader* (London: Arnold, 1998), p. xi.

19 See Denis McQuail, *Mass Communication Theory*, 3rd edn (London: Sage Publications, 1994), for an overview of media research traditions.

20 Stuart Hall, Dorothy Hobson, Andrew Love, and Paul Willis (eds), *Culture, Media, Language: Working Papers in Cultural Studies, 1972–79* (Boston: Unwin Hyman, 1980).

21 John Hartley and John Fiske, *Reading Television* (London: Methuen, 1978).

22 Martin Barker and Kate Brooks, "On Looking into Bourdieu's Black Box," in *Approaches to Audiences*, ed. Dickinson et al., pp. 218–32.

23 David Buckingham, "Dissin' Disney: Critical Perspectives on Children's Media Culture," *Media, Culture and Society*, 19, 2 (Apr. 1997), pp. 285–93, at p. 291. Alan Bryman, *Disney and his Worlds* (London: Routledge, 1995), also notes that analyses of the Disney theme parks have been "fatally flawed" without the perspectives of park visitors (p. 184).

24 For example, see David Buckingham, *Moving Images: Understanding Children's Emotional Responses to Television* (Manchester: Manchester University Press, 1996). Edited collections that present overviews of this work include Henry Jenkins (ed.), *The Children's Culture Reader* (New York: New York University Press, 1998); C. Bazalgette and David Buckingham (eds), *In Front of the Children* (London: British Film Institute, 1995); David Buckingham (ed.), *Reading Audiences: Young People and the Media* (Manchester: Manchester University Press, 1993). For a critique of this body of research, see David Buckingham, "Children and Television: A Critical Overview of the Research," in *Approaches to Audiences*, ed. Dickinson et al., pp. 131–46.

25 Michael Real, *Mass-Mediated Culture* (Englewood Cliffs, N.J.: Prentice-Hall, 1973).

26 Ibid., p. 84.

27 Kay Stone, "Things Walt Disney Never Told Us," *Journal of American Folklore*, 88 (1975), pp. 42–50.

28 Jill May, "Walt Disney's Interpretation of Children's Literature," *Language Arts*, 58, 4 (1981), pp. 463–72.

29 This unpublished study was conducted with the assistance of Mark Phillips.

30 Janet Wasko, Mark Phillips, and Eileen Meehan, *Dazzled by Disney?: The Global Disney Audience Project* (London: University of Leicester Press, 2001).

31 The author obtained approval from the students to use excerpts (anonymously) from some of these assignments.

32 In marketing research, it has been suggested that consumers above median usage of a given product – the "heavy half" – account for a disproportionate percentage of product purchases, like 80–90 percent of total volume. This is sometimes called the 80–20 rule. See Dik Warren Twedt, "Some Practical Applications of 'Heavy-Half' Theory," in *Market Segmentation: Concepts and Applications*, ed. James F. Engel, Henry F. Fiorillo, and Murray A. Cayley (New York: Holt, Rinehart, Winston, 1972).

33 The examples used to illustrate these archetypes have been drawn from a variety of sources, including the Disney student confessions previously

discussed, articles in the popular press, website material, and personal interviews by the author.

34 Reiger has distributed a biographical sheet to the press with this information.

35 "Tattoo Enthusiast Takes His Shirt Off to Disney," Associated Press, 16 Feb. 1993.

36 http://disney.go.com/disneyatoz/fan/july.html, 9 July 1999.

37 The Walt Disney Company, *1998 Fact Book*, p. 8.

38 Another option is Aladdin's magic carpet. Despite the promotional promise of a Disney wedding that makes your dreams come true, there are a number of restrictions: weddings cannot be held when the park is open; you cannot wear your wedding gown in the park during the regular business day; and Mickey, Minnie, and the other characters are not permitted anywhere near the pavilion, although they can appear at the receptions. Kathy and Wilson Craig Kelly, "A Wedding Album from Walt Disney World Vows, Coach and a Castle," *USA Today*, 25 June 1997, p. 1E. Interestingly, about two-thirds of the wedding couples are from Japan.

39 Robert Heide and John Gilman, *Disneyana: Classic Collectibles 1928–1958* (New York: Hyperion, 1995), p. 7.

40 Ibid., pp. 11–12.

41 Richard deCordova, "The Mickey in Macy's Window: Childhood, Consumerism, and Disney Animation," in *Disney Discourse: Producing the Magic Kingdom*, ed. Eric Smoodin (New York: Routledge, 1994), pp. 203–13.

42 The terms "Donaldism" and "Donaldist" were first coined by Jon Gisle in *Donaldismen – en muntert-videnskabelig studie over Donald Duck og hans verden* (Oslo: Fakkel, 1973). For an interesting bibliography on Carl Barks, see http://www/seriesam.com/barks.

43 Search engines survey, 29 June 1999: sites with "Disney" in title (includes Disney company sites and other commercial sties) – Alta Vista, 1,679,820; Yahoo, 22 categories, 999 sites; HotBot, 266,340; Infoseek, 9,484,012.

44 For a discussion of fans and audience labor, see Eileen Meehan, "Commodity Audience, Actual Audience: The Blindspot Debate," in *Illuminating the Blindspots: Essays Honoring Dallas W. Smythe*, ed. Janet Wasko, Vincent Mosco, and Manjunath Pendakur (Norwood, N.J.: Ablex Publishing, 1993), pp. 378–97.

45 Barker and Brooks, "On Looking," p. 225, refer to the difficulty of investigating cinema-goers who invest little interest in their cinema experiences.

46 "The Mousetrap: Inside Disney's Dream Machine," *New Internationalist*, Dec. 1998.

47 Safran's video was sponsored by the Australian Broadcasting Company in its *Race Around the World* series designed to support amateur video producers.

48 Groups participating in the boycott included the American Family Association, Focus on the Family, and Concerned Women for America. Other groups launched pro-Disney crusades, including the Human Rights Campaign. An interesting primer on the boycott is Richard D. Land and Frank

D. Yorker, *Send a Message to Mickey: The ABC's of Making Your Voice Heard at Disney* (Nashville, Tenn.: Broadman & Holman Publishers, 1998).

49 At the end of a list of such issues, one of the sites exclaims: "AS YOU CAN SEE FROM THE ABOVE LINKS, DISNEY IS MORE THAN A COMPANY WHO PROMOTES HOMOSEXUALITY" (from the Official Disney Boycott Site, www.laker.net/webpage/Boycott.htm).

50 For instance, more than one (leftist) colleague sent the author references to citations about this issue from one of the boycott sites.

51 Craig Yoe and Janet Morra-Yoe (eds), *The Art of Mickey Mouse* (New York: Hyperion, 1991), inside book jacket notes. This volume includes 110 examples of well-known artists' interpretations of "the world's favorite mouse."

52 Susan Willis, "Disney World: Public Use/Private State," *Southern Atlantic Quarterly* 92, 1 (1993), pp. 119–37.

53 Karen Klugman, "Reality Revisited," *Southern Atlantic Quarterly*, 92, 1 (1993), pp. 7–25.

54 Charlie Christensen, *Arne Anka* (Stockholm: Tago Förlag, 1989). At least two other collections featuring Arne Anka were produced: *Bombad Och Säkt* and *Arne Anka Del III*.

55 Jamie Malanowski, "When Disney Ran America: A Speculative History of the Near Future," *Spy*, June 1991, pp. 36–43; Peter David , "But I Digress," *Comic Buyer's Guide*, no. 998, 1 Jan. 1993.

56 See, e.g. Henry Jenkins, *Textual Poachers: Television Fans and Participatory Culture* (New York: Routledge, 1992).

57 Similar findings have been reported by Condit and Barker (see Bryman, *Disney and his Worlds*, p. 187).

Chapter 8 Living Happily Ever After?

1 Quoted, without source, by Kathy Merlock Jackson, *Walt Disney: A Bio-Bibliography* (Westport, Conn.: Greenwood Press, 1993), p. 68.

2 Cited in the *New Internationalist*, Dec. 1998, p. 11.

3 Susan Davis, personal correspondence.

4 Neil Postman, *The Disappearance of Childhood* (New York: Vintage Books, 1994).

5 Carl Hiassen's *Team Rodent: How Disney Devours the World* (New York: Ballantine, 1998) is an especially good example of a work that acknowledges the company's scope and power, while celebrating its failures.

6 Henry A. Giroux, *The Mouse that Roared: Disney and the End of Innocence* (Lanham, Md.: Rowan & Littlefield, 1999), p. 170.

Index